4/20	DATE DUE	

SHAKESPEARE
AN ILLUSTRATED DICTIONARY

SHAKESPEARE
AN ILLUSTRATED DICTIONARY

Stanley Wells

OXFORD UNIVERSITY PRESS

Copyright © Kaye & Ward Ltd, 1978

First published in Great Britain
by Kaye & Ward Ltd, London, 1978
First published in the United States
by Oxford University Press, New York, 1978
First issued in Great Britain
as an Oxford University Press paperback, Oxford, 1981

British Library Cataloguing in Publication Data
Wells, Stanley
Shakespeare.
1. Shakespeare, William – Dictionaries, indexes, etc.
I. Title
822.3'3   PR2892   81-9535
ISBN 0-19-871074-7 (UK pbk.)
ISBN 0-19-520054-3 (USA)

First American printing, 1981

This printing (last digit): 9 8 7 6 5 4 3 2 1

Printed in the United States of America

PREFACE

This volume is intended as a companion and guide to reading Shakespeare's plays and to experiencing them where they belong, in the theatre. Each play has a separate entry giving the basic information about its date, sources, and first publication, followed by a selective account of the history of its theatrical presentation. Other entries are concerned with Shakespeare's life, his contemporaries, his interpreters, creative artists who have come under his influence, and other topics likely to interest those who enjoy Shakespeare's works, and who want to know more about him and them. Selectivity has been essential. It would have been possible, for example, to fill the volume with entries for Shakespeare's theatrical interpreters alone. I have tried to choose the great figures of the past along with those who are most active as Shakespeare performers at present. The section on Further Reading (pp. 215–16) points to additional sources of information. An asterisk indicates that there is a separate entry in the dictionary for the topic so marked. The volume also includes a finding list of the characters in Shakespeare's plays.

Normally, quotations from early printed books and documents are given in modernized form. Quotations from Shakespeare are from Peter Alexander's edition (1951). In selecting illustrations I have benefited from the knowledge and experience of Mrs Marian Pringle, Miss Eileen Robinson and Miss Mary White, librarians at the Shakespeare Centre, Stratford-upon-Avon.

S.W.W.

ACKNOWLEDGMENTS

The author and publishers would like to thank the following for permission to reproduce photographs in the text:

The Bodleian Library, Oxford for photographs on pages 111, 143 and 183

The British Library for the photograph on page 62

The Fitzwilliam Museum, Cambridge for the photograph on page 190

The Folger Shakespeare Library for photographs on pages 20, 35, 54 and 65

Ontario House for the photograph on page 168

The Harvard Theatre Collection (Angus McBean collection) and the Governors of the Royal Shakespeare Theatre, Stratford-upon-Avon for the photographs on pages 32, 64, 100, 128, 176 and 179

Joe Cocks Photographer for photographs on pages 23, 64, 67, 80, 125 and 131

Holte Photographics for photographs on pages 2, 7, 31, 39, 53, 58, 66, 74, 87 and 180

The National Portrait Gallery, London for photographs on pages 17, 26, 45, 47, 72, 76, 84, 86 and 162

The Governors of the Royal Shakespeare Theatre, Stratford-upon-Avon for photographs on pages 33, 92, 110, 113, 129, 169 and 171

The Shakespeare Birthplace Trust, Stratford-upon-Avon for photographs on pages 3, 4, 11, 12, 15, 16, 17, 18, 21, 22, 27, 36, 37, 41, 43, 46, 47, 49, 50, 51, 52, 60, 61, 66, 70, 73, 75, 77, 80, 88, 89, 95, 98, 103, 104, 107, 115, 117, 118, 120, 134, 135, 136, 137, 139, 141, 142, 150, 151, 152, 161, 163, 170, 173, 175, 182, 184 and 188

The Shakespeare Institute, University of Birmingham for photographs on pages 8, 56, 73, 83, 90, 114, 124, 127, 145 and 155

The Tate Gallery, London for photographs on pages 19, 93 and 108

Crown Copyright, Victoria and Albert Museum for the photograph on page 34

The Walker Art Gallery, Liverpool for the photograph on page 79

The Public Record Office for the photograph on page 111

The Chapter of the College of Arms for the photograph on page 6

The photograph on page 148 is reproduced by the gracious permission of Her Majesty the Queen

The photograph on page 146 is reproduced by courtesy of the Trustees The National Gallery, London

The University of London Library for the photograph on page 164

The illustration on page 14 is reproduced by courtesy of Mrs Eva Reichmann

CONTENTS

A

Act-and-scene divisions. None of the quarto⋆ editions of Shakespeare's plays issued before the First Folio⋆ appeared, in 1623, is divided into scenes, and only one, *Othello*,⋆ printed in 1622, is divided into acts.

In the Folio, six plays are undivided; *Hamlet*⋆ is only partially divided; eleven plays are divided into acts only; the remaining eighteen are divided into acts and scenes. Some of the divided plays are ones which had been printed without divisions in quarto.

There is reason to suspect that Shakespeare himself did not divide his plays into acts and scenes, though there is also evidence, such as the placing of the Choruses⋆ in *Henry V*⋆ and *Pericles*,⋆ that he wrote with some consciousness of the conventional five-act structure.

The divisions marked in modern editions are basically those established by the early eighteenth-century editors, Nicholas Rowe⋆ and Alexander Pope.⋆

Actresses. No professional actresses appeared on the English stage until after the Restoration, in 1660. Female roles in Shakespeare's plays were written for boy actors.⋆

Admiral's Men. A theatre company, known first as Lord Howard's Men, under the patronage from 1576/7 to 1603 of Charles, Lord Howard, first Earl of Nottingham, who became Lord High Admiral in 1585. On James I's⋆ accession, they became Prince Henry's Men (1603–12), and after that the Elector Palatine's, or Palsgrave's, Men (1613–25).

They were the main rivals to Shakespeare's company, the Lord Chamberlain's (later King's) Men.⋆ From about 1589, perhaps earlier, to 1597, and 1600 to 1605, their leading actor was Edward Alleyn,⋆ Richard Burbage's⋆ chief rival. Their principal financier was Philip Henslowe,⋆ who owned the Rose Theatre, built in 1587, where the company mainly played from 1594 till they moved to his Fortune Theatre⋆ in 1600. This burned down in 1621. The company, greatly harmed, survived only till 1625.

Advice to the Players, Hamlet's. Hamlet's speeches to the actors, III.ii.1–43.

Age of Kings, An. A BBC television serial based on Shakespeare's English history plays (see Histories), directed by Peter Dews, and transmitted in 1961.

Alexander, Peter (1894–1969). British scholar whose edition of Shakespeare appeared in 1951.

Alleyn, Edward (1566–1626). Leading actor of the Admiral's Men.★ He was famous particularly as Marlowe's★ Faustus, Tamburlaine, and Barabas. He retired from 1597 to 1600, then returned to the stage till 1605, after which he continued as theatre manager. He was married first to Philip Henslowe's★ stepdaughter, Joan, then (in 1623) to John Donne's daughter, Constance.

All for Love. See Dryden, John, and *Antony and Cleopatra*.

All's Well that Ends Well. Shakespeare's comedy was first printed in the First Folio★ (1623). Its date is uncertain. It was not directly mentioned by Francis Meres★ in 1598, but is sometimes identified with his *Love's Labour's Won.*★ Resemblances to *Measure for Measure*★ cause it most often to be dated 1602–3. It is based on a story from Boccaccio's★ *Decameron*, probably in Painter's★ translation.

It has never been a favourite with audiences. Its first recorded performance is in 1741. Subsequent performances tended to emphasize the role of Parolles. J. P. Kemble★ tried, with little success, to restore the balance of the play at Drury Lane★ in 1794. A musical version was played at Covent Garden★ in 1832, and Samuel Phelps★ presented the original at Sadler's Wells★ in 1852. Barry Jackson★ produced a modern-dress version at Birmingham Repertory Theatre in 1927, with the young Laurence Olivier★ as Parolles. The most brilliant, if eccentric, production of modern times was Tyrone Guthrie's,★ given at Stratford, Ontario,★ in 1957,

Dame Edith Evans as the Countess of Roussillon, with Donald Eccles as her steward, in Tyrone Guthrie's production of *All's Well that Ends Well*, Stratford-upon-Avon, 1959 and again at Stratford-upon-Avon in 1959, with Edith Evans★ as the Countess.

All's Well that Ends Well has perhaps suffered by being labelled, since about 1900, a problem play.★ It has some excellent acting roles, some good comedy, and some fine, if rather rarified, poetry. It awaits a major production.

Anne Hathaway's Cottage. See Hathaway, Anne. The house was bought by the Shakespeare Birthplace Trust★ in 1892, and is maintained as a showplace.

Anne Hathaway's Cottage as it is today

Antony and Cleopatra. Shakespeare's Roman tragedy was first printed in the First Folio★ (1623). It had been entered in the Stationers' Register★ in 1608, and is usually dated 1606-7. The main source is Plutarch's★ *Lives of the Noble Grecians and Romans*. Shakespeare's wording is often close to North's★ translation. No early performance is recorded.

Dryden★ treated the subject in his *All for Love* (1678), with some debt to Shakespeare, and this probably had the effect of keeping Shakespeare's play off the stage. David Garrick★ revived it in a version prepared by Edward Capell,★ in 1759, without success. J. P. Kemble's★ acting version of 1813 incorporated passages from *All for Love*. It too failed, as did W. C. Macready's★ performances in 1833. The play had little success generally on the nineteenth-century stage.

Beerbohm Tree★ presented a spectacular revival in 1906. Robert Atkins's★ Old Vic★ production of 1922 successfully abandoned realistic settings in favour of a bare stage. The play has continued to prove intractable, though Stratford-upon-Avon productions by Glen Byam Shaw★ (1953) with Michael Redgrave★ and Peggy Ashcroft,★ by Trevor Nunn★ (1972) with Richard Johnson and Janet Suzman, and the St James's, London, production (1951) with Laurence Olivier★ and Vivien Leigh, have enjoyed some success, as did a New York production of 1947 with Godfrey Tearle and Katharine Cornell.

Cleopatra's death : an engraving from Nicholas Rowe's edition (1709)

The play's relative failure on the stage may be regarded as the failure of directors to find a workable style for its presentation; critically, it has aroused much interest, and it contains some of Shakespeare's greatest dramatic poetry, along with some of his most fascinating touches of characterization.

Apocryphal plays. A number of plays attributed to Shakespeare in his own time and since are now not generally accepted as his. These include six plays added to the second issue (1664) of the Third Folio★: *The London Prodigal,★ Thomas, Lord Cromwell,★ Sir John Old-castle,★ The Puritan,★ A Yorkshire Tragedy,★* and *Locrine.★* Other plays which were attributed to Shakespeare in the seventeenth and eighteenth centuries include *The Birth of Merlin, The Merry Devil of Edmonton, Mucedorus,★ The Second Maiden's Tragedy, Fair Em,* and *Arden of Feversham. Edward III★* may be partly by Shakespeare.

Apollonius of Tyre. The hero of a romantic tale, well-known in the Middle Ages and the Renaissance, and often retold. Shakespeare uses it in the framework of *The Comedy of Errors★* and as the main tale of *Pericles.★*

Arcadia, The. A lengthy prose romance by Sir Philip Sidney,★ based on Greek romances. It exists in two forms: the 'old' *Arcadia,* and an incompleted revision, the 'New' *Arcadia.* Shakespeare drew on it for the Gloucester sub-plot of *King Lear.★*

Arden edition. A one-play-per-volume edition of Shakespeare's works under the general editorship first of W. J. Craig, from 1891 to 1906, then of R. H. Case, from 1906 to 1924. The new Arden edition★ was intended as a revision of it.

Arden, Mary (d. 1608). Youngest daughter of Robert Arden of Wilmcote near Stratford-upon-Avon; married Shakespeare's father, John,★ about 1557; died in 1608. See Mary Arden's House.

Armin, Robert (c. 1568–1615). An actor and writer who seems to have joined Shakespeare's company, the Lord Chamberlain's Men,★ by 1599. The author of a book called *Foole upon Foole* (1600), he specialized in comic roles, and may have succeeded Will Kemp.★ No Shakespearian roles can certainly be assigned to him, but it seems likely that he played Dogberry, Touchstone, Feste, and Lear's Fool.

Arms, Shakespeare's. Shakespeare's father approached the Heralds' Office about a coat-of-arms shortly after becoming bailiff of Stratford-upon-Avon in 1568, but did not proceed far. He (or perhaps his son on his behalf) renewed the application in 1596. Sir William Dethick, Garter King-of-Arms, granted the request. Two rough drafts survive.

The shield was to be 'gold on a bend sables, a spear of the first steeled argent, and for his crest or cognizance a falcon, his wings displayed argent, standing on a wreath of his colours, supporting a spear gold, steeled as aforesaid, set upon a helmet with mantles and tassels as hath been accustomed and doth more plainly appear depicted on this margin'.

A rough sketch of the shield and crest appears on both drafts. The motto, which Shakespeare is not known to have used, is 'Non Sans Droit' – 'Not Without Right'. The grant of arms gave to John Shakespeare* and his family the status of gentlefolk.

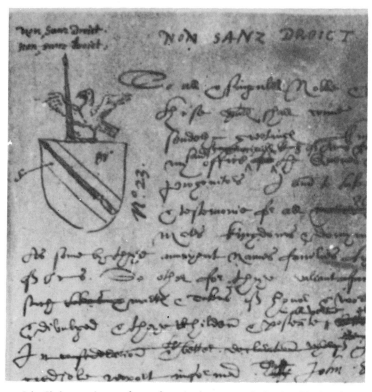

John Shakespeare's coat of arms, from the document assigning it to him (1596)

In 1599, John Shakespeare applied for the right to impale his arms with those of his wife's family, the Ardens, but this seems not to have been allowed. His right to arms was challenged in 1602, but the official reply was that he was 'a magistrate in Stratford-upon-Avon. A Justice of Peace, he married a daughter and heir of Arden, and was of good substance and habilité.'

Arne, Thomas (1710–78). Composer of delightful settings of songs from several of Shakespeare's plays, and of the music for Garrick's* Ode for the Jubilee of 1769.

Arras. A curtain or wall-hanging which appears to have been used on the Elizabethan stage, as for the eavesdropping Polonius (*Hamlet*,⋆ III.i) and the snoring Falstaff (*I Henry IV*,⋆ II.iv).

Ashcroft, Dame Peggy (b. 1907). English actress who has played many of Shakespeare's heroines, including Desdemona (Savoy, 1930, with Paul Robeson), Imogen (Old Vic,⋆ 1932, Stratford-upon-Avon, 1957), Juliet (Old Vic, 1932, New Theatre, with Laurence Olivier⋆ and John Gielgud⋆ alternating as Romeo and Mercutio), Portia (Queen's, 1935, Stratford-upon-Avon, 1953), Viola (Phoenix, 1938 and Old Vic, 1950), Ophelia (Haymarket,⋆ with Gielgud, 1944), and (all at Stratford-upon-Avon) Beatrice (1950, etc.), Cordelia (1950), Cleopatra (with Michael Redgrave,⋆ 1953), Rosalind (1957), Katherina (1960), Paulina (1960), Queen Margaret (in *The Wars of the Roses*,⋆ 1963, etc.), and Queen Katherine (1969).

Peggy Ashcroft as Cleopatra in Glen Byam Shaw's production of *Antony and Cleopatra*, Stratford-upon-Avon, 1953

Ashland, Oregon. See Oregon Shakespeare Festival.

As You Like It. Shakespeare's pastoral comedy, first printed in the First Folio⋆ (1623), is first heard of in the Stationers' Register⋆ in 1600, and was probably written not long before. It is based directly on Thomas Lodge's⋆ prose romance *Rosalynde*, first printed in 1590. Shakespeare adapted the story and added the characters of Jaques, Touchstone, Audrey, William, and Sir Oliver Martext.

No early performances are certainly recorded. In 1723 parts of the play were used in an odd compilation by Charles Johnson, *Love in a Forest*, which also draws on *A Midsummer Night's Dream*⋆ and other plays. Shakespeare's play was revived in 1740 by Charles Macklin,⋆ with songs by Thomas Arne.⋆ Since then it has been regularly performed, usually in picturesque settings, and often during the past hundred years in the open-air. Many leading actresses, including Dorothea Jordan,⋆ Ada Rehan,⋆ Mary Anderson, Edith Evans,⋆ Peggy Ashcroft,⋆ Margaret Leighton, and Vanessa Redgrave have

7

As You Like It: Vanessa Redgrave as Rosalind in Michael Elliott's production, Stratford-upon-Avon, 1961

excelled in the demanding role of Rosalind. In 1967 Clifford Williams directed an all-male version with the National Theatre* company at the Old Vic.

As You Like It is a play in which ideas are never far below the surface. It portrays contrasting attitudes to life, using an original technique of tolerant juxtaposition rather than presentation by intrigue or argument. The style of both its verse and its prose is exceptionally limpid and unforced, and though Rosalind is the dominating character, other roles, especially Jaques, Touchstone, Audrey, Corin, and William, offer opportunities for creative acting.

Atkins, Robert (1886–1972). English actor and director much associated with Shakespeare's plays at the Old Vic,* Stratford-upon-Avon, the Regent's Park* Open-Air Theatre, and elsewhere.

Aubrey, John (1626–97). His posthumously published *Brief Lives* include gossip about Shakespeare, some of it from William Beeston, son of Christopher, a member of Shakespeare's company. He describes Shakespeare as 'a handsome, well-shaped man: very good company, and of a very ready and pleasant smooth wit', and says that he was 'the more to be admired [because] he was not a company keeper . . . wouldn't be debauched, and if invited to, writ he was in pain.' From him comes the statement that Shakespeare 'had been in his younger years a schoolmaster in the country', as well as the suggestion that William Davenant* was Shakespeare's natural son.

Authorship. The first suggestion that Shakespeare did not write the plays attributed to him appears to have been made by the Rev. James Wilmot, who ascribed them to Francis Bacon around 1785. He did not publish his conclusion. The next appearance of the idea is in a book called *The Romance of Yachting*, published in 1848 by an eccentric New York lawyer, Colonel Joseph C. Hart. He was influenced by a denigratory life of Shakespeare in Dionysius Lardner's *Cabinet Cyclopaedia*, which found that the plays 'absolutely teem with the grossest impurities, – more gross by far than can be found in any contemporary dramatist.' Hart fantasized that Shakespeare 'purchased or obtained surreptitiously' other men's plays which he then 'spiced with obscenity, blackguardism and impurities.' He did not identify the original author.

The first extended attempt to prove Bacon's authorship was in an article by Delia Bacon, also an American, published in 1856. Later that year she spent a night in Holy Trinity Church★ with the intention of opening Shakespeare's grave, but abandoned the plan. Her theory was elaborated in her book *The Philosophy of the Plays of Shakespeare Unfolded* (1857).

The 'anti-Stratfordian' movement, as it has come to be called, developed. An English Bacon Society, producing a periodical, was founded in 1885, and an American Society followed in 1892. Much intellectual effort and learning have been expended in the attempt to find cryptograms and other clues to authorship in the texts and other places, such as the Droeshout engraving. The movement has had some distinguished adherents, including Mark Twain and Sigmund Freud.★

In more recent years splinter groups have attempted to replace Shakespeare with many different names, including those of the Earl of Derby, the Earl of Essex,★ Queen Elizabeth,★ Christopher Marlowe,★ the Earl of Oxford,★ and the Earl of Rutland.★ An excellent account of the whole topic is given in Part Six of S. Schoenbaum's *Shakespeare's Lives* (1970).

There is much factual evidence that William Shakespeare of Stratford-upon-Avon wrote the plays published as his in the First Folio★ of 1623. Attempts to displace him have been based usually on snobbery (the idea that a humble man from the country would not have been equipped to write the plays), the desire for self-advertisement, or mere folly.

B

Bacon, Delia. See Authorship.
Bacon, Francis. See Authorship.
Bad quarto. A technical term devised by the bibliographer A. W. Pollard to refer to pirated early texts of Shakespeare's plays, that is, ones not printed from an authoritative manuscript. These include the

first quartos* of *Romeo and Juliet** (1597), *Henry V* *(1600), *The Merry
Wives of Windsor** (1602), and *Hamlet** (1603). These texts seem to
have been reconstructed from memory by some of the actors, and are
corrupt in varying degrees. The theory that they are based on short-
hand transcripts is now discredited. Though they have no textual
authority they may assist in the effort to establish a true text, especially
in their stage directions which sometimes give us our only evidence
as to pieces of stage business.

> *Ham.* To be, or not to be, I there's the point,
> To Die, to sleepe, is that all? I all:
> No, to sleepe, to dreame, I mary there it goes,
> For in that dreame of death, when wee awake,
> And borne before an euerlasting Iudge,
> From whence no passenger euer retur'nd,
> The vndiscouered country, at whose sight
> The happy smile, and the accursed damn'd.
> But for this, the ioyfull hope of this,
> Whol'd beare the scornes and flattery of the world,
> Scorned by the right rich, the rich cursed of the poore?
> The widow being oppressed, the orphan wrong'd,
> The taste of hunger, or a tirants raigne,
> And thousand more calamities besides,
> To grunt and sweate vnder this weary life,
> When that he may his full *Quietus* make,
> With a bare bodkin, who would this indure,
> But for a hope of something after death?.
> Which puszles the braine, and doth confound the sence,
> Which makes vs rather beare those euilles we haue,
> Than flie to others that we know not of.
> I that, O this conscience makes cowardes of vs all,
> Lady in thy orizons, be all my sinnes remembred.

Hamlet's 'To be or not to be . . .' as it appeared in the 'bad quarto' of 1603

Balakirev, Mily Alexeievich (1837–1910). The Russian composer wrote an overture (1859) *King Lear* and published an extended suite of incidental music for the play in 1904.

Baptism, Shakespeare's. The baptism of 'Gulielmus filius Johannes Shakspere' is recorded in the Stratford-upon-Avon Parish Register on 26 April 1564. The Register is a transcript dated 1600.

The entry of Shakespeare's birth in the Stratford-upon-Avon Parish Register

Barker, Harley Granville. See Granville-Barker, Harley.

Barry, Elizabeth (c. 1658–1713). English actress, mistress of the Earl of Rochester; she acted with Thomas Betterton,★ and played Cordelia in Nahum Tate's★ version of *King Lear*,★ Mrs Ford in *The Merry Wives of Windsor*,★ Queen Katherine in *Henry VIII*,★ and Lady Macbeth.

Barry, Spranger (1717?–77). Irish actor, chief rival of David Garrick,★ with whom he acted in his later years; most successful as Romeo, Hamlet, Othello, Macbeth, Lear, and Richard III. A female admirer, comparing him with Garrick as Romeo, said, 'Had I been Juliet to Garrick's Romeo – so ardent and impassioned was he, I should have expected he would have *come up* to me in the balcony; but had I been

Juliet to Barry's Romeo – so tender, so eloquent, and so seductive was he, I should certainly have *gone down* to him!' In Lear, however, Barry was said to be 'every inch a King', but Garrick 'every inch King Lear!'

Spranger Barry as Lear, with his wife, Mrs Dancer, as Cordelia in Tate's adaptation of *King Lear*; an anonymous engraving from the *Universal Museum*, September 1767

Bartlett, John (1820–1905). American compiler of a *Complete Concordance to Shakespeare's Dramatic Works and Poems*, published in 1894, standard until the publication of Spevack's★ more truly 'complete' work.

Barton, John (b. 1928). Associate Director of the Royal Shakespeare Company,★ whose work includes distinguished productions of *The Taming of the Shrew*★ (1960), *Love's Labour's Lost*★ (1965), *All's Well that Ends Well*★ (1967), *Coriolanus*★ (1968), *Troilus and Cressida*★ (1968, 1976), *Twelfth Night*★ (1969), *Measure for Measure*★ (1970), *Othello*★ (1971) and *Much Ado About Nothing*★ (1976). He adapted the texts of the early history plays to make *The Wars of the Roses*★ (1963 etc.), which he directed with Peter Hall,★ and also adapted *King John*★ (1974), omitting much, and inserting many passages from *The Troublesome Reign*,★ some lines from John Bale's *King John* (written in the 1530s), and many lines of his own composition.

Basse, William (1583?–1653?). English poet, author of a manuscript sonnet-epitaph on Shakespeare written before 1623, beginning:

> Renowned Spenser, lie a thought more nigh
> To learnèd Chaucer, and rare Beaumont, lie
> A little nearer Spenser to make room
> For Shakespeare in your three-fold, four-fold tomb.

Baylis, Lilian (1874–1937). See Old Vic.

Bear. One of the more surprising stage directions in Shakespeare occurs in *The Winter's Tale*,★ III.iii.59, when Antigonus is required to 'Exit, pursued by a bear', which devours him.

Beaumont, Francis (c. 1584–1616). English dramatist, collaborator with John Fletcher★ and author of independent plays. *The Woman Hater* (c. 1606) quotes a phrase from *Hamlet* in a comic context, and in *The Knight of the Burning Pestle* (c. 1607) are lines which appear to be an early allusion to *Macbeth*.★ They are spoken by Jasper 'with his face mealed', and evidently refer to the appearance of Banquo's ghost, and to record a piece of stage business – the dropping of the cup – used by many later actors. They are:

> When thou art at thy table with thy friends,
> Merry in heart, and filled with swelling wine,
> I'll come in midst of all thy pride and mirth,
> Invisible to all men but thyself,
> And whisper such a sad tale in thine ear
> Shall make thee let the cup fall from thy hand,
> And stand as mute and pale as death itself. (V.i.26–32)

Bed-trick. The deceptive substitution of one woman in a man's bed for another, a common motif of romance literature, used by Shakespeare in both *All's Well that Ends Well*★ and *Measure for Measure.*★

Beerbohm, Max (1872–1956). English satirical writer and artist who reviewed many productions of Shakespeare's plays (see Stanley Wells, 'Shakespeare in Max Beerbohm's Theatre Criticism', *Shakespeare Survey*★ *29*, 1976), and drew several cartoons featuring Shakespeare, including one alluding to the authorship★ controversy.

Beethoven, Ludwig van (1770–1827). Beethoven's overture 'Coriolan' (1807) was written for a play 'after Shakespeare' by a Viennese playwright, H. Collin, but he may have had Shakespeare's play in mind. The slow movement of his first string quartet, Opus 18 No. 1, is said to have been inspired by the last scene of *Romeo and Juliet*,★ and when asked the meaning of the first movement of his piano sonata in D minor, Opus 31 No. 2, he replied 'Read Shakespeare's *The Tempest*.'

Bell, John (1745–1831). A London publisher who brought out an edition of Shakespeare's plays (printed 1773–5) based on the prompt-books of the Theatres Royal, edited and introduced by Francis Gentleman, which is invaluable to the theatre historian. The plays not in the theatres' repertoires are also printed, in complete texts with Gentleman's suggestions for omissions. The edition is accompanied with two plates for each play, one illustrating an actor as one of the characters, the other portraying a scene from the play. The plates were published separately, and are not necessarily included in sets of the plays. Bell also published a conventional edition, based on the text of Samuel Johnson★ and George Steevens,★ in 1788.

Caricature by Max Beerbohm: William Shakespeare, his method of work.

Belleforest, François de (1530–83). French writer; his continuation of Pierre Boaistuau's translation of Matteo Bandello's *Novelle*, as *Histoires Tragiques* (1559–82), includes a version of a legend from Saxo Grammaticus★ which influenced *Hamlet*★ (perhaps indirectly), and a story which may have influenced *Much Ado About Nothing*.★

Bellini, Vincenzo (1801–35). The Italian composer wrote a successful opera, *I Capuletti ed i Montecchi* (1830), based on *Romeo and Juliet*.★

Belott, Stephen. See Mountjoy, Christopher.

Benson, Sir Francis (Frank) Robert (1858–1939). Actor-manager who ran a company which presented most of Shakespeare's plays, mainly in the English provinces, including Stratford-upon-Avon, from 1883 to 1919. He produced the plays simply and with few cuts. He gave a full text of *Hamlet*★ at the Lyceum★ Theatre, London, in 1900. In 1906 his company gave the English history plays (omitting *1 Henry IV*) at Stratford-upon-Avon, where he managed the Festival from 1888 to 1919. Among his own best roles were Hamlet, Richard II (the subject of a fine review by C. E. Montague), Richard III, Petruchio, and Caliban.

Benthall, Michael (1919–74). English director who worked at Stratford-upon-Avon (1947–51) and directed the Old Vic Theatre★

F. R. Benson as Richard II: a stained glass window designed by Vernon Spreadbury for the picture gallery of the Shakespeare Memorial Theatre, Stratford-upon-Avon

15

from 1953 to 1958, during which time all Shakespeare's plays were given, many of them directed by Benthall.

Benson, John (d. 1667). A London publisher who brought out an edition of Shakespeare's *Poems* in 1640. It omits *Venus and Adonis*★ and *The Rape of Lucrece*★ and includes many non-Shakespearian poems along with inauthentic versions of most of the Sonnets.★

Berlioz, Hector (1803–69). French composer greatly influenced by Shakespeare, especially in his fantasia for chorus and orchestra on *The Tempest* (1830, incorporated into *Lélio*, 1832); his concert overture *King Lear* (1831); his dramatic symphony *Romeo and Juliet* (1839); his choral and orchestral pieces *The Death of Ophelia* (originally for voice and piano) and 'Funeral March for Hamlet' (1848); his comic opera *Beatrice and Benedict* (1862), and, less directly but no less profoundly, his opera *The Trojans* (1858).

Bernard, Sir John (1605–74). Second husband of Shakespeare's grand-daughter, Elizabeth Hall.★

Bernhardt, Sarah (1834–1923). French actress who made an early success as Cordelia in a translation of *King Lear*,★ and later played Hamlet. She was sixty-five at the time. Max Beerbohm,★ reviewing the performance, wrote, 'Her friends ought to have restrained her. The native critics ought not to have encouraged her. The custom-house officials at Charing Cross ought to have confiscated her sable doublet and hose . . . the only compliment one can conscientiously pay her is that her Hamlet was, from first to last, *très grande dame*.'

Sarah Bernhardt as Hamlet, Adelphi Theatre, London, 1899

Bestrafte Brudermord, Der. See *Fratricide Punished*.

Betterton, Thomas (1635–1710). The leading actor of the Restoration period, also involved with theatre management. After a short period with Thomas Killigrew★ and the King's Men, he joined William Davenant★ and the Duke's

Men, and in 1661 played Hamlet with them 'beyond imagination', according to Pepys.★ He went on playing Hamlet until he was over seventy, and his other Shakespeare roles included Brutus, Macbeth, Mercutio, Sir Toby Belch, Lear, Henry VIII, Othello, and Falstaff.★

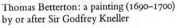

Thomas Betterton: a painting (1690–1700) by or after Sir Godfrey Kneller

Master Betty as Hamlet: an engraving by J. Alais

Betty, Master William (1791–1874). Known as the 'Young Roscius', he had a brief period of sensational popularity from 1803 to 1808, playing Romeo, Hamlet, Richard III, and Macbeth, among other roles.

Bible. Shakespeare's plays show a familiar acquaintance with both the Geneva Bible (1560) and the Bishops' Bible (1568). The standard study is Richmond Noble's *Shakespeare's Biblical Knowledge and Use of the Book of Common Prayer*, 1935.

Birmingham Shakespeare Library. See Shakespeare Memorial Library, Birmingham.

Birthday, Shakespeare's. Shakespeare was baptized on 26 April 1564, probably only a few days after his birth, traditionally celebrated on St George's Day, 23 April, the date of his death. The annual celebrations at Stratford-upon-Avon include a flag-unfurling ceremony, a procession including diplomatic representatives of many nations, a luncheon at which the Immortal Memory of William Shakespeare is toasted by a distinguished speaker, a performance of one of the plays, a church service with a special sermon, and a lecture.

Birthplace, Shakespeare's. When Shakespeare was born, in 1564, his father owned two adjacent houses in Henley Street, Stratford-upon-Avon, and another in Greenhill Street. Legal records show that he was living in Henley Street in 1552 and as late as 1597. There is no reason to suppose that he lived elsewhere during this period, so the Henley Street property is likely to be that in which Shakespeare was born.

Shakespeare's Birthplace as it is now

When Shakespeare died, his sister, Joan Hart, was living in the western part of the property, and he left her a life-tenancy in it for an annual rent of one shilling. His grand-daughter left both houses to Joan's descendants, who lived in the western one and rented the other. They sold the property in 1806, when the western wing became a butcher's shop. The property was bought as a public trust (see Shakespeare Birthplace Trust) in 1847.

Bishop, Sir Henry Rowley (1786–1855). English composer who worked with Frederick Reynolds* on musical versions of several of

Shakespeare's plays at Covent Garden,* and also wrote incidental music. His best-known setting of Shakespeare is 'Lo, here the gentle lark', words from *Venus and Adonis** introduced into *The Comedy of Errors** (1819).

Blackfriars Gatehouse. In March 1613 Shakespeare bought a house in the Blackfriars, in the eastern part of the City of London, close to the theatre, for £140. He appears not to have lived in it, and to have bought it as an investment.

Blackfriars Theatre. A disused monastery in the Blackfriars area of London, used sporadically as a theatre by children's companies between 1576 and 1608, when it was acquired for the King's (formerly Lord Chamberlain's*) Men, who used it as a winter house from autumn 1609 to 1642. It was a 'private'* theatre, roofed, with higher admission charges than the 'public' theatres, and holding only about 700 spectators. It was demolished in 1655.

Blake, William (1757–1827). The English poet and artist produced more than twenty highly imaginative pictorial treatments of Shakespearian themes.

Blake's drawing illustrating 'Pity, like a naked, new-born babe . . .', *Macbeth*, I.7.21ff

Blank verse. Unrhymed verse, with five iambic feet to a line, a measure introduced into England by the Earl of Surrey (c. 1517–47), the poet, which became the basic verse form of Elizabethan drama.

Bloch, Ernest (1880–1959). The Swiss composer of an opera (1910), *Macbeth*, based on Shakespeare's play.

Blocking entry. An entry in the Stationers' Register★ which seems designed to establish a claim to the right of printing a work rather than as an immediate preliminary to printing it. Several of Shakespeare's plays were entered in this way.

Boccaccio, Giovanni (1313–75). Italian writer best known for his *Decameron* (1353), a collection of one hundred tales, some of them translated by William Painter in his *Palace of Pleasure* (1567), which includes the story of Giletta of Narbonne, used by Shakespeare for *All's Well that Ends Well.*★

Bohemia, sea-coast of. Shakespeare's attribution in *The Winter's Tale*★ of a sea-coast to Bohemia has often been held against him. It troubled Sir Thomas Hanmer★ so much that he supposed it to be a mistake for Bithynia, a reading which Charles Kean★ adopted in his acting version.

Booth, Edwin (1833–93). American actor and manager, son of Junius Brutus Booth, successful also in London. He excelled as Hamlet, Iago, Brutus, and Lear.

Booth, Junius Brutus (1796–1852). English tragedian, at first an imitator of Edmund Kean;★ he worked in America from 1821, and toured regularly. His Shakespeare roles included Richard III, Shylock, Iago, Hamlet, Macbeth, Lear, Othello, and Cassius. He was the father of three actors: Junius, Edwin, and John Wilkes, who assassinated Abraham Lincoln.

Bouncing Knight, The. See *Henry IV, Part One.*

Bowdler, Miss Henrietta Maria (1754–1830). Sister of Dr Thomas Bowdler,★ and the editor of the

Edwin Booth as Hamlet; an anonymous lithograph

first anonymous edition of the *Family Shakespeare*, in which twenty of Shakespeare's plays were published, expurgated, in 1807. She also published best-selling sermons and religious poems and essays.

Bowdler, Dr Thomas (1754–1825). Notorious as the editor of an expurgated ('bowdlerized') edition of Shakespeare. Twenty of the plays appeared in the *Family Shakespeare* in 1807. This was issued anonymously, and was the work of Bowdler's sister, Henrietta.* Thomas Bowdler expurgated the remaining plays for the second edition, of 1818. His principle was that 'If any word or expression is of such a nature that the first impression it excites is an impression of obscenity, that word ought not to be spoken nor written or printed; and, if printed, it ought to be erased.' His edition was often reprinted.

THE

FAMILY SHAKSPEARE,

In Ten Volumes;

IN WHICH
NOTHING IS ADDED TO THE ORIGINAL TEXT;
BUT THOSE WORDS AND EXPRESSIONS
ARE OMITTED WHICH CANNOT WITH PROPRIETY
BE READ ALOUD IN A FAMILY.

BY

THOMAS BOWDLER, Esq. F.R.S. & S.A.

VOL. I.

CONTAINING

TEMPEST;
TWO GENTLEMEN OF VERONA;
MERRY WIVES OF WINDSOR;
TWELFTH-NIGHT: OR, WHAT YOU WILL.

LONDON:
PRINTED FOR LONGMAN, HURST, REES, ORME, AND BROWN,
PATERNOSTER-ROW.
1818.

The titlepage of Bowdler's expurgated edition of Shakespeare (1818)

He also published (posthumously) Edward Gibbon's *History of the Decline and Fall of the Roman Empire, for the use of Families and Young Persons, reprinted from the original text with the careful omissions of all passages of an irreligious or immoral tendency* (1826).

Boy Actors. No professional actresses appeared on the English stage before 1660. All the female roles in Shakespeare's plays were originally played by male actors. This is no doubt one explanation of the popularity of plots in which girls dress up as boys. Younger roles, such as Juliet, Hero, Viola, Rosalind, Desdemona, Marina, and Miranda, were probably played by boys. Older women, such as Juliet's Nurse, Mistress Quickly, Mistress Overdone, Lady Macbeth, and Volumnia, may have been given to young men.

Boy actors underwent a rigorous training as apprentices to senior members of the acting companies, and there is no reason to suppose that they lacked expertise. In Shakespeare's time there were also companies composed exclusively of boys, which at times constituted serious rivals to the adult companies. A passage in *Hamlet*★ (II.ii.335–358) alludes to their success.

Boydell's Shakespeare Gallery. Alderman John Boydell (1719–1804) commissioned paintings of scenes from Shakespeare by the leading British artists of the day, including Henry Fuseli,★ William Hogarth,★ Sir Joshua Reynolds, George Romney, Robert Smirke, Richard Westall, and Francis Wheatley. A gallery for their exhibition was

'Shakespeare Nursed by Tragedy and Comedy', painted by George Romney for Boydell's Shakespeare Gallery, and engraved by Benjamin Smith

opened in Pall Mall, London, in 1789. About 170 paintings were completed, and many of them engraved, but Boydell had money troubles, and the collection was sold by auction in 1805. There is an account of the venture in Chapter 5 of W. M. Merchant's *Shakespeare and the Artist* (1959).

Boys from Syracuse, The. A musical, loosely related to *The Comedy of Errors*,★ by Richard Rodgers and Lorenz Hart, staged 1938, filmed 1940.

Bradley, Andrew Cecil (1851–1935). Critic, Professor of Poetry at Oxford, 1901–6, author of *Shakespearean Tragedy* (1904), essays on *Antony and Cleopatra*★ and 'The Rejection of Falstaff' published in *Oxford Lectures on Poetry* (1909), and a British Academy lecture on *Coriolanus*.★ Although he has been criticized for treating Shakespeare's characters too much as if they were real people, his writings are classics of criticism.

Bridges, Robert (1844–1930). English poet laureate, author of an essay 'On the Influence of the Audience', published in Vol. 10 (1907) of the Shakespeare Head Press edition of Shakespeare, which accuses Shakespeare of pandering to the supposed stupidity and 'moral bluntness' of his audiences.

Bridges-Adams, William (1889–1965). English director of the festival seasons at the Shakespeare Memorial Theatre,★ Stratford-upon-Avon, from 1919 to 1934.

Britten, Benjamin (1913–76). English composer whose settings for Shakespeare include the opera *A Midsummer Night's Dream* (1960).

Brook, Peter (born 1925). English theatre director. Most of his Shakespeare productions have been given initially at Stratford-upon-Avon; they include *Romeo and Juliet*★ and *Love's Labour's Lost*★ (1947), *Measure for Measure*★ and *The Winter's Tale*★ (both with Gielgud,★ 1951), *Titus Andronicus*★ (with Olivier★) and *Hamlet*★ (1955), *King Lear*★ (with Scofield,★ 1962), and *A Midsummer Night's Dream*★ (1970).

Peter Brook's production of *A Midsummer Night's Dream*, Stratford-upon-Avon, 1970: David Waller as Bottom, Sara Kestelman as Titania, and the Fairies

Brooke, Arthur (d. 1563). English author of the long poem, *The Tragical History of Romeus and Juliet* (1562), on which Shakespeare based *Romeo and Juliet*.★

Burbage, James (c. 1530–97). A joiner who became an actor with the Earl of Leicester's Men and, in 1576, built the Theatre★; father of Cuthbert (1566–1636, also a theatre owner) and Richard.★

Burbage, Richard (c. 1567–1619). Son of James; leading actor in Shakespeare's company throughout his career; known to have played, probably at their first performances, Richard III, Hamlet, King Lear, and Othello. An elegy ascribed to 'Jo Fletcher' includes the lines:

> He's gone, and with him what a world are dead,
> Which he revived, to be revivèd so.
> No more young Hamlet, old Hieronimo,
> King Lear, the grievèd Moor, and more beside,
> That lived in him, have now forever died . . .

He was a painter (see Rutland, Francis Manners); an anecdote about him and Shakespeare is told by John Manningham.★

C

Cambridge Shakespeare. An edition in nine volumes, prepared by W. G. Clark, J. Glover, and W. A. Wright, published from 1863 to 1866. It includes footnotes recording variant readings from all editions before 1700 and from selected later editions. It was reprinted in one volume as the Globe Shakespeare in 1864, without footnotes but with act, scene, and line numbering which became the standard form of reference. A second edition of the full-scale work, revised by Wright, appeared in 1891–3.

Cancel. A bibliographical term referring to a leaf which is substituted for one removed by the printers because of an error or other reason for change. The first quarto★ of *Troilus and Cressida*★ has a title page which exists in both cancelled and uncancelled states.

Capell, Edward (1713–81). English scholar whose ten-volume edition of Shakespeare appeared in 1768; it is based on a careful collation of early editions, and he is the first editor to have realized the full importance of the good quartos.★

Cardenio. A lost play acted by the King's Men★ in 1613 and entered in the Stationers' Register* in 1653 as 'The History of Cardenio, by Mr. Fletcher and Shakespeare'. If it was printed, no copies are known. In 1727 Lewis Theobald* prepared for the stage a play, *The Double Falsehood*, which he claimed to be by Shakespeare and is based on the story of Cardenio and Lucinda in Cervantes's *Don Quixote*, which had appeared in English in 1612. Theobald stated that he had 'revised' the play and 'adapted [it] to the stage' from an old manuscript. He did not include it in his edition of Shakespeare. The story may have some foundation in truth.

Casson, Sir Lewis (1875–1969). English actor and producer, husband of Sybil Thorndike,* much associated with Shakespeare.

Castelnuovo-Tedesco, Mario (1895–1968). The Italian-born composer wrote operas based on *All's Well that Ends Well* (1958) and *The Merchant of Venice* (1961), overtures to seven of Shakespeare's plays, and settings to all of Shakespeare's songs.

Cast-off copy. To 'cast-off' printer's copy is to estimate in advance how many sheets will be required to print a given manuscript, and to estimate the amount of copy needed to fill a single sheet. The practice meant that work could be shared out among a number of men working simultaneously. It was adopted for the Shakespeare First Folio.* Mistakes could result in the spreading out of a small amount of material over a large space, or in the crowding, even omission, of lines. In *Titus Andronicus*,* for instance, at the foot of a page, a single line of verse is printed as two lines (III.i.95), whereas on the crowded last page of *Much Ado About Nothing*,* verse is printed as prose, words are omitted, and abbreviated forms are used to save space.

Catherine and Petruchio. An adaptation by David Garrick* of *The Taming of the Shrew*,* which first appeared in 1754 and held the stage for over a hundred years.

Censorship. In Shakespeare's time, plays had to be licensed for performance and, from 1607, for printing by the Master of the Revels.* An ordinance of 1559 required the censoring of 'matters of religion or of the governance of the estate of the common weal'. The absence of the deposition scene from the first three quartos* of Shakespeare's *Richard II** is presumably the result of censorship. In 1606, an Act 'to restrain abuses of players', known as the Profanity Act, required that 'any person or persons' who 'in any stage play, interlude, show, may-game, or pageant, jestingly or profanely speak or use the holy name of God or of Jesus Christ, or of the Holy Ghost or of the Trinity' should 'forfeit for every such offence by him or them committed ten pounds'. This is reflected in a number of Shakespeare's plays. For example, in the Folio★ text (1623) of *The Merry Wives of Windsor*,★ 'heaven' several times replaces 'God' in the quarto of 1602.

Chamberlain's Men. See Lord Chamberlain's Men.

Chambers, Sir Edmund Kerchever (1866–1953). English scholar, author of *The Medieval Stage* (2 vols., 1903), *The Elizabethan Stage* (4 vols., 1923), *William Shakespeare: A Study of Facts and Problems* (2 vols., 1930), and other works. His *Shakespeare* is an authoritative compilation of reference material, partially superseded by S. Schoenbaum's *William Shakespeare: A Documentary Life* (1975, compact edition, 1977).

Chandos portrait of Shakespeare. An early seventeenth-century portrait believed to have belonged to William Davenant,★ then to Thomas Betterton★; later in the possession of the Dukes of Chandos; given by the Earl of Ellesmere to the newly founded National Portrait Gallery in 1856. It may be an authentic portrait of Shakespeare. Many copies of it exist, including one made by Sir Godfrey Kneller for Dryden.★ It was frequently engraved, and became the dominant source of eighteenth-century images of Shakespeare.

The Chandos portrait

Chapman, George (c. 1560–1634). English poet, playwright, translator of Homer; sometimes conjecturally identified as the rival poet★ of Shakespeare's Sonnets.★

Charlecote House. See Lucy, Sir Thomas.

Chesterfield portrait of Shakespeare. An early variation on the Chandos★ portrait, perhaps by the Dutch painter Pieter Borseler, who worked in England in the 1660s and 1670s. It now hangs in the Shakespeare Centre,★ Stratford-upon-Avon.

The Chesterfield portrait

Chettle, Henry (c. 1560–c. 1607). English printer and writer, author of *Kind-heart's Dream* (1592), in which he expresses regret that, in preparing *Greene's Groatsworth of Wit* for the press, he did not 'moderate the heat' of Greene's★ reference to Shakespeare: 'I am as sorry as if the original fault had been my fault, because myself have seen his demeanour no less civil than he excellent in the quality he professes. Besides, divers of worship have reported his uprightness of dealing, which argues his honesty, and his facetious grace in writing, which approves his art.' It has been suggested, but not proven, that Chettle had in fact written the *Groatsworth* himself in order to stir up controversy.

Children's Companies. See Boy actors.

Chorus. Shakespeare makes varied use of chorus figures. *Romeo and Juliet*★ has a prologue to Acts I and II; *2 Henry IV*★ opens with a speech by Rumour, 'painted full of tongues'; each act of *Henry V*★ is introduced by a Chorus, who speaks some of the finest poetry in the play; in *Pericles*,★ too, Chorus has an extended role, in the figure of the poet, John Gower★; the gap of sixteen years in the action of *The Winter's Tale*★ is bridged by Time, as Chorus; and both *Henry VIII*★ and *The Two Noble Kinsmen*★ have introductory prologues.

The authenticity of the prologue to Act II of *Romeo and Juliet* is sometimes doubted, and the prologue to *The Two Noble Kinsmen* is usually attributed to Fletcher.★ (See also Epilogues.)

Chronicle play. A play based closely on material from chronicle sources of English history. See Holinshed and Halle.

Chronology. The precise dating, and the order of composition, of Shakespeare's plays have been a major concern of scholarship for many years, and are not likely ever to be finally determined. The two most important sources of evidence are the list of plays given by Francis Meres★ in his book, *Palladis Tamia*, of 1598, and the entries of plays in the Stationers' Register.★ Other clues are given by the dates of sources,★ contemporary allusions within and outside the plays, and stylistic evidence. The standard treatment of the subject is in E. K. Chambers's★ *William Shakespeare: A Study of Facts and Problems* (2 vols., 1930), but this should not be regarded as final. Particular doubt attaches to the relative order of the plays written before 1598, and we have no real evidence as to when Shakespeare began to write.

Cibber, Colley (1671–1757). English actor and playwright. His adaptation of *Richard III*★ had long-lasting influence. He also adapted *King John*,★ as *Papal Tyranny in the Reign of King John* (1737).

Cibber, Theophilus (1703–58). Son of Colley; see *Henry VI, Part Three*.

Cinthio, Giovanni Battista Giraldi (1504–73). Italian writer best known for *Hecatommithi* (1565), a collection of prose tales. *Othello*★ is fairly closely based on one of the tales. No translation is known to have existed, so Shakespeare may have read it in Italian. Another tale was used by Whetstone★ for *Promos and Cassandra*, a source of *Measure for Measure*.★

Clarke, Mary Cowden. See *Girlhood of Shakespeare's Heroines, The*.

Clemen, Wolfgang H. (b. 1909). German scholar and critic; Professor at the University of Munich, 1946–74; author of *The Development of Shakespeare's Imagery* (1951; original, German version, 1936), a seminal work of criticism; *A Commentary on Shakespeare's 'Richard III'* (tr. 1968); *Shakespeare's Dramatic Art* (1974), etc.

Clown. In Shakespeare's time this term could be used for a rustic fellow, not necessarily a conscious entertainer, but it is often equated with 'fool'.★ Modern criticism distinguishes between the naturally comic characters, or clowns, such as Launce, Bottom, Dogberry, etc., and the professional fools, or jesters, such as Touchstone, Feste, and Lear's Fool.

Cobbler of Preston, The. See *The Taming of the Shrew.*

Coghill, Nevill (b. 1899). Merton Professor of English at Oxford, 1952–66; author of *Shakespeare's Professional Skills* (1964); influential as director of Shakespeare's plays with the Oxford University Dramatic Society★ between 1934 and 1966.

Coleridge, Samuel Taylor (1772–1834). English poet, and the most influential of the Romantic critics of Shakespeare. His most important extended essay is 'The specific symptoms of poetic power elucidated in a critical analysis of Shakespeare's *Venus and Adonis* and *The Rape of Lucrece*', published as Chapter XV of *Biographia Literaria* (1817). His main concern was to demonstrate the organic unity of Shakespeare's plays. Most of his criticism has to be assembled from letters, marginalia, lecture notes, reports of lectures, and so on. It is collected by T. M. Raysor (*Coleridge's Shakespearean Criticism*, 2 vols., 1930; revised edn., Everyman's Library, 1960), and by Terence Hawkes (*Coleridge's Writings on Shakespeare*, 1959, reprinted as *Coleridge on Shakespeare*, 1969).

Collation. The process of comparing different copies of the same edition of a work, in order to discover alterations made during printing, or of comparing copies of different editions in order to discover variations. For example, the collation of a quarto★ of a Shakespeare play against the text in the Folio★ invariably reveals many differences, for which various explanations may be offered.

The word also means a formula to describe the make-up of a printed book.

Collier, John Payne (1789–1883). English scholar who forged many documents, annotations, poems, etc., apparently relating to Shakespeare. Any manuscript or copy of a book which he is known to have handled must be viewed with suspicion.

Collins, Francis (d. 1617). Shakespeare left him twenty marks and asked him to oversee his will.★ As an attorney, he drew up the will, which may be in his handwriting.

Colman, George (the Elder, 1732–94). English playwright and theatre manager who in 1763 revised *The Fairies*, Garrick's★ adaptation of *A Midsummer Night's Dream*,★ as *A Fairy Tale*, for Drury Lane,★ and who revised Nahum Tate's★ version of *King Lear*★ for Covent Garden★ in 1768, restoring many of Shakespeare's lines.

Combe family. Neighbours of Shakespeare in Stratford-upon-Avon. William (1551–1610) sold land to Shakespeare in 1602. His nephew John (c. 1560–1614), a usurer, left Shakespeare £5 and had other business dealings with the family, as did his brother, Thomas (d. 1609). Shakespeare left his sword to Thomas's younger son, also called Thomas (1589–1657).

Comedies. The Folio★ distinguishes fourteen of Shakespeare's plays as comedies. To these may be added *Cymbeline*,★ called a tragedy in the Folio,★ and *Pericles*,★ not included in the Folio. The plays are sometimes grouped as Early Comedies;★ Romantic Comedies;★ Problem Comedies (or Problem Plays★), or Dark Comedies; and Last Plays,★ or Romances.★

Comedy of Errors, The. Shakespeare's comedy, his shortest play, was first printed in the First Folio★ (1623), probably from the author's manuscript. Its date is uncertain, but it appears to have been performed at the Christmas revels of Gray's Inn (see Gesta Grayorum) in 1594. It is based on *The Menaechmi*, by Plautus,★ with additional material from Plautus's *Amphitruo* and, for the framework story, from the traditional tale of Apollonius of Tyre,★ which Shakespeare also used in *Pericles*.★ *The Comedy of Errors* and *The Tempest*★ are his only two plays which conform to the principles of the unities of plot, time, and place advocated by neo-classical theoreticians.

It was played at Court at Christmas 1604. The first recorded revival was in adaptation, as a farce called *Every Body Mistaken* (Lincoln's Inn Fields,★ 1716). Numerous subsequent adaptations have included *See if You Like It, or 'Tis All a Mistake* (Covent Garden,★ 1734), *The Twins*, by Thomas Hull (1762), J. P. Kemble's★ revision of this (1808), and Frederick Reynolds's★ musical version (Covent Garden, 1819).

Samuel Phelps★ revived the original play at Sadler's Wells★ in 1855, but, perhaps because of its brevity and its relative lightness, it has continued to be padded out with extraneous material, as in Trevor Nunn's★ musical version (Stratford, 1976), and to be treated as a vehicle for directorial inventiveness. Perhaps the most distinguished production of the play itself was Clifford Williams's (Stratford, 1962, etc.).

Although this is Shakespeare's only play with the word 'comedy' in its title, it is often labelled a farce as an excuse for evading the basis of real human emotion which Shakespeare is careful to provide for the comic complications of the action. It is a brilliantly constructed comedy which far transcends its sources and reveals Shakespeare's early mastery of theatrical and verbal techniques.

Comical Gallant, The. See Dennis, John.

'Commodity' speech. The Bastard's speech, *King John*,★ II.i.561–98, in which he comments ironically on the King of France's withdrawal of support from Prince Arthur under the temptation of 'commodity' (i.e. self-interest):

The Antipholus twins: Charles Kay and Ian Richardson in Clifford Williams's production, Stratford-upon-Avon, 1965

> That smooth-fac'd gentleman, tickling commodity,
> Commodity, the bias of the world . . .

Condell, Henry (d. 1627). An actor and shareholder in the same company as Shakespeare; with John Heminges,★ he was responsible for the publication of the First Folio.★ Shakespeare left him 26s. 8d. to buy a ring.

Cons, Emma. See Old Vic Theatre.

'Contention' plays. The bad quartos★ of *2* and *3 Henry VI*,★ printed as *The First Part of the Contention betwixt the Two Famous Houses of York and Lancaster* . . . (1594) and *The True Tragedy of Richard, Duke of York, and the Death of Good King Henry the Sixth, with the Whole Contention between the Two Houses Lancaster and York* . . . (1595, actually an octavo★). They were both reprinted in 1600 and 1619.

Cooke, George Frederick (1756–1811). English actor, famous as Richard III, Falstaff,★ Shylock, Henry VIII, etc.

Corambis. Name for Polonius in the 'bad' quarto★ (1603) of *Hamlet*.★

Coriolanus. Shakespeare's Roman★ tragedy was first printed in the First Folio★ (1623), and is usually dated 1607–8, mainly on stylistic evidence. It is based principally on Plutarch's★ *Lives of the Noble*

Coriolanus

Grecians and Romans in Sir Thomas North's★ translation. No early performances are recorded.

Nahum Tate's★ adaptation, as *The Ingratitude of a Commonwealth, or the Fall of Caius Martius Coriolanus*, was played in 1681, with little success. John Dennis's★ adaptation, *The Invader of his Country or The Fatal Resentment* (1719), was no better received. Shakespeare's play had a few revivals around the same time. In 1749 appeared James Thomson's *Coriolanus*, an independent play which Thomas Sheridan drew on in a spectacular adaptation of Shakespeare at Covent Garden★ in 1754, in which year Shakespeare's play, abbreviated, was given at Drury Lane.★ In 1789

Laurence Olivier as Coriolanus (III.i), in Peter Hall's production, Stratford-upon-Avon, 1959

J. P. Kemble★ also amalgamated Shakespeare and Thomson, at Drury Lane. His sister, Sarah Siddons,★ and he had lasting success as Volumnia and Coriolanus. Edmund Kean's★ attempt to restore Shakespeare in 1820 failed, but W. C. Macready★ had more success on various occasions from 1819 to 1839. Samuel Phelps★ gave the play four times at Sadler's Wells★ (1848, 1850, and March and September 1860). Edwin Forrest★ gave successful performances in New York in the later nineteenth century.

Benson's★ London revival of 1901 had Geneviève Ward as a powerful Volumnia, a role which she continued to play over about twenty years. Irving's★ Lyceum★ production, also of 1901, with Ellen Terry★ as Volumnia, failed. The aged William Poel★ offered a rewritten, Napoleonic version at the Chelsea Palace in 1931. In 1933–4 the play was given at the Comédie Française in an adaptation aimed at overthrowing democratic government; riots resulted. Laurence Olivier★ played the hero with great success at the Old Vic in 1938, with Sybil Thorndike★ as his mother, and again at Stratford-upon-Avon in 1959, with Edith Evans.★ In 1972 the play was directed at Stratford-upon-Avon by Trevor Nunn★ as one of a cycle of Roman plays★ with Ian Hogg as Coriolanus, succeeded by Nicol Williamson at the Aldwych in 1973. Terry Hands's 1977 Stratford-upon-Avon production had Alan Howard in the title-role. In 1963, an unfinished adaptation by Bertholt Brecht was given by the Berliner Ensemble. Günter Grass's play *The Plebeians Rehearse the Uprising* (Aldwych, 1970) shows Brecht rehearsing his *Coriolan*, and John Osborne wrote a 're-working' of Shakespeare's play as *A Place Calling Itself Rome* (1973).

Coriolanus has a reputation of being one of Shakespeare's less popular plays, partly because of its unsympathetic hero. It offers a long and unremittingly serious study of the relationship between individual personality and politics, and is a remarkable illustration of Shakespeare's capacity to understand and portray an alien culture.

Covent Garden Theatre. The first theatre in Covent Garden, in central London, was opened in 1732. A patent★ theatre, it was the chief rival to Drury Lane.★ It was rebuilt in 1787, and burned down in 1808. A new building also burned down, in 1856, having come to be used mainly for opera some years before. The present opera house was built in 1858.

Covent Garden Theatre: an oil painting by Henry Andrews (d. 1868) showing Charles Kemble as Henry VIII, Charles Young as Wolsey, and Fanny Kemble as Queen Katherine in *Henry VIII*, II.iv (1831)

Cowley, Richard (d. 1619). An actor in Shakespeare's company. His name is printed as a speech-prefix for Verges in *Much Ado About Nothing*,★ suggesting that Shakespeare had him in mind as he wrote.

Crabtree, Shakespeare's. An anonymous letter-writer in the *British Magazine*, 1762, tells the story that the landlord of the White Lion in Stratford-upon-Avon took him to Bidford-on-Avon, some miles away, and showed him 'in the hedge a crabtree called "Shakespeare's Canopy", because under it our poet slept one night; for he, as well as Ben Jonson, loved a glass for the pleasure of society; and he, having heard much of the men of that village as deep drinkers and merry fellows, one day went over to Bidford to take a cup with them. He enquired of a shepherd for the Bidford drinkers, who replied they were absent, but the Bidford sippers were at home: "and, I suppose", continued the shopkeeper, "they will be sufficient for you"; and so indeed they were. He was forced to take up his lodging under that tree for some hours.' See also Villages, the Shakespeare.

Craig, (Edward) Gordon (1872–1968). English actor and influential stage designer, son of Ellen Terry,★ author of several books on the theatre.

Gordon Craig: a model made for a production of *Hamlet* at the Moscow Arts Theatre, 1911, showing the use of screens characteristic of his theatre designs

Craig, Hardin (1875–1968). American scholar, author of *The Enchanted Glass* (1936), a book concerned with ideas in the Elizabethan period, and editor of a complete edition of Shakespeare (1951).

34

Crane, Ralph (1550(60?)–c. 1632). A scribe who worked mainly for lawyers but also for theatre companies. Some of his scribal characteristics, particularly the 'massing' of entries (i.e. the listing at the head of a scene of all the characters who appear in it) are found in certain plays of the First Folio,★ which he may have helped to prepare for the press.

Crowne, John (c. 1640–1703). English playwright who made adaptations of the *Henry VI*★ plays.

Cushman, Charlotte (1816–76). American actress who became well known as Lady Macbeth, Volumnia, Gertrude, Emilia, and Queen Katherine. She also played male roles, such as Romeo (restoring Shakespeare's text in place of Garrick's★), Hamlet, and Cardinal Wolsey.

Cymbeline. Shakespeare's romance was first printed in the First Folio★ (1623), with the title '*The Tragedie of Cymbeline*'. The play is usually dated 1609–10, mainly on stylistic grounds. The historical part is based on Holinshed's★ *Chronicles*. The wager plot derives from Boccaccio's★ *Decameron*, per-

Charlotte Cushman as Romeo with her sister, Susan, as Juliet; an anonymous engraving

haps indirectly through a pamphlet of 1560, *Frederick of Jennen*. The Belarius story may come from an anonymous play, printed in 1589, *The Rare Triumphs of Love and Fortune*. The authenticity of the vision scene (V.iv) has often been questioned, but is nowadays generally defended.

Simon Forman,★ who died in 1611, recorded seeing a performance without saying when, and the play was presented at Court in 1634. An adaptation by Thomas D'Urfey, *The Injured Princess or The Fatal Wager*, was written about 1673 and held the stage. Shakespeare's play was revived in 1746. David Garrick★ put on a revised version in 1761, and frequently played Posthumus, a role later taken by John Philip Kemble,★ with Mrs Siddons★ as a notable Imogen.

The character of Imogen was idealized by nineteenth-century readers and audiences. Swinburne said that 'in Imogen we find half-glorified already the immortal godhead of womanhood', and Tennyson (who is said to have died with a copy of the play open on his lap) shared his opinion. The most distinguished representatives of the role after Mrs Siddons were Helena Faucit★ and Ellen Terry.★

Cymbeline, III.vii: Imogen comes from the cave. A drawing by Francis Hayman engraved by H. F. B. Gravelot for Thomas Hanmer's edition, 1743–4

Twentieth-century productions have not generally been very successful. Bernard Shaw,★ who wrote fascinating letters to Ellen Terry about her preparation to play Imogen, also wrote his own version of the last act, which has occasionally been performed. Peggy Ashcroft★ played Imogen at Stratford-upon-Avon in 1957, and Vanessa Redgrave in 1962. A considerably shortened version at Stratford-upon-Avon in 1974 had Susan Fleetwood as an affecting Imogen.

Cymbeline is a fantasy, highly elaborated in both style and action, experimental in its technique, which achieves some brilliant effects but remains puzzling in its design. The song 'Hark, hark the lark' has become independently famous in Schubert's★ setting, and the dirge ('Fear no more the heat of the sun') is also well known apart from the rest of the play.

D

Daly, Augustin (1838–99). American director whose London Theatre (Daly's) opened in 1893 with a performance of *The Taming of the Shrew*★ given by his company led by Ada Rehan,★ to whom much of his success was due. He took many liberties with the texts of Shakespeare, and Shaw★ wrote caustic reviews of his spectacular productions, but admired Ada Rehan, especially as Kate, in *The Taming of the Shrew*★, and Rosalind, in *As You Like It.*★

Daly's production of *A Midsummer Night's Dream* (New York, 1888; London, 1895): the arrival at Athens, from the 'panoramic illusion of the passage of Theseus's barge to Athens' inserted before the last act, and described by Shaw as 'more absurd than anything that occurs in the tragedy of Pyramus and Thisbe'

Daniel, Samuel (1562–1619). English poet and dramatist, author of a popular sonnet-cycle, *Delia* (1592), a closet drama, *The Tragedy of Cleopatra* (1593), *The Civil Wars* (first four books 1595, complete version, as *The Civil Wars between the Houses of Lancaster and York* 1609), etc. Shakespeare's *Richard II*★ seems to have been influenced by *The Civil Wars*, and Shakespeare may have drawn on Daniel's *Cleopatra* in *Antony and Cleopatra.*★

Dark Lady of the Sonnets. The woman referred to, and addressed, in many of Shakespeare's Sonnets★ 127–54, and possibly in others. Many attempts have been made to identify her with a real person, such as Mary Fitton,★ one of Queen Elizabeth's maids of honour. A. L. Rowse's suggestion of Emilia Lanier,★ put forward in his *Shakespeare the Man* (1973), is no more plausible than the rest.

Davenant, Sir William (1606–68). English poet, playwright, and theatre manager whose father was a vintner at the Crown Tavern, Oxford. He wrote many plays and masques, and was appointed Poet Laureate in 1638. A royalist, he took part in the Civil War.

At the Restoration, in 1660, he and Thomas Killigrew★ both received patents enabling them to form an acting company and to manage a theatre. Davenant established the Duke's Men,★ performing first in the old Salisbury Court Theatre and, from 1661, at the Lincoln's Inn Fields Theatre,★ under the patronage of the Duke of York. The right to perform Shakespeare's plays was divided between Davenant and Killigrew.

Davenant was largely responsible for carrying into the public theatres the staging techniques used at Court before the Restoration, greatly influencing the future development of the English theatre. He adapted some of Shakespeare's plays to the taste of his age: *Macbeth*★ (1663), *The Two Noble Kinsmen*★ (as *The Rivals*, 1644), *The Tempest*★ (with Dryden,★ as *The Enchanted Isle*, 1667), and *Measure for Measure*,★ into which he interpolated scenes from *Much Ado About Nothing*,★ to make *The Law Against Lovers* (1662). The first two were particularly influential.

According to John Aubrey,★ Davenant boasted that he was Shakespeare's natural son.

Davies, John, of Hereford (c. 1565–1618). English poet and writing-master. His *Scourge of Folly* (c. 1610) includes a cryptic epigram 'To our English Terence, Mr. Will Shakespeare':

> Some say, good Will, which I in sport do sing,
> Hadst thou not played some kingly parts in sport,
> Thou hadst been a companion for a king,
> And been a king among the meaner sort.
> Some others rail; but, rail as they think fit,
> Thou hast no railing, but a reigning wit;
> And honesty thou sow'st, which they do reap,
> So to increase their stock which they do keep.

Davies, Richard (d. 1708). An Oxford man who in 1688 inherited papers belonging to a Gloucestershire clergyman, William Fulman, including notes on Shakespeare. Davies added the first account of Shakespeare's deer-stealing from Sir Thomas Lucy,★ and the statement that Shakespeare 'died a papist'.

Death-mask. See Kesselstadt Death Mask.

Death of Shakespeare. See Ward, John.

Decameron. See Boccaccio, Giovanni.

Dedications. The only works bearing dedications by Shakespeare are *Venus and Adonis*★ (1593) and *The Rape of Lucrece*★ (1594), both addressed to Henry Wriothesley,★ 3rd Earl of Southampton. The Sonnets★ bear a publisher's dedication to Mr. W.H. The First Folio★ is dedicated by Heminges★ and Condell★ to William and Philip Herbert,★ Earls of Pembroke and Montgomery.

'Degree' speech. Ulysses's speech in *Troilus and Cressida*★ (I.iii.75–137), which expounds the common notion of a hierarchical principle binding the universe and preventing it from falling back into chaos. The idea is discussed in relation to Shakespeare by Hardin Craig★ in *The Enchanted Glass* (1936) and by E. M. W. Tillyard★ in *The Elizabethan World Picture* (1943).

Dench, Judi (b. 1934). English actress, whose Shakespeare roles have included Ophelia (Old Vic,★ 1957), Juliet (Old Vic, 1960), and (all with the Royal Shakespeare★ Company) Isabella and Titania (1962), Hermione and Perdita (doubled) and Viola (1969), Portia (1971), and Beatrice and Lady Macbeth (1976).

Dennis, John (1657–1734). English dramatist and critic, who adapted *The Merry Wives of Windsor*★ in 1702 as *The Comical Gallant*. His Epistle to this is the source of the legend that the play was written 'at the command' of Queen Elizabeth,★ 'and by her direction, and she was so eager to see it acted that she commanded it to be finished in fourteen days'.

Judi Dench as Viola in John Barton's production of *Twelfth Night* (Royal Shakespeare Company, 1969)

39

Two years later Dennis improved the story by saying that Elizabeth commanded Shakespeare to write the play 'in ten days' time'. Nicholas Rowe★ elaborated further: 'She was so well pleased with that admirable character of Falstaff, in the two Parts of *Henry the Fourth*, that she commanded him to continue it for one play more, and to show him in love.'

In 1710, Charles Gildon★ conflated the anecdotes: 'the Queen ... who had obliged him to write a play of Sir John Falstaff in love and which I am very well assured he performed in a fortnight.'

Dennis also adapted *Coriolanus*★ as *The Invader of his Country* (1719).

de Quincey, Thomas (1785–1859). English essayist who wrote the article on Shakespeare in the seventh edition (1838) of the *Encyclopaedia Britannica*, and a famous essay (1823) 'On the Knocking at the Gate in *Macbeth*'.

Dering manuscript. A manuscript version of *1* and *2 Henry IV*★ written about 1613 and revised about 1623, by Sir Edward Dering (1598–1644), probably for private performance. It is (except for *Sir Thomas More*★) the earliest known manuscript of a Shakespeare play.

de Witt, Johannes. A Dutchman who visited the Swan Theatre★ in 1596. His drawing of it, done from memory and surviving only in an early copy, is our only detailed picture of the interior of an Elizabethan theatre. He also described it, in Latin, saying that it held three thousand people.

Diana. A Spanish prose romance by Jorge de Montemayor (c. 1521–61), translated into French by Nicholas Colin (1578) and into English by Bartholomew Yonge (1592, not published till 1598). *The Two Gentlemen of Verona*★ is based, perhaps indirectly, on a section of it.

Dibdin, Charles (1745–1814). English composer of music for the Garrick★ Jubilee in 1769, including a cantata, 'Queen Mab, or the Fairies' Jubilee', and the songs 'The Warwickshire Lad' and 'Sweet Willy O'.

Dickens, Charles (1812–70). The great English novelist's works include many allusions to Shakespeare. He was deeply interested in the theatre, and himself performed Justice Shallow in *The Merry Wives of Windsor*.★ He sponsored an appeal to endow a curatorship of Shakespeare's Birthplace,★ and to this end organized amateur theatrical performances with casts including distinguished literary figures, but the project was unsuccessful.

Digges, Leonard (1588–1635). English poet and translator, stepson of Thomas Russell★; probably known to Shakespeare. He contributed a

A playbill for a performance given by Dickens and distinguished friends

poem in Shakespeare's memory to the First Folio,★ and another to the 1640 edition of Shakespeare's *Poems*,★ in which he praises Shakespeare above Jonson★ for his theatrical success:

> let but Falstaff come,
> Hal, Poins, the rest, you scarce shall have a room,
> All is so pestered. Let but Beatrice
> And Benedick be seen, lo, in a trice
> The Cockpit galleries, boxes, all are full
> To hear Malvolio, that cross-gartered gull.

Dorset Garden Theatre, London. Known as the second Duke's House because it was planned by William Davenant* for the Duke of York's Men,* this fine theatre, designed by Christopher Wren, opened in 1671 and was directed initially by Thomas Betterton* and Henry Harris. It was used for many Shakespeare performances, but declined after the King's* and The Duke's Men combined, in 1682, making Drury Lane* their headquarters. It is last heard of in 1706.

Double Falsehood, The. See *Cardenio*.

Dowden, Edward (1843–1913). Professor of English at Trinity College, Dublin, author of *Shakspere: A Critical Study of his Mind and Art* (1875), an attempt to trace the growth of Shakespeare's 'intellect and character from youth to full maturity'. His *Shakspere Primer* (1877) includes the well-known division of Shakespeare's career into periods labelled 'In the Workshop', 'In the World', 'Out of the Depths', and 'On the Heights'.

Dowland, John (1563–1626). Lutenist, and one of the greatest of English song composers. There is a complimentary allusion to him in a poem by Richard Barnfield which was included in *The Passionate Pilgrim*,* ascribed to Shakespeare.

Drayton, Michael (1563–1631). Warwickshire poet, author of the long topographical poem *Polyolbion* (1612, 1622), probably a friend of Shakespeare (see Ward, John). He was treated by Dr John Hall.* In a poem published in 1627 he wrote:

> And be it said of thee,
> Shakespeare, thou hadst as smooth a comic vein,
> Fitting the sock, and in thy natural brain,
> As strong conception, and as clear a rage,
> As anyone that trafficked with the stage.

Droeshout, Martin (1601–c. 1650). Engraver of the frontispiece portrait of Shakespeare in the First Folio.* Droeshout was only fifteen when Shakespeare died, and the engraving must be from an unknown drawing, but, except for the bust on the monument,* it is the only portrait with any convincing claim to authenticity (see Portraits of Shakespeare). It exists in three states, with only slight variants.

Drolls. Brief adaptations of comic scenes extracted from popular plays made during the closing of the theatres, 1642–1660. A collection, including some based on Shakespeare, was published in 1672 by Francis Kirkman as *The Wits, or Sport upon Sport*. Its frontispiece, possibly depicting an improvised stage, shows characters from several different plays.

Droeshout's engraving of Shakespeare, printed on the title page of the First Folio (1623)

Frontispiece of Kirkman's *The Wits* (1662)

Drummond, William, of Hawthornden. See Jonson, Ben.

Drury Lane Theatre. A theatre between Bridge Street and Drury Lane, London, was opened by Thomas Killigrew★ in 1663. It burned down in 1672, and was replaced by a new Theatre Royal designed by Christopher Wren, opened in 1674. David Garrick★ managed it from 1747 to 1776. Rebuilt and enlarged in 1794, it burned down in 1809. The present theatre opened in 1812, and continued as a patent★ theatre till 1843. It has seen many great Shakespeare performances.

Dryden, John (1631–1700). The great English poet, dramatist, and critic wrote the first important criticism of Shakespeare, mainly in the *Essay of Dramatic Poesy* (1688), the *Essay on the Dramatic Poetry of the Last Age* (1672), and the Preface to *Troilus and Cressida* (1679), an adaptation of Shakespeare's play. He collaborated with William Davenant★ in an adaptation of *The Tempest,★ The Enchanted Isle* (1667); and his tragedy *All for Love* (1677) derives partly from *Antony and Cleopatra.★*

Duffett, Thomas (fl. 1673–8). English playwright whose *Empress of Morocco* (c. 1673) has an Epilogue burlesquing the production of the witch scenes in William Davenant's★ adaptation of *Macbeth★* as performed at Dorset Garden Theatre, London,★ in 1673. His *The Mock-Tempest, or The Enchanted Castle* (1674) is a full-scale burlesque of the production, also at the Dorset Garden Theatre, of Shadwell's★ operatic version of *The Tempest.★*

Dugdale, Sir William (1605–86). English antiquary. His *Antiquities of Warwickshire* (1656) includes the first representation of Shakespeare's monument.★

Duke's Men. See Davenant, William.

Dvorak, Antonin (1841–1904). The Czech composer wrote a concert overture, 'Othello' (1891).

E

Early Comedies, Shakespeare's. Shakespeare's earliest comedies are *The Two Gentlemen of Verona,★ The Comedy of Errors,★ The Taming of the Shrew,★* and *Love's Labour's Lost.★ A Midsummer Night's Dream★* is also sometimes classed as an early comedy.

Education, Shakespeare's. See Grammar School, Stratford-upon-Avon.

Edward III. Anonymous history play, entered in the Stationers'

Register* in 1595, published 1596, first ascribed to Shakespeare in 1656. Kenneth Muir (*Shakespeare as Collaborator*, 1960), thinks that Shakespeare may have partially revised someone else's work.

Elgar, Sir Edward (1857–1934). English composer whose 'symphonic study', 'Falstaff' (1913), is one of the greatest orchestral works inspired by Shakespeare.

Elizabeth I, Queen of England (1533–1603). Though thrifty, she was a great patron of literature and drama. Her enjoyment of plays helped the theatre companies against the opposition of the City fathers. Shakespeare's company often performed for her at Court. Two phrases in *A Midsummer Night's Dream*,* 'a fair vestal, throned by the west', and 'the imperial Vot'ress' (II.i.158,163) are often interpreted as allusions to her. She appears on stage, as an infant, at the climax of *Henry VIII*,* written some ten years after her death.

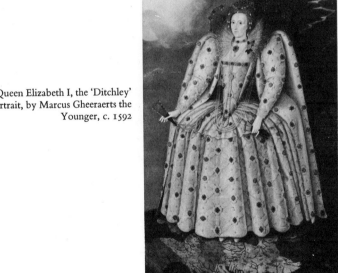

Queen Elizabeth I, the 'Ditchley' portrait, by Marcus Gheeraerts the Younger, c. 1592

She was sensitive about comparisons between herself and Richard II, and Shakespeare's company was in some trouble about performing *Richard II** on the eve of the Essex* rebellion, in 1601. For the legend that *The Merry Wives of Windsor** was written at her command, see Dennis, John.

Elizabethan Stage Society. See Poel, William.

Emerson, Ralph Waldo (1803–1882). The American transcendentalist had scruples about the morality of Shakespeare's plays, but his essay 'Shakspere; or, the Poet' in *Representative Men* (1850) also reveals great admiration for him.

Epilogue. Conventionally an apology and request for applause spoken at the end of a performance by a main character. Shakespeare's plays with epilogues are *A Midsummer Night's Dream,*★ *As You Like It,*★ *Henry V,*★ *Twelfth Night*★ (a song), *All's Well that Ends Well,*★ *Troilus and Cressida,*★ *Pericles,*★ *The Tempest,*★ *2 Henry IV,*★ and *Henry VIII.*★

Epitaph, Shakespeare's. Shakespeare's gravestone, in the chancel of Holy Trinity Church,★ Stratford-upon-Avon, close to his monument,★ bears simply the epitaph:

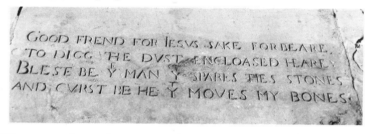

GOOD FREND FOR IESVS SAKE FORBEARE,
TO DIGG THE DVST ENCLOASED HARE.
BLESE BE Y MAN Y SPARES THES STONES
AND CVRST BE HE Y MOVES MY BONES.

The curse refers to the practice of removing bones to a charnel house in order to make more burial space available in the church. There is a late seventeenth-century tradition that Shakespeare wrote his own epitaph. The gravestone is, according to Halliwell-Phillipps,★ a mid-eighteenth-century replacement for the original one, which had decayed.

Essex, Robert Devereux, 2nd Earl of (1566–1601). A favourite of Queen Elizabeth.★ He married Sir Philip Sidney's★ widow in 1590, and was a naval commander and Earl Marshal. He commanded the English troops in Ireland in 1599, and this appears to be the occasion of one of Shakespeare's few explicitly topical allusions,★ in the Chorus to Act V of *Henry V:*★

> Were now the General of our gracious Empress –
> As in good time he may – from Ireland coming,
> Bringing rebellion broached on his sword,
> How many would the peaceful city quit
> To welcome him! (ll. 30–34)

The Earl of Essex, a portrait by an unknown artist, after Marcus Gheeraerts the Younger

Edith Evans as Cressida in the first recorded English production of *Troilus and Cressida*, directed by William Poel in 1912–13; photographed outside the Shakespeare Memorial Theatre, Stratford-upon-Avon, 1913

In fact the expedition failed, and Elizabeth banished Essex from Court. He plotted a rebellion, on the eve of which his followers arranged a special performance by the Lord Chamberlain's Men★ of *Richard II*,★ hoping that the play about the deposition of a monarch who was often associated with Elizabeth would arouse support. The rebellion failed, and Essex was executed on 25 February 1601. The previous evening, Shakespeare's company played before the Queen.

Evans, Dame Edith (1888–1976). English actress, especially distinguished in Restoration comedy, Shaw, and high comedy roles. She played Cressida in the first professional English stage performance of *Troilus and Cressida*,★ directed by William Poel★ for the Elizabethan Stage Society in 1912. Her other performances in Shakespeare included Helena in *A Midsummer Night's Dream*★ (Drury Lane,★ 1924), Juliet's Nurse (Old Vic,★ 1926, New York, 1934, New Theatre, 1935, Stratford-upon-Avon, 1961), Rosalind (Old Vic, 1936, New, 1937), Katherina (New, 1937), Cleopatra (Piccadilly, 1946), Queen Katherine (Old Vic, 1958), Countess of Rousillon and Volumnia (Stratford-upon-Avon, 1959),

47

and Queen Margaret (Stratford-upon-Avon, 1961).

Evans, Maurice (b. 1901). English actor, naturalized American in 1941. His Shakespeare roles include Richard II (Old Vic,★ 1934, New York, 1937, etc.), Hamlet (Old Vic, 1934, New York, 1938, etc.), Romeo (New York, 1935), etc.

Every Body Mistaken. See *Comedy of Errors, The.*

F

Facsimiles. The best available photographic facsimile of the First Folio★ is *The Norton Facsimile of the First Folio of Shakespeare* (1968), prepared by Charlton Hinman. It is made from the best-printed pages from thirty different copies.

A series of facsimiles of the quarto★ editions of Shakespeare's plays was initiated by the Shakespeare Association★ under the editorship of W. W. Greg★ in 1939, and was taken over by Oxford University Press with Charlton Hinman and Richard Proudfoot as later editors. It is not yet complete.

Fair copy. A final, corrected (but not necessarily entirely correct) manuscript such as a dramatist might submit to a theatre company, as distinct from the draft or 'foul papers'.★

Fairies, The. See *A Midsummer Night's Dream* and Smith, John Christopher.

Fairy Queen, The. An adaptation of *A Midsummer Night's Dream*★ presented by Thomas Betterton★ at Dorset Garden Theatre★ in 1692. It has a fine musical score by Henry Purcell,★ but the words set to music are not by Shakespeare.

Fairy Tale, A. See *A Midsummer Night's Dream.*

Falstaff. Shakespeare's greatest character appears in three plays: *1 Henry IV,*★ *2 Henry IV,*★ and *The Merry Wives of Windsor*★; his death is described in *Henry V,*★ II.iii. Shakespeare derived some hints for him from Sir John Oldcastle★ in the anonymous *Famous Victories of Henry V,*★ and there is evidence within the plays that Falstaff originally had that name and that it was changed because of objections by Oldcastle's descendants, the Lords Cobham.

Falstaff has always been a popular character, and has been a source of inspiration to creative artists. There are, for example, famous tributes by Dr Johnson,★ William Hazlitt,★ and J. B. Priestley; a novel by Robert Nye (1976); and many paintings and sculptures. He is the central figure of operas by Nicolai,★ Verdi,★ and Vaughan Williams,★ and the subject of a fine symphonic study (1913) by Edward Elgar.★ He is also the subject of much popular art: china figurines, inn-signs, and so on, showing the extent to which he has passed into folk mythology.

Herbert Beerbohm Tree as Falstaff in *Henry IV, Part One*, Haymarket Theatre, 1896

Famous Victories of Henry V, The. An anonymous chronicle play, registered 14 May 1594, surviving in an edition of 1598, perhaps written by 1588; a possible source for Shakespeare's *1* and *2 Henry IV*★ and *Henry V*.★

Faucit, Helena (1817–1898). English actress who played many Shakespeare roles. She married Sir Theodore Martin, and wrote *On Some of Shakespeare's Female Characters* (1885; enlarged edition, 1891), which includes some remarkable memories of her performances, especially as Hermione, with W. C. Macready.★

Fauré, Gabriel (1845–1924). The French composer wrote a suite, 'Shylock' (1889), for a French version of *The Merchant of Venice*★; it has two songs and four orchestral pieces.

Field, Richard (1561–1624). Printer of *Venus and Adonis*★ in 1593, *The Rape of Lucrece*★ in 1594, and *Love's Martyr*★ (which includes 'The Phoenix and the Turtle'★) in 1601. He was born in Stratford-upon-Avon, so may well have had some personal acquaintance with Shakespeare. In *Cymbeline*★ (IV.ii.378) the disguised Imogen calls herself by a version of his name – Richard Du Champ.

Films. Most of Shakespeare's plays have been filmed, in many different countries, and sometimes in radical adaptations. Information about some of the more important films is given under the names of the directors and actors concerned, including Grigori Kozintsev, Laurence Olivier, and Orson Welles.

There are studies by Robert Hamilton Ball, *Shakespeare on Silent Film* (1968), and Roger Manvell, *Shakespeare and the Film* (1971).

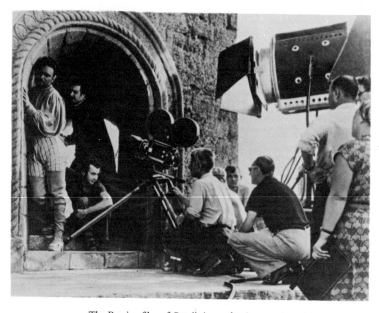

The Russian film of *Othello* in production, 1956

Finzi, Gerald (1901–56). The English composer wrote a fine Shakespearian song-cycle, 'Let us Garlands Bring' (1942).

Fitton, Mary (c. 1578–1647). One of Queen Elizabeth's ★maids of honour; she became the mistress of William Herbert,★ Earl of Pembroke, and has sometimes been thought to be the Dark Lady of the Sonnets.★

Fletcher, John (1579–1625). English playwright who collaborated with Shakespeare in, probably, *The Two Noble Kinsmen,*★ *Cardenio,*★ and *Henry VIII,*★ and succeeded him as principal dramatist to the

King's Men,★ collaborating with other dramatists including Francis Beaumont.★

Florio, John (1553?–1625). English-born translator, of Italian descent, educated at Oxford, tutor of Henry Wriothesley,★ 3rd Earl of Southampton. Shakespeare knew his translation of Montaigne,★ and may have known him.

Florizel and Perdita. An adaptation by David Garrick★ of *The Winter's Tale*,★ made in 1756, which uses mainly the last two acts of the play. It held the stage for the rest of the century, and influenced later versions, including J. P. Kemble's.★

Flower, Charles Edward (1830–92). Founder and benefactor of the Memorial Theatre★ at Stratford-upon-Avon, which opened in 1879. His descendants have continued to be actively concerned with the theatre's business.

Flower portrait of Shakespeare. The earliest painting of Shakespeare, resembling, and probably deriving from, the Droeshout★ engraving. It is painted over a fifteenth-century Italian Madonna and Child. Mrs Charles Flower gave it to the Picture Gallery of the Stratford-upon-Avon theatre, where it now hangs.

Folger, Henry Clay (1857–1930). American oil millionaire and book collector who founded the Folger Shakespeare Library in Washington, rich in materials for Shakespearian research, especially editions of the plays.

The 'Flower' Portrait

Folio, the First. A folio is a book made of sheets of paper folded only once, and thus of large size. The first collected edition of Shakespeare's plays is the First Folio, of 1623. It was put together by his colleagues, John Hemminges★ and Henry Condell,★ 'without ambition either of self-profit or fame, only to keep the memory of so worthy a friend and fellow alive as was our Shakespeare'.

The volume was printed and published by William and Isaac Jaggard,★ with Edward Blount as an additional publisher. It includes sixteen plays not previously printed, and two others (*3 Henry VI*★ and *The Taming of the Shrew*★) previously printed only in doubtful texts. It also provides superior texts of some of the previously printed plays. *Pericles*★ is omitted. Probably about 1,000 copies of the Folio were printed; between 230 and 240 survive. It sold originally for £1.

Hemminges and Condell supplied an Address 'To the great variety of readers', and dedicated the volume to William and Philip Herbert,★ Earls of Pembroke and Montgomery. The preliminary matter includes the commendatory poem by Ben Jonson.★

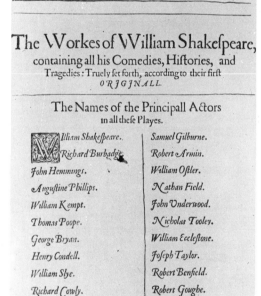

A page from the First Folio (1623), listing the principal members of Shakespeare's company, the Lord Chamberlain's Men

The principal studies of the First Folio are W. W. Greg's★ *The Shakespeare First Folio* (1955) and Charlton Hinman's *The Printing and Proof-reading of the First Folio of Shakespeare* (1963). Several facsimiles have been published. The most important for scholarly purposes is *The Norton Facsimile* (1968), prepared by Charlton Hinman and using the best pages from thirty different copies.

Folios, the Second, Third, and Fourth. The First Folio★ was re-printed in 1632, 1663, and 1685. These reprints have no independent authority. *Pericles*★ and six apocryphal plays, *The London Prodigal*★. *Thomas, Lord Cromwell,*★ *Sir John Oldcastle,*★ *The Puritan,*★ *A Yorkshire Tragedy,*★ and *Locrine,*★ were added in the second issue (1664) of the Third Folio.

Fool. A type-character, related to the domestic fools kept in royal and noble households. There were wise fools – intelligent men employed as entertainers – and natural fools – idiots kept for amusement. Shakespeare's fools are mostly 'wise'; they include Touchstone, Feste, Lavache, Thersites, and Lear's Fool. Useful studies are Enid Welsford's *The Fool* (1935), which covers the type from classical to modern times, and R. H. Goldsmith's *Wise Fools in Shakespeare* (1955). See also Clowns.

Michael Williams as the Fool and Donald Sinden as Lear in Trevor Nunn's production of *King Lear* (Stratford-upon-Avon, 1976), in which the character of the Fool was projected through the image of a broken-down old music-hall comedian.

Forbes-Robertson, Sir Johnston (1853–1937). English actor, best known as Romeo, Macbeth, Othello, and Hamlet, whom he played in an early silent film (1913). His stage production of *Hamlet*★ (1897) restored passages that had frequently been omitted, including much of the concluding episode, after Hamlet's death, and is the subject of a classic review by Bernard Shaw.★

Forgeries. See Ireland, William Henry and Collier, John Payne.

Forman, Simon (1552–1611). English doctor and astrologer; he kept a 'Bocke of Plaies', containing accounts of visits to performances of *Macbeth*★ on 20 April 1611, *The Winter's Tale*★ on 15 May 1611, *Cymbeline*★ (undated), and a play about Richard II which seems not to be Shakespeare's. He made partial summaries of the plots, and drew morals. His voluminous casebooks, written partly in code, include the references to Emilia Lanier★ on which A. L. Rowse based his theory that she was the Dark Lady of the Sonnets.★

Forrest, Edwin (1806–72). American tragedian, of heroic build, notably principally as Othello, Lear, and Coriolanus. He also frequently played Hamlet, Macbeth, and Richard III. He had a notorious feud with the English actor W. C. Macready★ which culminated in the Astor Place Riot of 1849, in New York, in which thirty-one people were killed.

Edwin Forrest in 1836;
an engraving by
H. Meyer from an
original by J. W. Childe

Fortune Theatre. Built in Finsbury, London, by the Admiral's Men★ in 1600. The contract survives, and gives the external and internal dimensions, with much other information, but unfortunately says that the stage was to be 'contrived and fashioned like unto the stage of the said playhouse called the Globe', for which we have no detailed information. The Fortune was square, the walls eighty feet long on the outside, fifty-five feet on the inside, and forty-two feet high. It was popular till it burned down in 1621.

Foul papers. A dramatist's original, manuscript drafts, as distinct from a fair copy.★

Fratricide Punished. As *Der Bestrafte Brudermord*, a German version of *Hamlet*★ surviving in a text of 1710, of uncertain relationship to the original play.

Freeman, Thomas (c. 1590–?). English poet. His collection of epigrams *Run and a Great Cast* (1614) includes a sonnet addressed to Shakespeare, with the lines:

> Virtue's or vice's theme to thee all one is;
> Who loves chaste life, there's *Lucrece* for a teacher;
> Who list read lust there's *Venus and Adonis*,
> True model of a most lascivious lecher.
>
> . . .
>
> Then let thine own works thine own worth upraise,
> And help t'adorn thee with deservèd bays.

Freud, Sigmund (1856–1939). The great Austrian psychiatrist used characters of Shakespeare as illustrations in his writings, and wrote papers on some of them. He did not believe in Shakespeare's authorship of the works.

Fuller, Thomas (1608–61). His *Worthies of England* (pub. 1662) includes early comment on Shakespeare, including a comparison between Shakespeare, the 'English man of War', and Jonson,★ the 'Spanish great galleon'.

Fulman, William. See Davies, Richard.

Furness, Horace Howard (1833–1912). An American scholar who founded the New Variorum edition of Shakespeare with his own edition of *Romeo and Juliet*★ in 1871 (see Variorum). The work was continued by his son, H. H. Furness Jr. (1865–1930). In 1936 the editorship was assumed by a committee of the Modern Language Association of America, and work continues. The volumes in the series are uneven in quality, and some are seriously out of date, but they gather together much information that is not easily found else-where.

Fuseli, Henry (Johann Heinrich Füssli; 1724–1825). Swiss painter who came to England in 1764. He did many paintings illustrative of Shake-speare's plays, some of actors, including David Garrick,★ and some highly imaginative. He contributed to Boydell's Shakespeare Gallery.★

David Garrick and Mrs Pritchard as Macbeth and Lady Macbeth after the murder of Duncan (II.ii), a watercolour drawing by Henry Fuseli of about 1766

G

Garrick, David (1717–79). English actor, playwright, and manager of Drury Lane★ Theatre from 1747 to 1776. Throughout his career he was specially associated with Shakespeare, and did much to revive his popularity. His greatest roles included Benedick, Richard III, Hamlet, Romeo, King Lear, and Macbeth.

He restored many passages of the plays that had been traditionally omitted, while making new adaptations such as *Catherine and Petruchio*★ (from *The Taming of the Shrew*★), *Florizel and Perdita*★ (from *The Winter's Tale*★), and his own version of *Hamlet*.★ He wrote a dying speech for Macbeth and a final duologue between Romeo and Juliet. In 1769 he organized a remarkable Jubilee at Stratford-upon-Avon, helping to establish the town as a centre of Shakespearian pilgrimage.

There are a biography by Carola Oman (1958), an important study by Kalman Burnim, *David Garrick, Director* (1961), and several accounts of the Jubilee including Johanne M. Stochholm's *Garrick's Folly* (1964).

Gascoigne, George (c. 1539–77). A versatile English writer; see *Supposes*.

Gastrell, the Rev. Francis. As a retired vicar, he bought the rebuilt New Place★ in 1753. He had the mulberry tree★ cut down in 1758, and demolished the house in the following year because of a disagreement over the rates.

Genest, the Rev. John (1764–1839). English author of *Some Account of the English Stage from the Restoration in 1660 to 1830* (10 vols., Bath, 1832), an important early work of reference.

Gentleman, Francis. See Bell, John.

George III, King of England (1738–1820). Fanny Burney recorded his opinion of Shakespeare in 1785. 'Was there ever such stuff as great part of Shakespeare? only one must not say so! But what think you? – What? Is there not sad stuff? What? – What? I know it's not to be said! but it's true. Only it's Shakespeare, and nobody dare abuse him.'

German, Sir Edward (1862–1936). The English composer wrote incidental music for several Shakespeare plays, including *Henry VIII*★ (Lyceum,★ 1892), from which the dances are often performed.

Gesta Grayorum. Records of Gray's Inn printed in 1688, which include an account of the Christmas revels of 1594 when 'A Comedy of Errors, like to Plautus his *Menaechmi*, was played by the players.' This was almost certainly Shakespeare's play performed by his company. The exceptional shortness of the play has led to the conjecture that it was written for this occasion.

Ghost characters. Characters such as the 'Innogen' described in the first stage direction in both the quarto★ and Folio★ texts of *Much Ado About Nothing*★ as Leonato's wife, mentioned again in the first stage direction of Act II, who says nothing, takes no part in the action, and is neither addressed nor mentioned by any other character.

Gielgud, Sir John (b. 1904). English actor and director, a member of the Terry family, especially renowned for his speaking of verse. His many Shakespeare roles have included Romeo (Old Vic,★ 1929, New, 1935), Hamlet (Old Vic, 1929, Queen's, 1930, New, 1934, St James, 1936, Lyceum,★ 1939, Haymarket,★ 1944), Richard II (Old Vic, 1929, Queen's, 1937, etc.), King Lear (Old Vic, 1940, Stratford-upon-Avon, 1950, etc.), Prospero (Old Vic, 1940, Stratford-upon-Avon, 1957, National Theatre Company,★ 1974), Angelo (Stratford-upon-Avon, 1950), Benedick (Stratford-upon-Avon, 1950, etc.), Leontes (Phoenix, 1951), Othello (Stratford-upon-Avon, 1961), and Julius Caesar (National Theatre, 1977). He has frequently appeared in a solo anthology of selections from Shakespeare, *Ages of Man*, and in films of Shakespeare's plays.

John Gielgud as Prospero, with Brian Bedford as Ariel, in Peter Brook's production of *The Tempest*, Stratford-upon-Avon, 1957

Gilbert, Sir William Schwenck (1836–1911). See *Rosencrantz and Guildenstern*.

Gildon, Charles (1665–1724). English critic and dramatist. He simplified Davenant's★ adaptation of *Measure for Measure,*★ *The Law Against Lovers*, as *Measure for Measure; or Beauty the Best Advocate* (1700), interpolating Purcell's★ opera *Dido and Aeneas* between the acts. In 1710 he issued a volume of Shakespeare's poems fraudulently made to look like a seventh volume of Rowe's★ edition of the *Works* (1709).

Girlhood of Shakespeare's Heroines, The. A book by Mary Cowden Clarke (1809–98), published in three volumes (1851–2), often maligned as an extreme instance of the critical tendency to treat

Shakespeare's characters as real people, but in fact an imaginative work of fiction based on these characters. With her distinguished husband, Charles (1787–1877), she edited the plays (1864–8).

Globe edition. See Cambridge Shakespeare.

Globe Playhouse Trust. Formed by the actor and director Sam Wanamaker in 1971 with the prime object of rebuilding a Globe playhouse on Bankside, London. The Trust also organizes Summer Schools and other activities.

Globe Theatre. Built on Bankside, London, by the Lord Chamberlain's Men★ in 1598 from timbers of the dismantled Theatre.★ Shakespeare was a principal shareholder, and here most, if not all, of his plays written from 1599 were performed. Thomas Platter★ saw a play about Julius Caesar, probably Shakespeare's, there on 21 September 1599. It was accidentally destroyed by fire on 29 June 1613 during a performance of *Henry VIII*★; various accounts survive, including one by Sir Henry Wotton.★

It was immediately rebuilt, and was open again by 30 June 1614. A contemporary, John Chamberlain, described the new theatre as 'the fairest that ever was in England'. It can be seen in Hollar's★ panorama. This building was, for safety, tiled instead of thatched. It was pulled down in 1644.

There are two valuable studies by C. Walter Hodges, *The Globe Restored* (2nd edition, enlarged, 1968), and *Shakespeare's Second Globe* (1973).

Golding, Arthur (1576?–1605?). Translator whose version of Ovid's★ *Metamorphoses* (1567) in fourteeners (fourteen-syllabled lines) was used by Shakespeare, particularly in *The Tempest*,★ where Prospero's speech 'Ye elves of hills, brooks, standing lakes, and groves' (V.i.33–57), in particular, is indebted to it.

Good quarto. An edition of a play in quarto★ printed from an authoritative manuscript, as distinct from a bad quarto.★

Gounod, Charles (1818–93). The French composer's opera *Roméo et Juliette*, based on Shakespeare's play, was written in 1867 and revised for the Paris Opera in 1888, with the addition of a ballet.

Gower, John (c. 1330–1408). English poet whose long poem *Confessio Amantis* includes a version of the tale of Apollonius of Tyre,★ which may have been a source for Shakespeare's use of this story in the framework plot of *The Comedy of Errors*★ and in *Pericles*,★ in which Gower is himself represented, and his style imitated, in the figure of the Chorus.★

Gower memorial. Lord Ronald Gower, a sculptor, made and presented to Stratford-upon-Avon a group of bronze statues commemorative of Shakespeare which stood on the lawn south of the theatre from 1888 to 1933, when it was moved to its present position by the canal basin.

A seated figure of Shakespeare mounted on a plinth is surrounded by figures of Henry V (as History), Falstaff★ (as Comedy), Lady Macbeth (as Tragedy), and Hamlet (as Philosophy). Behind each figure is a plinth with a mask bearing symbolic vegetation. Henry V has English roses and French lilies, Falstaff, hops and grapes, Hamlet, ivy and cypress, and Lady Macbeth, poppies and peonies.

The Gower Memorial

'Grafton' portrait of Shakespeare. A portrait of someone aged twenty-four in 1588. This, and a vague resemblance to the Droeshout★ engraving, are all that connect it with Shakespeare. It was found in an inn in County Durham, and had for long been in a farmhouse in the village of Grafton, Northants. It now hangs in the John Rylands Library, Manchester.

Grammar School, Stratford-upon-Avon. Known in Shakespeare's day as the King's New School; now the King Edward the Sixth School for Boys. The early schoolroom is next to the Guild Chapel,★ above the former Guildhall. It was a good school, with well-qualified masters. Names of sixteenth-century pupils do not survive. Shakespeare probably went to it from the age of seven or eight, leaving when he was about fifteen or less. His principal master would have been Thomas Jenkins.★

The curriculum was mainly classical. Works of literature including Roman comedies, Ovid's★ *Metamorphoses*, and other books known to have influenced Shakespeare were studied. Shakespeare portrays a Latin lesson in *The Merry Wives of Windsor*,★ IV. i.

Granville-Barker, Harley (1877–1946). English actor, director, play-

Shakespeare's schoolroom

Granville-Barker's production of *The Winter's Tale*, IV.iv, at the Savoy Theatre, London, 1912; Cathleen Nesbitt as Perdita

wright, and scholar. He played Richard II for William Poel,★ and his famous productions of *The Winter's Tale*,★ *Twelfth Night*★ (both 1912) and *A Midsummer Night's Dream*★ (1914) at the Savoy Theatre, London, carried over into the professional theatre some of Poel's ideals of a return to the basic principles of Elizabethan staging. He was more of a textual purist than Poel, though less austere in the visual aspects of his staging. After these productions he virtually retired from the theatre, but his *Prefaces* to many of Shakespeare's plays (1927 onwards) have done much to increase understanding of the principles of Shakespeare's stagecraft, in both theatre and study.

Greene, Robert (1558–92). English writer, educated at Cambridge. His romantic comedies *James IV* (c. 1590–91) and *Friar Bacon and Friar Bungay* (c. 1589–92) may have influenced Shakespeare, and his prose romance *Pandosto* (1588?) is the main source of *The Winter's Tale*.★ The earliest undoubted allusion to Shakespeare in London, and the earliest in print, is in *Greene's Groatsworth of Wit* (1592), written in the last months of his life and published posthumously: 'there is an upstart crow beautified with our feathers that, with his "tiger's heart wrapped in a player's hide", supposes he is as well able to bombast out a blank verse as the best of you; and, being an absolute *Johannes Factotum*, is in his own conceit the only Shake-scene in a country.'

Robert Greene's attack on Shakespeare (1592)

This parodies a line from *3 Henry VI*,★ I.iv.137: 'O tiger's heart wrapp'd in a woman's hide!' The passage, enigmatic like much Elizabethan literary satire, shows resentment that the actor Shakespeare is offering competition to established playwrights; it has also been interpreted as an accusation of plagiarism. The book was prepared for the press by Henry Chettle,★ who apologized for the Shakespeare reference in his *Kind-heart's Dream* (1592), though he has been suspected of writing the *Groatsworth* himself.

Greene, Thomas. See Welcombe enclosures.

Greet, Sir Ben (1857–1936). English actor-manager. In 1886 he gave the first of his many open-air performances of Shakespeare plays, forming a company with which he toured England and America for many years. In 1914 his company became the nucleus of the Shakespeare company at the Old Vic Theatre,★ London, where, with Lilian Baylis,★ he presented many of the plays from 1915 to 1918. After this he gave many performances of Shakespeare for schoolchildren in the London area, and also worked in both Paris and America.

Greg, Sir Walter Wilson (1875–1959). English bibliographer, Shakespeare scholar, author of *The Shakespeare First Folio* (1955), *The Editorial Problem in Shakespeare* (1942), and major bibliographical studies of the drama of Shakespeare's time.

Groundlings. Hamlet's word for the spectators who spent one penny to stand on the ground in the open space around the apron stages of Elizabethan theatres: 'O, it offends me to the soul to hear a robustious periwig-pated fellow tear a passion to tatters, to very rags, to split the ears of the groundlings, who, for the most part, are capable of nothing but inexplicable dumb shows and noise.' (III.ii.11–16.)

Guild Chapel, Stratford-upon-Avon. The fifteenth-century chapel of the Guild of the Holy Cross, dating from the thirteenth century and dissolved in 1547. It was across the road from New Place,★ and next to the Grammar School.★

Guthrie, Sir Tyrone (1900–71). English director of plays at Stratford-upon-Avon and the Old Vic,★ specially associated with the Festival Theatre at Stratford, Ontario★; he directed many Shakespeare plays in a brilliant and idiosyncratic fashion.

The Guild Chapel as it is now, showing part of the Grammar School to the right

(*Below*) The Duke of Florence reviews his troops: an episode inserted by Tyrone Guthrie before III.iii in his Stratford-upon-Avon production of *All's Well that Ends Well* (1959)

H

Hackett, James Henry (1800–71). American actor, distinguished as an imitator. He played Richard III in imitation of Edmund Kean,* and noted Kean's playing of the role in detail. He was the leading American Falstaff* of his time. In 1863 he published *Notes and Comments upon Certain Plays and Actors of Shakespeare.*

Hall, Elizabeth (1608–70). Shakespeare's grand-daughter, only child of John* and Susanna Hall, baptized 21 February 1608. Shakespeare bequeathed to her almost all of his plate. She married Thomas Nash* in 1626. When her father died, in 1635, they moved into New Place.*

James Hackett as Falstaff in *The Merry Wives of Windsor*; engraved from a daguerrotype

Her husband died in 1647. He left New Place and other property to his cousin, Edward Nash, but Elizabeth and her mother contested the will and retained the property.

She married John (later Sir John) Bernard on 5 June 1649, in which year her mother died. Some time afterwards the Bernards moved to his estate in Abington, Northamptonshire, where she died in 1670. She directed that New Place be offered for sale to Edward Nash, but he did not buy it, and it was sold in 1675 to Sir Edward Walker, passing from him into the Clopton family.

Elizabeth had no children. With her death, Shakespeare's direct family came to an end.

Hall, John (1575–1635). Entered Queens' College, Cambridge, 1589; B.A., 1593; M.A., 1597; studied medicine in France; settled in Stratford-upon-Avon about 1600. He married Shakespeare's elder daughter, Susanna,* on 5 June 1607. Their daughter, Elizabeth,* was baptized on 21 February 1608.

He was a distinguished physician, and had to pay £10 on refusing a knighthood from Charles I in 1626. One of his medical diaries, written in Latin, was translated and printed in 1657 as *Select Observa-*

tions on English Bodies. He was a devout Christian, with Puritan sympathies, presented Holy Trinity Church★ with a carved pulpit, and was a churchwarden.

The Halls are said to have lived in Hall's Croft★; they certainly lived in New Place★ after Shakespeare's death. John is buried in the chancel of Holy Trinity Church, close to his father-in-law.

Hall, Sir Peter (b. 1930). English Director of the Royal Shakespeare Theatre,★ 1960–68, and of the National Theatre★ (from 1973). He has directed many of Shakespeare's plays, including, at Stratford-upon-Avon, *Love's Labour's Lost*★ (1956), *Cymbeline*★ (1957), *Twelfth Night*★ (1958, etc.), *A Midsummer Night's Dream*★ and *Coriolanus*★ (1959), *The Two Gentlemen of Verona*★ and (with John Barton★) *Troilus and Cressida*★ (1960), *Romeo and Juliet*★ (1961), *The Wars of the Roses*★ (with John Barton, 1963), *Richard II*,★ *1* and *2 Henry IV*,★ *Henry V*★ (1964); *Hamlet*★ (1965), and *Macbeth*★ (1967), as well as *The Tempest*★ (National Theatre Company,★ 1973), and an uncut *Hamlet*★ (National Theatre,★ 1975).

Halle, Edward (c. 1498–1547). English author of *The Union of the*

Select Observations
ON
ENGLISH
BODIES:
OR,
Cures both Empericall and Historicall, performed upon very eminent Persons in desperate Diseases.

First, written in Latine by Mr. *John Hall* Physician, living at *Stratford* upon *Avon* in *Warwick-shire*, where he was very famous, as also in the Counties adjacent, as appeares by these Observations drawn out of severall hundreds of his, as choyseft.

Now put into English for common benefit by *James Cooke* Practitioner in *Physick* and *Chirurgery*.

London, Printed for *John Sherley*, at the Golden Pelican, in Little-Britain. 1657

The title page of the posthumously published translation into English of some of John Hall's medical notes

(*Right*) Peter Hall's production of *Twelfth Night*, Stratford-upon-Avon, 1958; Dorothy Tutin as Viola and Eric Porter as Malvolio in the revival of 1960

Two Noble and Illustre Families of Lancaster and York, completed and published after his death by Richard Grafton in 1548, much of which was incorporated by Holinshed★ into his *Chronicles*. Halle's influence on Shakespeare's early history plays is probably greater than Holinshed's.

Halliwell, later Halliwell-Phillipps, James Orchard (1820–89). English bibliophile and scholar, author of a *Life of William Shakespeare* (1848), *Outlines of the Life of Shakespeare* (1881, final revision 1887), editor of the *Works* (16 vols., 1853–65). He published many other writings concerned with Shakespeare.

Hall's Croft. A fine Tudor house in Old Town, Stratford-upon-Avon, maintained since 1949 as a showplace by the Shakespeare Birthplace Trust.★ Tradition says that Shakespeare's daughter, Susanna,★ and her husband John Hall★ lived there, but the present name of the house has not been traced before the mid-nineteenth century.

Hall's Croft

Hamlet. Shakespeare's tragedy was entered in the Stationers' Register★ on 26 July 1602 and first printed in 1603, advertised as having been 'divers times acted by his Highness' servants in the City of London, as also in the two Universities of Cambridge and Oxford, and elsewhere'.

This is a bad quarto,★ probably put together from the memories of a few of the actors. A good text appeared in 1604, said to be 'enlarged to almost as much again as it was, according to the true and perfect copy', and probably printed from Shakespeare's manuscript. The version in the Folio★ is somewhat shorter, and probably derives from a prompt★ copy. Most modern editors base their texts on the 1604 quarto, with some help from the Folio.

Hamlet was probably written about 1600–1, based on a lost play known as the *Ur-Hamlet*.★ Richard Burbage★ was almost certainly the first Hamlet, and many allusions to the play vouch for its contemporary success. Davenant★ revived it in 1661, omitting much but not radically revising it. Thomas Betterton,★ aged twenty-six, played Hamlet, and continued to do so for nearly fifty years. David Garrick★ took the role from 1742 till his retirement in 1776. In 1772 he played in his own radical revision, designed to rescue 'that noble play from all the rubbish of the fifth act'. It was not published, and the manuscript was lost until 1934.

J. P. Kemble★ was the most famous Hamlet of the Romantic period, succeeded by Edmund Kean★ and W. C. Macready.★ During the nineteenth century the play was much shortened, and the curtain generally went down on Hamlet's own last line. The Frenchman Charles Fechter gave his naturalistic interpretation in London in 1861. Henry Irving's★ production achieved an unparalleled run of 200 performances at the Lyceum★ in 1874–5. J. Forbes-Robertson★ restored Fortinbras to the text in 1897, and F. R. Benson★ gave a complete text at the Lyceum in 1900. Barry Jackson★ presented the play in modern dress in 1925. John Gielgud,★ perhaps the greatest Hamlet of the twentieth century, first played the part at the Old Vic★ in 1930. Laurence Olivier★ acted in Tyrone Guthrie's★ production in 1937; his film of a heavily abbreviated text appeared ten years later.

The most famous American Hamlets have been Edwin Booth,★ who played the role from 1853 to 1891, and John Barrymore (1922).

Only a few of the most distinguished performers of Hamlet are mentioned here. The role has appealed, not only to most actors, but also to many actresses. The play has been the world's most popular tragedy, above all because of its vivid portrayal of the struggles of its young and vulnerable hero to come to terms with his own destiny. It has provoked an enormous amount of critical comment and has inspired many other works of art, including operas by Ambroise Thomas★ (1868) and Humphrey Searle (1968), music by Tchaikovsky,★

Berlioz,* and Liszt,* a ballet by Robert Helpmann, and many paintings. Grigori Kozintsev's* film (1964) had music by Shostakovitch.*

Handwriting, Shakespeare's. The only certain examples are six
signatures,* along with the words 'by me' before the last signature on
the will. But three pages of *Sir Thomas More** may also be in Shakespeare's hand.

Hanmer, Sir Thomas (1677–1746). A country gentleman, Speaker of
the House of Commons in 1714, and the fourth editor of Shakespeare.
His six-volume edition (1743–4) is of little textual importance, but is
finely printed and handsomely illustrated by Hubert Gravelot and
Francis Hayman.*

Harsnett, Samuel (1561–1631). Scholar; Archbishop of York, 1629–
31; his *A Declaration of Egregious Popish Impostures* (1603) is echoed in
*King Lear** and *The Tempest.**

Hart, William. See Shakespeare, Joan.

Harvey, Gabriel (1545?–1630?). English scholar, barrister, and con-
troversialist. A note written, probably, between 1598 and 1601 in his
copy of an edition of Chaucer alludes to Shakespeare: 'The younger
sort takes much delight in Shakespeare's *Venus and Adonis*; but his
Lucrece, and his tragedy of *Hamlet, Prince of Denmark*, have it in them
to please the wiser sort . . . [Sir Edward Dyer's *Amaryllis*] and Sir
Walter Raleigh's *Cynthia*, how fine and sweet inventions! Excellent
matter of emulation for Spenser, Constable, France, Watson, Daniel,
Warner, Chapman, Silvester, Shakespeare, and the rest of our flower-
ing metricians . . .'

Hathaway, Anne (1555 or 1556–1623). Shakespeare's wife, whom he
married on 27 November 1582, when she was twenty-six, and by
whom he had three children. Her family were landowners in Shottery,
a village close to Stratford-upon-Avon, and lived in Hewland, an
Elizabethan farmhouse bought by Anne's brother, Bartholomew, in
1610, and known since the late eighteenth century as Anne Hathaway's
Cottage.*

We know scarcely anything about Shakespeare's relations with his
wife. Their children were Susanna* and the twins Hamnet* and
Judith.* Shakespeare appears to have left Anne in Stratford-upon-
Avon when he went to London, but he retained interests in his home
town (see e.g. New Place).

In his will, Shakespeare left Anne only his second-best bed. The
exact significance of this is uncertain. Sometimes it has been interpreted
as a derisory gesture. But it may be that, by local custom, Anne

would have automatically had a life interest in one-third of the estate, as well as the right to continue to live in New Place,★ and thus, presumably, to occupy the best bed if she wished.

She died on 6 August 1623 and is buried in Holy Trinity Church,★ next to her husband. The inscription on the gravestone states that when she died she was 'of the age of 67 years'; this is the only evidence as to her date of birth.

Haydn, Franz Josef (1732–1809). The great Austrian composer wrote a well-known setting for voice and piano of 'She never told her love', from *Twelfth Night*.★

Hayman, Francis (1708–86). An English artist and scene painter who designed most of the illustrations for Hanmer's★ edition of Shakespeare (1743–4).

A drawing by Francis Hayman illustrating *Romeo and Juliet*, V.iv, engraved by H. F. B. Gravelot for Thomas Hanmer's edition, 1743–4

Haymarket Theatre, London. Built in 1720, it came to be known as 'the Little Theatre in the Hay'. In 1766 it became a Theatre Royal, and plays could legally be presented there in the summer months. It was demolished in 1820, and the present building on the site opened in 1821. Herbert Beerbohm Tree★ presented elaborate Shakespeare productions there from 1887 to 1897, and John Gielgud★ acted there in *Hamlet*★ and other plays in 1944–5.

Hazlitt, William (1778–1830). English essayist and critic. His reviews of Edmund Kean's★ early London performances include some of his best writing on the theatre. His *The Characters of Shakespear's Plays* (1817), which incorporates passages from his reviews, has had great popularity.

Heavens. The cover or canopy over the stages in some Elizabethan theatres, sometimes supported by pillars. Descents could be made from it, and it may have been painted with a representation of the sky.

Hell-mouth. The trap-door in the stages of Elizabethan theatres, deriving its name from the use to which it was put in medieval miracle plays.

Heminges, John (d. 1630). An actor in Shakespeare's company through most, if not all, of Shakespeare's career, and in later years apparently their business manager. Shakespeare left him 26s. 8d. to buy a mourning ring. With Henry Condell,★ he was responsible for the preparation of the First Folio.★

Henry IV, Part One. The second play in Shakespeare's second historical tetralogy was entered in the Stationers' Register★ on 25 February 1598, and printed twice the same year. Only an eight-page fragment of the first edition survives. The quarto★ was reprinted in 1599, 1604, 1608, 1613, and 1622. The 1613 edition, from which the oaths had been removed (see Censorship), was reprinted in the First Folio.★ The play was probably written about 1596–7. It takes up the historical story from the end of *Richard II*,★ and is based on Holinshed's★ *Chronicles* with material from *The Famous Victories of Henry V*,★ in which Shakespeare found the name Sir John Oldcastle,★ which he originally gave to Falstaff.★ The change of name seems to be the result of protests from Oldcastle's descendant, William Brooke, Lord Cobham.

The play has always been successful, mainly because of Falstaff. It was popular before 1640 (see Digges, Leonard), and was adapted as a droll,★ *The Bouncing Knight*, while the theatres were closed. Thomas Betterton,★ who played Hotspur in 1682, appeared as Falstaff in 1700. James Quin★ took on the role in 1722 and played it till his retirement in 1751. J. P. Kemble★ revived the play carefully in 1803–4 at Covent Garden,★ playing Hotspur, a role which W. C. Macready★ took from

1815 to 1847. Samuel Phelps★ played both Hotspur and, later, Falstaff.

The play's popularity waned
during the Victorian period, but
Beerbohm Tree★ revived it at the
Haymarket★ in 1896, and later,
playing Falstaff. Robert Atkins★
was much associated with it, as producer and actor, playing Falstaff,
from the 1920s to the 1950s. Ralph
Richardson★ was a great Falstaff in
an Old Vic★ production at the New
Theatre in 1945, with Laurence
Olivier★ as Hotspur. Orson
Welles★ played the role on both
stage and film. The play has been
given at Stratford-upon-Avon as
part of a cycle of Elizabethan
histories in 1951, 1962, and 1975.

King Henry IV: an electrotype from
the alabaster effigy on his tomb in
Canterbury Cathedral, c. 1408–27

Henry IV, Part Two. The third play in Shakespeare's second historical tetralogy was entered in the Stationers' Register★ on 23 August
1600 and printed in the same year. III.i was accidentally omitted, but
included in a second issue. The play was not reprinted until 1623, in
the First Folio,★ which includes several additional passages. It was
probably written about 1597–8. Like Part One, it is based mainly on
Holinshed's★ *Chronicles*, with additional material from *The Famous
Victories of Henry V.*★

The play has been generally less popular than Part One; sometimes
the two plays have been conflated, usually with emphasis on Falstaff.★
James Quin★ played Falstaff in both Parts. Theophilus Cibber★ presented his adaptation, *The Humourists*, in 1754, playing Pistol. An
elaborate production at Covent Garden★ in 1761–2 celebrated the
coronation of George III,★ and there was another coronation production, for George IV, at Covent Garden in 1821. Samuel Phelps★
played both the King and Shallow at Sadler's Wells★ in 1853, and
later. F. R. Benson★ played Part Two more often than Part One.
Barry Jackson★ presented both parts in a single day at Birmingham
Repertory Theatre on 23 April 1922. The Old Vic★ production of
1945 had Ralph Richardson★ as a great Falstaff and Laurence Olivier★
as Shallow. It has been played at Stratford-upon-Avon as part of a

cycle of history plays in 1901, 1906, 1951, 1964, and 1975.

The relative unpopularity of Part Two may be the result of its having a less clearly defined structure than Part One, but it offers a more profound, if more pessimistic, portrayal of human beings under the pressures of war and time, and the Gloucestershire scenes are among Shakespeare's greatest dramatic achievements.

Henry V. The fourth play in Shakespeare's second historical tetralogy was entered in the Stationers' Register★ on 4 August 1600 and printed in a bad quarto★ the same year. This text was reissued in 1602 and (falsely dated 1608) in 1619 (see Jaggard, William). A good text appeared in the First Folio★ (1623). A line in the Chorus★ to Act V seems to refer to the Earl of Essex's★ campaign in Ireland, which would date its composition between 27 March and 28 September 1599. It is based mainly on Holinshed's★ *Chronicles*.

Aaron Hill's radical adaptation, omitting the comic scenes and adding romantic complications, was played at Drury Lane★ in 1723. Shakespeare's play seems to have been revived first at Goodman's Fields in 1735, and was played frequently in London after that. J. P. Kemble★ played the King with great success in his own revision from 1789 to 1811; W. C. Macready★ took over from 1819 to 1839. His

Ralph Richardson as Falstaff and Laurence Olivier as Justice Shallow in John Burrell's production of *Henry IV, Part Two*, for the Old Vic at the New Theatre, London, 1945

Henry V: Laurence Olivier in his film of the play, 1944

1839 version was pictorially spectacular, as was Charles Kean's★ production at the Princess's in 1859, in which his wife played the Chorus as Clio, the muse of history. He interpolated a pageant of Henry's entry into London after Agincourt. F. R. Benson★ and Lewis Waller were successful as Henry in the early twentieth century. The play has had special appeal in time of war. Laurence Olivier's★ popular film appeared in 1944. The play has been given at Stratford-upon-Avon as part of a cycle of history plays in 1901, 1906, 1951, 1975, and 1977.

Until comparatively recent times, *Henry V* was regarded as a great patriotic play. Modern criticism, perhaps defensively, has discerned ironic attitudes in Shakespeare's presentation of the hero.

Henry VI, Part One. The first play in Shakespeare's first historical tetralogy was first printed in the First Folio★ (1623). Its authorship has often been disputed, and George Peele,★ in particular, has been thought to have had a hand in it. Its date is uncertain; some scholars have thought that it may have been written later than Parts Two and Three. There is an apparent allusion to it in *Pierce Penniless*, by Thomas Nashe,★ published in 1592. It is firmly based on Holinshed's★ *Chronicles* and Halle's★ *Union of the Two Noble and Illustre Families of Lancaster and York*. One of the characters is Joan of Arc, portrayed here, as in Holinshed, as a loose-living witch. The patriotic tone of the play may well be related to the defeat of the Spanish Armada in 1588.

Alan Howard as Henry VI in Terry Hands's production of the three parts of *Henry VI*, Stratford-upon-Avon, 1977

This play may be the 'Harey the vj' listed by Henslowe★ as having been performed by Strange's Men at the Rose on 3 March 1592, and played thirteen times more that year and twice again the following January. Only one revival in the eighteenth century is recorded, at Covent Garden★ on 13 March 1738, and only one in the nineteenth, in 1899, at Stratford-upon-Avon, where F. R. Benson★ gave it again, along with the other two Parts, in 1906. Robert Atkins★ produced it at the Old Vic★ on 29 January 1923 only, with the first part of Part Two. It was given successfully as part of a complete cycle of the histories in California at the Pasadena Community Playhouse in 1935, and, directed by Douglas Seale, at the Birmingham Repertory Theatre and the Old Vic in 1953, as part of the trilogy. This production was repeated at the Old Vic in 1957. John Barton★ included much of the play in his text for Peter Hall's★ *The Wars of the Roses*★ at Stratford-upon-Avon in 1963, and it was included in the B.B.C. television series, *An Age of Kings*,★ in 1961. Terry Hands directed all three Parts in an important revival at Stratford-upon-Avon in 1977.

Henry VI, Part Two. The second play in Shakespeare's first historical tetralogy first appeared in a corrupt text in 1594 (see 'Contention' plays). It is usually dated 1590–91, and is freely based on Holinshed's★ *Chronicles* and Halle's★ *Union of the Two Noble and Illustre Families of Lancaster and York*. For its later history, see *Henry VI, Part Three*.

Henry VI, Part Three. The third play in Shakespeare's first historical tetralogy was first printed in a corrupt text in 1595 (see 'Contention' plays). It is alluded to in Robert Greene's★ *Groatsworth of Wit*, written by September 1592, and is usually dated shortly before this. It is based on Holinshed's★ *Chronicles*

The Death of Cardinal Beaufort (*Henry VI, Part Two*, III.iii), a painting by Sir Joshua Reynolds (1723–92) engraved by Caroline Watson

and Halle's★ *Union of the Two Noble and Illustre Families of Lancaster and York*, and is so closely related to Part Two that the plays were probably intended to be given consecutively.

John Crowne★ adapted the first three acts of Part Two as *Henry the*

Sixth, the First Part, and parts of both plays in *The Misery of Civil War,* both in 1680 (acted 1681). Ambrose Philips's *Humphrey, Duke of Gloucester,* given at Drury Lane★ in 1723, uses only about thirty lines of Part Two. Theophilus Cibber's★ *Historical Tragedy of the Civil Wars in the Reign of King Henry VI,* given once only at Drury Lane★ in the same year, draws on both Parts, as well as on Crowne and on *Henry V.*★ J. H. Merivale also drew on both Parts in his *Richard, Duke of York* in which Edmund Kean★ appeared at Drury Lane★ in 1817–18.

Shakespeare's Part Two was given at the Surrey Theatre, London, in 1864. F. R. Benson★ gave it at Stratford-upon-Avon in 1899, 1901, and 1909, and included all three Parts in a history cycle of seven plays in 1906. Robert Atkins★ reduced the three plays to two at the Old Vic★ in 1923. Douglas Seale directed all three at the Birmingham Repertory Theatre in 1951–3, and they were repeated with great success at the Old Vic in 1957. John Barton★ adapted them as two plays for Peter Hall's★ *The Wars of the Roses,*★ played at Stratford-upon-Avon and London

King Henry VI: an early sixteenth-century portrait, by an unknown artist

in 1963–4. The plays were included in the B.B.C. television series *An Age of Kings*★ in 1961, and Terry Hands directed them in an important revival at Stratford-upon-Avon in 1977.

Henry VIII. This play was first published in the First Folio★ (1623). It is generally, though not unanimously, believed that Shakespeare collaborated in its composition with John Fletcher.★ There is no external evidence about this. The Globe Theatre★ burned down during a performance (possibly the first) of *Henry VIII* on 29 June 1613. The event was described in a letter by Sir Henry Wotton,★ who refers to the play as *All is True.* The main source is Holinshed's★ *Chronicles,* supplemented by Halle's★ *Union of the Two Noble and Illustre Families of Lancaster and York.*

The second recorded performance was given at the second Globe Theatre on 29 July 1628, at the request of the then Duke of Buckingham, who left after the Buckingham of the play went to his execution.

Henry VIII: the trial of Queen Katherine (II.iv), a painting by George Henry Harlow (1787–1819) otherwise known as 'The Kemble Family'. It shows Mrs Siddons as the Queen, J. P. Kemble as Cardinal Wolsey, Stephen Kemble as Henry VIII, Charles Kemble as Cromwell, and Fanny Kemble as a page. Painted in 1817 after Mrs Siddons's retirement, it does not portray a specific production.

After the Restoration, Thomas Betterton★ played the King, giving the role up only in 1709, the year before he died. The play was frequently revived during the eighteenth century. A Drury Lane★ production of 1727 celebrated George II's coronation with an elaborate procession which was repeated for many years afterwards. John Philip Kemble★ revived the play at Drury Lane in 1788 with Sarah Siddons★ as Queen Katharine, a role in which she excelled and continued to appear till 1816. Kemble frequently played Wolsey as, later, did W. C. Macready,★ Samuel Phelps,★ and, in 1855, Charles Kean★ in his own spectacular production at the Princess's, with a real barge and an elaborate panoramic view of London. Henry Irving★ also played Wolsey, with Ellen Terry★ as Katharine, in 1892.

Nineteenth-century productions generally cut the play heavily, especially in the last two acts. Beerbohm Tree★ acted Wolsey in 1910. Since then, less emphasis has been placed on this character. Sybil Thorndike★ excelled as Katharine at the Empire in 1925. Tyrone Guthrie★ directed the play at Sadler's Wells★ in 1933, with Charles

Laughton as Henry, in 1949 at Stratford-upon-Avon, with Anthony Quayle★ as Henry, and in 1951 at the Old Vic,★ in honour of the coronation of Elizabeth II. Michael Benthall's★ Old Vic production in 1958 had John Gielgud★ as Wolsey and Edith Evans★ as Katharine. Trevor Nunn★ directed a Brecht-influenced production at Stratford-upon-Avon in 1969, with Donald Sinden as Henry and Peggy Ashcroft★ as Katharine.

Henry VIII is not one of Shakespeare's most popular plays, but its fine acting roles and opportunities for spectacle have kept it alive in the theatre.

Henslowe, Philip (d. 1616). English theatre manager, stepfather of Edward Alleyn's★ wife, associated especially with the Admiral's Men.★ His papers, including the *Diary* (really an account or memorandum book), are a uniquely valuable source of information about theatre practice in his time. They include detailed lists of performances and takings from 1592 to 1603, records of transactions with and for actors, playwrights, and the Master of the Revels,★ notes about costumes and properties, etc. They could only be more valuable if they related to Shakespeare's company. They have been edited by W. W. Greg★ (3 vols., 1904–8), and by R. A. Foakes and R. T. Rickert (1961).

Herbert, Philip, Earl of Montgomery, later 4th Earl of Pembroke (1584–1650). Dedicatee, with his brother, William,★ of the First Folio.★

Herbert, William, 3rd Earl of Pembroke (1580–1630). Dedicatee, with his brother, Philip,★ of the First Folio★; sometimes identified as the Mr. W.H. of the Sonnets.★

Heywood, Thomas (c. 1570–1641). English dramatist, poet, and prose-writer; see *The Passionate Pilgrim*.

Histories. The Folio★ distinguishes ten of Shakespeare's plays as Histories. These are the English history plays: *King John,★ Richard II,★ 1* and *2 Henry IV,★ Henry V,★ 1, 2,* and *3 Henry VI,★ Richard III,★* and *Henry VIII.★* The plays about Roman history are grouped with the Tragedies.★

Eight of Shakespeare's English history plays fall naturally into two groups. In *1, 2,* and *3 Henry VI* and *Richard III* he dramatizes a consecutive sequence of events, and in *Richard II, 1* and *2 Henry IV* and *Henry V,* which he wrote later, he does the same with an earlier historical period. Each group of four plays is often referred to as a tetralogy, though the degree to which Shakespeare thought of them as sequences is disputed.

Hogarth, William (1697–1764). The English artist's best-known illustration of Shakespeare is his fine oil-painting of David Garrick★ as Richard III (1745). There are also an early drawing, 'Falstaff Examining his Recruits' (c. 1728), and a painting of 'A Scene from *The Tempest*' (c. 1735).

Hogarth's painting of Garrick as Richard III awaking from his dream (V.iii)

Holinshed, Raphael (c. 1529–c. 1580). English chronicler whose publisher asked him to compile a history of the world. What he produced in 1577 was *The Chronicles of England, Scotland, and Ireland*. He wrote the history of England (borrowing extensively from Edward Halle★), and included a 'Description of England' by William Harrison, as well as material by other writers.

Shakespeare drew on Holinshed, probably in the greatly enlarged edition of 1587, for his history★ plays, and for *Macbeth*,★ *Cymbeline*,★ and *King Lear*.★ Richard Hosley has edited *Shakespeare's Holinshed* (1968).

Holland, Hugh (d. 1633). English poet; author of a commendatory poem in the First Folio.★

Hollar, Wenceslaus (1607–77). An engraver from Prague whose 'Long

View' of London from the Bankside was etched in Antwerp in 1647 and based on sketches made while he lived in London from about 1636 to 1642 or later. It is the most detailed panorama of early London, and includes a representation of the second Globe Theatre,* its name mistakenly reversed with that of the Bear-baiting house.

Part of Hollar's *Long View of London* (Amsterdam, 1647), showing the second Globe Theatre and the Beargarden, with their names interchanged

Holst, Gustav (1874–1934). The English composer wrote an opera, *At the Boar's Head* (1925), based on *1* and *2 Henry IV*,* and using much folk-music.

Holy Trinity Church. Parish church of Stratford-upon-Avon, dating mainly from the fourteenth century; the steeple is an eighteenth-century addition. In this fine church Shakespeare was baptized* and buried.

Humourists, The. See *Henry IV, Part Two*.

Hunsdon, Lord. See Lord Chamberlain's Men.

Huntington Library. Henry E. Huntington (1850–1927) endowed a library and art gallery at San Marino, California, as a public trust. The library is rich in Renais-

(*Right*) Holy Trinity Church (the spire is an eighteenth-century addition)

sance, including Shakespearian, research materials.

Hut. A room above the canopy⋆ in at least some Elizabethan theatres, in which stage hands could operate machinery for ascents and descents and create sound effects. Alongside it appears to have been a platform from which three trumpet calls were sounded to announce a performance, and a flag flew above it during a performance.

Hutt, William (b. 1920). Canadian actor and director who has been associated with the Stratford, Ontario⋆ Festival since its opening in 1953. Roles he has played there include Polonius (1957), Jaques (1959), Prospero (1962, 1976), Pandarus (1963), Richard II (1964), Brutus (1965), Enobarbus (1967), Duke Vincentio (1969, etc.). He has also directed for the company.

I

Illustrations of Shakespeare's plays. The only illustration of a Shakespeare play surviving from his own time is in the Longleat manuscript.⋆ Some information about the many later drawings and paintings inspired by the plays is given under the names of individual artists.

Image cluster. Certain images seem regularly to have led Shakespeare's mind along a train of associated ones. Walter Whiter,⋆ in his *Specimen of a Commentary on Shakespeare* (1794), showed that flattery suggested dogs, which suggested sweetmeats. The phenomenon was more fully discussed by E. A. Armstrong in his *Shakespeare's Imagination: A Study of the Psychology of Association and Inspiration* (1946), and is used by Kenneth Muir as evidence of authorship in his *Shakespeare as Collaborator* (1960).

Imagery. Both the verse and the prose in Shakespeare's plays contain images which can serve various purposes, and the imagery can also extend to visual and auditory effects.

The study of Shakespeare's imagery goes back to the late eighteenth century (see Whiter, Walter), but first became dominant in the 1930s, under the influence of the movement known as the New Criticism, and forming a reaction against study of the plays centred on character criticism.

Caroline Spurgeon's⋆ pioneering *Shakespeare's Imagery and What it Tells Us* (1935) identifies prominent image patterns in a number of the plays, and, less happily, extends the investigation to an attempt to define Shakespeare's personality and temperament through deductions from his imagery.

W. H. Clemen's★ *The Development of Shakespeare's Imagery* (1936, translated 1951) is a more truly critical study, revealing how recurrent imagery can convey meaning, and also showing how metaphor takes over from simile as a vehicle of imagery in Shakespeare's later plays.

Many other critics have used the study of imagery as an instrument in the critical examination of the plays, notably G. Wilson Knight.★

Induction. Part of a play which lies outside, but leads into, the main action. The most obvious example in Shakespeare is the opening episode of *The Taming of the Shrew.*★ The First Folio★ also gives this label to Rumour's speech which introduces *2 Henry IV.*★

Ingratitude of a Commonwealth, The. See *Coriolanus.*

Injured Princess, The, or The Fatal Wager. See *Cymbeline.*

Inner Stage. Many plays of Shakespeare's time call for an area at the back of the stage where characters may be revealed, from which a bed may be put forth (as in *Othello,*★ V.ii), or which could suggest at least the opening of a cave (as in *Cymbeline,*★ III.iii). Some historians have believed that there was an inner stage area at the back of the main acting area, and the term 'inner stage' (not found in Elizabethan times) was created to describe it. The general current belief is that while some theatres, at least, may have had a large door or a curtain at the back of the stage which could open to reveal an area where characters or properties could be revealed, this was no more than an extension of the main platform, on which all the main action would take place. An alternative theory suggests that one or more curtained booths were set against the back wall, and that they could open to reveal characters or properties.

Inns of Court. Four London law colleges: Gray's Inn, the Middle Temple,★ the Inner Temple, and Lincoln's Inn. The first two particularly were famous for their masques and revels. *The Comedy of Errors*★ was played at Gray's Inn in 1594, and *Twelfth Night*★ at the Middle Temple in 1602. It has been conjectured of more than one Shakespeare play that it was specifically written to be performed at an Inn of Court, but there is no external evidence.

Inn Yards. The rectangular yards of inns, surrounded by galleries or balconies, were sometimes used for theatrical performances during the sixteenth century. A stage could be set up against one wall, and some inns were taken over entirely for this purpose. A City of London regulation of 1576 referred to 'evil practices of incontinency in great inns having chambers and secret places adjoining to their open stages and galleries.' This may have encouraged James Burbage★ to build the Theatre★ in 1576, but performances continued to be given in inns from time to time.

International Shakespeare Association. An association founded after the World Shakespeare Congress★ in Vancouver in 1971, to further the development of Shakespeare interests and to advise on the planning of other World Shakespeare Congresses. A second one was held in April 1976, in Washington, D.C., under the auspices of the Association, along with the Shakespeare Association of America★ and the Folger Shakespeare Library.★

The headquarters of the International Shakespeare Association are at the Shakespeare Centre,★ Stratford-upon-Avon.

Invader of his Country, The. See Dennis, John, and *Coriolanus*.

Ireland, William Henry (1775–1835). A London lawyer's clerk who forged many documents purporting to relate to Shakespeare, including a letter to Anne Hathaway★ with a lock of her hair. He also wrote a Shakespeare play, *Vortigern*. The papers were published late in 1795 (dated 1796), deceiving many eminent persons, but in March 1796 Edmond Malone★ published an *Inquiry* demonstrating that they were inauthentic. A few days later, *Vortigern* was given its single performance, at Drury Lane.★ Later that year, Ireland published *An Authentic Account of the Shakespear Manuscripts*, admitting his responsibility.

Irving, Sir Henry (1838–1905). The greatest actor–manager of his time: his first major success was as Hamlet in a production of 1874. From 1878 to 1902 he owned and managed the Lyceum Theatre,★ London, appearing in many Shakespearian roles, including Richard III, Hamlet, Shylock, Othello, Iago, Romeo, Benedick, Macbeth, Wolsey, Lear, Iachimo, and

Sir Henry Irving as King Lear at the Lyceum Theatre, 1892; a drawing by Bernard Partridge from the souvenir programme

Coriolanus. His leading lady was Ellen Terry,★ and his productions were prepared with great care for visual effect. He was at his best in roles requiring the presentation of intellectuality, such as Hamlet and Iago. In 1895 he became the first actor to be knighted.

Irving, Washington (1783–1859). American writer whose *Sketch-Book* (1819–20) includes an account of a visit to Shakespeare's Birthplace.★

Italic hand. A style of handwriting beginning to come into use in Shakespeare's time; it eventually displaced the secretary hand,★ and is closer to modern handwriting.

J

Jackson, Sir Barry (1879–1961). Founder in 1913 of the Birmingham Repertory Theatre, where the many Shakespeare productions included influential modern-dress★ versions of *Cymbeline*★ (1923), *Hamlet*★ (1925–6), and *Macbeth*★ (1928). He directed the Shakespeare Memorial Theatre★ at Stratford-upon-Avon from 1945 to 1948.

Jaggard, William (1569–1623). Printer, with his son Isaac (1595–1627), of the First Folio★ (1623), and also (independently) of *The Passionate Pilgrim*★ (1599). In 1619, with Thomas Pavier, he issued a collection of ten Shakespearian and pseudo-Shakespearian plays. After they started to appear, the Lord Chamberlain ordered the Stationers' Company not to reprint any of the King's Men's★ plays without the actors' consent, and this is probably why some of the editions are falsely dated 1600.

James I, King of England (1566–1625). The only child of Mary Queen of Scots, he became James VI of Scotland in 1567 and in 1589 married Princess Anne of Denmark. He succeeded Queen Elizabeth I★ in March 1603, and gave his royal patent to Shakespeare's company, the Lord Chamberlain's Men,★ making them the King's Men. In 1604 Shakespeare was one

King James I: a portrait (1621) by Daniel Mytens

of nine members of the company to whom James gave four-and-a-half yards of red cloth for livery to walk in the Coronation procession.

Many of Shakespeare's plays were acted at Court during James's reign, and *Macbeth*★ seems especially relevant to James's interests. Attempts have been made to identify him and members of his family more or less closely with characters in a number of Shakespeare's other plays, but the evidence is speculative.

Janssen, Gheerart (fl. 1600–23). Son of a Dutch sculptor who emigrated from Amsterdam to London about 1567. The family had a workshop in Southwark, London, and Gheerart made Shakespeare's monument.★

Jenkins, Thomas. Schoolmaster of Stratford-upon-Avon Grammar School,★ 1575–9.

Jig. A satirical, song-and-dance entertainment customarily performed as an after-piece at certain theatres in Shakespeare's time. In 1612 the Middlesex justices of the peace made an order suppressing jigs because they provoked breaches of the peace. Very few examples survive.

Johnson, Charles. See *As You Like It*.

Johnson, Robert (c. 1583–1633). Lutenist and composer who wrote music for many of the King's Men's★ masques and plays. His only Shakespeare settings known to have survived are of 'Full Fathom Five' and 'Where the Bee Sucks', from *The Tempest*,★ and appear to have been written for a Court performance in 1612 or 1613 during the celebrations of Princess Elizabeth's marriage.

Johnson, Samuel (1709–84). The great English essayist, biographer, poet, editor, lexicographer, and conversationalist first published proposals for a new edition of Shakespeare in 1745, then again in 1756, but his edition, with its famous Preface, did not appear until 1765. His Shakespeare criticism is conveniently gathered together in W. K. Wimsatt's *Dr. Johnson on Shakespeare* (1969).

Jonson, Ben (1572–1637). Shakespeare's most distinguished contemporary playwright. There are some certain and some possible allusions to Shakespeare in a number of his plays. His *Conversations with William Drummond*, of 1618–19, include informal comments, such as 'That Shakespeare wanted art'. The First Folio★ includes his lines 'To the Reader', placed opposite the portrait of Shakespeare, and his famous verse eulogy 'To the Memory of my Beloved, the Author Master William Shakespeare, and what he hath left us', in which he refers to Shakespeare's 'small Latin and less Greek', but declares 'He was not of an age, but for all time!' In his 'Ode to Himself', written c. 1629, he alludes to the 'mouldy tale' of *Pericles*,★ and in notebooks, published as *Timber: or Discoveries Made upon Men and Matter*, wrote 'the players have often mentioned it as an honour to Shakespeare that in his writing, whatsoever he penned, he never blotted out line. My answer hath been, would he had blotted a thousand . . . I loved the man, and do honour his memory (on this side idolatry) as much as any. He was, indeed, honest, and of an open and free nature; had an excellent fancy, brave notions, and gentle expressions, wherein he flowed with that facility, that sometime it was necessary he

Ben Jonson: a portrait by an unknown artist after Abraham Blyenberch

should be stopped . . . But he redeemed his vices with his virtues. There was ever more in him to be praised than to be pardoned.' Shakespeare is known to have acted in Jonson's plays *Every Man in his Humour* (1598) and *Sejanus* (1603).

Jordan, Dorothea (1762–1816). Irish actress who became the mistress of the Duke of Clarence, later King William IV. She excelled in comedy, and her best Shakespeare performances were as Rosalind, Viola, and Imogen.

Jordan, John (1746–1809). A self-educated wheelwright, poet, and antiquarian, born at Tiddington, near Stratford-upon-Avon, who collected (and elaborated) anecdotes about Shakespeare (see Villages, the Shakespeare), and concerned himself with the Shakespeare properties. He appears to be responsible for the identification of Mary Arden's House,★ and assisted Edmond Malone★ with his investigations into the 'spiritual testament'★ of John Shakespeare.★

Jubilee. See Garrick, David.

Julius Caesar. Shakespeare's Roman tragedy, based fairly closely on the translation of Plutarch★ by Sir Thomas North,★ was first printed in the First Folio★ (1623), but there is an apparent reference to a performance of it at the Globe★ on 21 September 1599 in a notebook of Thomas Platter.★ It has been a popular play in the theatre. After the Restoration, it was played, with little alteration, by the King's Com-

The death of Caesar: Mark Dignam as Caesar, John Wood as Brutus, in Trevor Nunn's production, Stratford-upon-Avon, 1972

pany.★ Thomas Betterton★ played Brutus frequently from 1684 to 1709. An adaptation published in 1719 and acted at Drury Lane★ continued to influence performances for a century.

Though David Garrick★ did not put the play on while he was manager of Drury Lane, it was played regularly at Covent Garden★ until 1767, after which there were only eight more London performances until 1780, and then none until J. P. Kemble's★ revival at Covent Garden in 1812, with Kemble as Brutus. W. C. Macready★ played first Cassius then Brutus, and Samuel Phelps★ was a distinguished Brutus.

Performances by the Duke of Saxe-Meiningen's company at Drury Lane in 1881 were famous for the handling of the crowd scenes. Beerbohm Tree★ played Mark Antony in a spectacular production at Her Majesty's in 1898, many times revived. During the twentieth century, *Julius Caesar* has been played frequently at Stratford-upon-Avon and the Old Vic.★ A modern-dress version at the Embassy Theatre, London, in 1939 set it in Mussolini's Italy. John Gielgud★ was a powerful Cassius at Stratford-upon-Avon in 1950 and in Joseph Mankiewicz's film (1952), which also had James Mason as Brutus and Marlon Brando as Mark Antony. Gielgud also played Caesar at the National Theatre★ in 1977. In America in the later part of the nineteenth century Edwin Booth and Laurence Barrett frequently played together as Brutus and Cassius. Orson Welles* used modern dress in his successful New York production (1937), in which he played Brutus.

Julius Caesar is a powerful, male-dominated drama of the political life in which Shakespeare returns to a consideration of the functions and responsibilities of rulers and of the consequences of usurpation s··ch as had preoccupied him in the English history plays. Its demonstration of the uses and abuses of rhetoric is part of his constant concern with language. At the same time, the inward portrayal of Brutus looks forward to the even more profound examinations of men under stress that were to follow in the great tragedies.

K

Kean, Charles (1811–68). Son of Edmund, educated at Eton; married Ellen Tree. In 1850 he began to manage the Princess's Theatre, where for nine years he presented and acted in spectacular productions of Shakespeare's plays with great attention to accuracy of historical detail.

Thomas Grieve's design for Charles Kean's production of *The Winter's Tale*, IV.iv (described in the acting edition as 'the extravagant merriment of a Dionysia'), Princess's Theatre, London, 1856

Kean, Edmund (1787–1833). One of the greatest of English actors. His first triumph was as Shylock at Drury Lane★ in 1814, when William Hazlitt★ luckily happened to be present. His Shakespeare roles also included Hamlet, Richard III, Macbeth, Othello, and Lear. He lived recklessly, and in his later years became unreliable.

Keeling, William. Captain of *Dragon*, an East India Company ship which in 1607, along with *Hector* and *Consent*, journeyed to the East Indies. His journal tells of performances of Shakespeare's plays on the High Seas, off Sierra Leone: 5 September: 'I sent the interpreter, according to his desire, aboard the *Hector* where he broke fast, and after came aboard me, where we

Edmund Kean as Richard III: an engraving by C. Turner from a painting by J. J. Halls

gave the tragedy of *Hamlet*'; 30 September: 'Captain Hawkins [of the *Hector*] dined with me, where my companions acted *King Richard the Second*'; 31 March 1608: 'I invited Captain Hawkins to a fish dinner, and had *Hamlet* acted aboard me; which I permit to keep my people from idleness and unlawful games, or sleep.'

Kemble, Charles (1775–1854). English actor, brother of John Philip, who played a wide range of Shakespeare roles. He followed his brother as manager of Covent Garden★ where in 1823, with the help of J. R. Planché,★ he put on a production of *King John*★ which inaugurated the fashion for accuracy in historical detail.

Kemble, Frances (Fanny) Anne (1809–93). Charles's★ daughter, who at the age of nineteen had a great success at Covent Garden★ as Juliet to her father's Mercutio. She played Portia, Beatrice, Lady Macbeth, and other leading roles. In 1832 she went with her father to America where she married Pierce Butler, a plantation owner. She divorced him because of her aversion to slavery in 1848, and in later years gave many readings in England and America, as well as writing several books.

Kemble, John Philip (1757–1823). Brother of Sarah Siddons,★ manager of Drury Lane★ from 1788 to 1802, and of Covent Garden★ from 1803 till his retirement in 1817. He produced and acted in many of Shakespeare's plays, and was best in stately and declamatory roles. He was successful as Hamlet, King John, Macbeth, Othello, Brutus, and Coriolanus.

Kemp, Will. Actor with the Lord Chamberlain's Men★ from 1594 to 1599; listed as one of the 'principal actors' in the First Folio.★ Famous as a comedian; his name appears in the stage directions to the second quarto★ of *Romeo and Juliet*★ as Peter, and in the 1600 quarto of *Much Ado About Nothing*★ as Dogberry, suggesting that Shakespeare wrote these parts for him. In 1600, for a bet, he morris-

John Philip Kemble as Coriolanus, an oil painting (1798) by Sir Thomas Lawrence (1769–1830)

danced from London to Norwich, nearly one hundred miles, and wrote a book about it. There is no record of him after 1603.

Will Kemp: from the title page of *Kemp's Nine Days' Wonder, Performed in a Dance from London to Norwich*, published in 1600

Kesselstadt Death Mask. A death mask once in the possession of the Kesselstadt family, who lived in and near Cologne. The mask was found in a junk-shop at Mainz in 1849, and was said to resemble a picture dated 1637, traditionally supposed to represent Shakespeare lying in state, which also had belonged to the Kesselstadt family. Otherwise the mask has nothing to connect it with Shakespeare beyond the fact that it is dated 1616. The date is probably false: no other death masks of non-royal persons are known to have been made at that time.

Killigrew, Thomas (1612–83). Like Sir William Davenant,★ he was a dramatist and theatre manager who was active before the closing of the theatres, in 1642, and who was granted a patent in 1660 enabling him to form an acting company and to manage a theatre. Killigrew established the King's Men,★ playing for a short time in Vere Street, then, in 1663, in the Theatre Royal, Drury Lane.★ The right to perform Shakespeare's plays was divided between Killigrew and Davenant (see Patent Theatres).

King John. Shakespeare's play was first printed in the First Folio★ (1623), probably from his manuscript. It was mentioned by Francis Meres★ in 1598, and probably dates from a few years earlier. In structure, though not in language, it is closely based on an anonymous play, *The Troublesome Reign of John, King of England,*★ printed in 1591. Shakespeare greatly reduced the anti-Catholic bias of his source.

The first recorded production of *King John* was at Covent Garden★ in 1737. In the same year, Colley Cibber★ adapted it as *Papal Tyranny in the Reign of King John*, reverting to the anti-Catholic position of the source play. Cibber's version was performed at Covent Garden in 1745, when it was of topical interest because of Jacobite risings. David Garrick★ played Shakespeare's *King John* at Drury Lane★ five nights later. In 1800 Richard Valpy, headmaster of Reading School, prepared a version which incorporated some of Cibber's alterations, and this had a few performances at Covent Garden in 1803.

King John was popular in the nineteenth century. John Philip Kemble★ appeared frequently as the King from 1783 to 1817, often with Sarah Siddons★ as a great Constance. A production at Covent Garden in 1823 is important because Charles Kemble,★ who played the Bastard, commissioned J. R. Planché★ to design historically accurate costumes and settings. This inaugurated the trend in methods of staging Shakespeare which was rapidly to become dominant for the rest of the century. W. C. Macready★ mounted the play spectacularly in 1842. Samuel Phelps* staged it at Sadler's Wells* in 1844, and again at Drury Lane, with great success, in 1865. The archaeological style of production reached its peak with Charles Kean* at the Princess's Theatre in the 1850s; he gave *King John* in 1852 and 1858. Beerbohm Tree's* spectacular production at Her Majesty's in 1899 included an elaborate dumb-show of the signing of Magna Carta, an episode that Shakespeare failed to provide.

King John, IV.i: Hubert (portraying J. P. Kemble) and Arthur; an oil painting by George Henry Harlow (1787–1819)

King John's theatrical popularity has waned during the twentieth century, though there have been a number of productions in Stratford-upon-Avon, London, and elsewhere. The Old Vic* had Ralph Richardson* as the Bastard in 1931, Ernest Milton as the King and Sybil Thorndike* as Constance in 1941, and Richard Burton as the Bastard in 1953. Peter Brook* directed Paul Scofield* as the Bastard in Birmingham in 1945. At Stratford-upon-Avon, Robert Helpmann played the King in 1948, and Robert Harris in 1957, with Alec Clunes as the Bastard. There also, in 1974, John Barton* directed his very radical adaptation, omitting about 1200 lines of Shakespeare, and incorporating many lines from *The Troublesome Reign** and many more of Mr Barton's own composition.

The changing fortunes of the play are an interesting index to fluctuations in taste. So is the relative importance accorded to the King and the Bastard. Prince Arthur has often been played by a girl. Constance's lament over his absence (III.iv.93–105) – not over his death – has often been interpreted as a reflection of Shakespeare's grief for the death of his son, Hamnet,* in August 1596, but this requires a later date for the play's composition than is suggested by stylistic evidence.

King Lear. Shakespeare's tragedy was entered in the Stationers' Register* on 26 November 1607 'as it was played before the King's Majesty at Whitehall upon St. Stephen's Night at Christmas last by his Majesty's servants playing usually at the Globe on the Bankside.' It was printed in 1608 'for Nathaniel Butter . . . to be sold at his shop in Paul's Churchyard at the sign of the Pied Bull near St. Austin's Gate.' This text is known as the Pied Bull Quarto,* and is corrupt. It was reprinted, with corrections and additions, in 1619 (see Jaggard, William). The First Folio* text contains 100 lines not in Q1, which contains about 300 not in the Folio; it seems to have been based on a copy of Q1 (and, perhaps, Q2), corrected from a theatre copy.

The play's sources include an anonymous play, *The True Chronicle History of King Leir* (printed in 1605), Sidney's* *Arcadia** (for the Gloucester plot), and Samuel Harsnett's* *A Declaration of Egregious Popish Impostures*, published in 1604. It was probably written in late 1605 or early 1606.

A performance in Yorkshire in 1610 is recorded. In 1681, Nahum Tate's* adaptation was performed, with Thomas Betterton* as Lear, and published. Tate makes Edgar and Cordelia lovers, omits the Fool altogether, and gives the play a happy ending, with Lear, Kent, and

Lear and Cordelia: an early drawing by William Blake

Gloucester going into peaceful retirement. Tate's play kept Shakespeare's off the stage for a century and a half, though revisions by David Garrick* (1756) and George Colman* (1768) brought it closer to the original without restoring either the Fool or the tragic ending. Garrick was a great Lear. J. P. Kemble* played the part well from 1788, and Edmund Kean* was successful in 1820. In 1823 he acted in a version which restored the tragic ending, but it was not well received, and he soon reverted to Tate.

W. C. Macready* played Lear from 1834, restoring parts of Shakespeare, and in 1838 played in a text purged of Tate's rewritings, and including the Fool (played by a woman), though rearranged and abbreviated. Samuel Phelps* played Lear finely, in a much purer text and with a man as the Fool, at Sadler's Wells* in 1845 and later. Charles Kean's* version (1858) was, as usual, retrogressive. Henry Irving's* Lear at the Lyceum* (1892) cut much of the text and was not one of his most successful productions.

In the early years of the twentieth century, the play had comparatively few major productions. John Gielgud* played Lear in 1931, 1940 (co-directed by Harley Granville-Barker,* whose *Preface* (1927) had a great influence), and 1955. Donald Wolfit* was greatly admired in the role during the 1940s and '50s. Laurence Olivier* played Lear, with Alec Guinness as the Fool, at the New Theatre for the Old Vic* in 1946. Peter Brook's* Stratford-upon-Avon production of 1962, filmed in 1970, had Paul Scofield*as a fine Lear.

The first really distinguished American interpreter of the role was Edwin Forrest,* who played it over forty-five years from 1826. Edwin Booth* played first in Tate's adaptation, but gave impressive performances in the original play from 1870. Robert Mantell played Lear successfully from 1905, and Morris Carnovsky impressed at Stratford, Connecticut in 1963 and 1965. Grigori Kozintsev's* film version (1972) made a profound impression.

Reduced by Tate, and often regarded as unplayable, partly perhaps under the influence of Charles Lamb's* essay, 'On the Tragedies of Shakespeare Considered with Reference to their Fitness for Stage Representation' (1811), *King Lear*'s true stature has only been appreciated during the twentieth century, when, partly under the influence of Granville-Barker's *Preface*, it has come to be recognized as perhaps Shakespeare's most profound examination of the human condition.

King Leir, The True Chronicle History of. A play entered in the Stationers' Register* in 1594 and published anonymously in 1605; a source of *King Lear*.*

King's Men. See Lord Chamberlain's Men; also Killigrew, Thomas.

Kirkman, Francis. See Drolls.

Kiss Me, Kate. A musical by Cole Porter (1893–1964) based on *The Taming of the Shrew*.★

Kittredge, George Lyman (1860–1941). Harvard scholar, revered by his pupils, versatile in his interests, who edited the whole of Shakespeare (1936) and published *Sixteen Plays* (1946) with excellent annotation.

Knight, G. Wilson (b. 1897). Professor of English at the Universities of Toronto and Leeds, author of studies of seminal importance in the criticism of Shakespeare's plays, including *The Wheel of Fire* (1930, enlarged 1949), *The Imperial Theme* (1931), *The Shakespearian Tempest* (1932), *The Sovereign Flower* (1958), and *Shakespeare and Religion: Essays of Forty Years*, 1967.

Knight of the Burning Pestle, The. See Beaumont, Francis.

Komisarjevsky, Theodore (1882–1954). Russian theatre director who emigrated to England in 1919 and directed some of Shakespeare's plays in a modern, fantasticated style at Stratford-upon-Avon and elsewhere. His best-known Stratford-upon-Avon productions were a 'steel' *Macbeth*★ (1933), *King Lear*★ with Randle Ayrton (1936), and *The Comedy of Errors*★ (1938–9).

[Logan

A set designed by Komisarjevsky for his 'steel' *Macbeth*, Stratford-upon-Avon, 1933

Kozintsev, Grigori (1905–73). Russian film director, best known in the West for his book *Shakespeare: Time and Conscience* (1967), and for his films of *Hamlet* (1964) and *King Lear* (1971).

Kyd, Thomas (1558–94). Author of the popular and influential play *The Spanish Tragedy* (c. 1587); the *Ur-Hamlet*★ is sometimes attributed to him.

L

Lamb, Charles (1775–1834). Author with his sister, Mary, of the well-known *Tales from Shakespeare* (1807); his criticism includes the essay 'On the Tragedies of Shakespeare Considered with Reference to their Fitness for Stage Representation' (1811), arguing that the plays suffer in performance, a view which may be related to the conditions of performance in his time.

Lampe, John Frederick (c. 1703–51). German musician who wrote a new version of *The Comick Masque of Pyramus and Thisbe*, by Richard Leveridge,★ which was performed at Covent Garden★ in 1745.

Lanier, Emilia (c. 1569–1645). English-born daughter of a musician, Baptista Bassano; wife of a composer, Alphonso Lanier. According to an entry in the notebooks of Simon Forman★ in 1597, she had been the mistress of Lord Hunsdon (see Lord Chamberlain's Men). A. L. Rowse has claimed her as the Dark Lady of the Sonnets.★

Last Plays. A term given to *Pericles*,★ *Cymbeline*,★ *The Winter's Tale*,★ and *The Tempest*,★ sometimes extended to include *Henry VIII*★ and *The Two Noble Kinsmen*.★

Law Against Lovers, The. William Davenant's★ adaptation of *Measure for Measure*,★ which includes Beatrice and Benedick from *Much Ado About Nothing*,★ performed in 1662 and not known to have been revived, though it was itself adapted by Charles Gildon.★

Leopold Shakespeare. A popular one-volume edition published in 1877 with an introduction by F. J. Furnivall and the text prepared by the German scholar Nikolaus Delius, dedicated to Prince Leopold, Queen Victoria's youngest son.

Leveridge, Richard (c. 1670–1758). English singer and composer who probably wrote some of the once-popular incidental music for *Macbeth*★ attributed to Matthew Locke,★ and who also composed several settings of lyrics by Shakespeare, as well as a burlesque of Italian opera, *The Comick Masque of Pyramus and Thisbe*, based on *A Midsummer Night's Dream*★ and performed at Lincoln's Inn Fields★ in 1716.

Lichtenberg, Georg Christoph (1742–99). A German scientist and philosopher who made two visits to England, in 1770 and 1774–5. His published letters from England to his friends at home include some vivid accounts of visits to the theatre, and especially of performances by Garrick.★

Liebesverbot, Das. See Wagner, Richard.

Lincoln's Inn Fields Theatre, London. Originally Lisle's Tennis Court, built in 1656 and converted into a theatre by Sir William Davenant★ in 1661, for the Duke's Men.★ It was the first public theatre to have a proscenium arch and to use variable scenery. On 28 August 1661, Pepys★ saw *Hamlet*★ there, 'done with scenes very well, but above all Betterton did the prince's part beyond imagination.' Davenant died in 1668, but his widow, along with Henry Harris and Thomas Betterton,★ continued to manage the theatre until the Dorset Gardens Theatre★ opened in 1671. Lincoln's Inn Fields became a tennis-court again, except for its use as a theatre by Killigrew's★ company in 1672–4, until 1695, when Betterton returned there. The building ceased to be used as a theatre in 1732, but was not demolished till 1848.

Linley, Thomas, the younger (1756–78). English composer, friend of Mozart, who died at the age of twenty-two. His compositions include a fine 'Ode on the Fairies, Aeriel Beings, and Witches of Shakespeare', performed at Drury Lane★ in 1776, and incidental music for a production of *The Tempest*★ at Drury Lane in 1777.

Location of scenes. With very few exceptions, the early editions of Shakespeare's plays do not indicate the locality of the action. Later editions frequently added indications, often influenced by pictorial and representational methods of staging. The current editorial trend is to omit scene locations.

Locke, Matthew (c. 1630–77). English composer of music for productions of *Macbeth*★ in the late seventeenth century, though some of the music for this play traditionally ascribed to him is probably by Richard Leveridge★ (c. 1670–1758). Locke also wrote music for *The Tempest*★ (1674) and a setting of 'Orpheus with his lute', from *Henry VIII*★ (published in 1673).

Locrine. An anonymous tragedy, entered in the Stationers' Register★ in 1594, published in 1595 as 'newly set forth, overseen and corrected by W.S.', and attributed to Shakespeare in the seventeenth century (see Apocryphal plays).

Lodge, Thomas (c. 1557–1625). English author of *Rosalynde;*★ his

Wit's Misery (1596) refers to an *Ur-Hamlet*★: 'the vizard of the ghost which cried so miserably at the Theatre, like an oyster-wife, "Hamlet, revenge!"'

London Prodigal, The. An anonymous play published in 1605 as by Shakespeare and included in the second issue of the Third Folio,★ no longer ascribed to Shakespeare.

Longleat manuscript. A single leaf in the library of the Marquess of Bath at Longleat, signed by Henry Peacham (c. 1576–1643), a teacher and artist. Usually dated 1594 or 1595, it bears a transcript of forty lines from various parts of *Titus Andronicus*★ and a drawing roughly illustrating the first scene.

The drawing is of exceptional interest as the first illustration to a

The Longleat drawing of *Titus Andronicus*, showing a mixture of sixteenth-century and classical costumes

Shakespeare play. Whether it is based on performance, public or private, is not known. Aaron is shown as a negro; the major characters wear Roman costume, but the attendants are clearly Elizabethan. The manuscript is discussed by J. Dover Wilson* in *Shakespeare Survey 1* (1948).

Lopez, Roderigo. A Jewish physician to Queen Elizabeth,* hanged for conspiracy in a plot against her in 1594. Gratiano's statement that Shylock's 'currish spirit / Govern'd a wolf ... hang'd for human slaughter' (*Merchant of Venice*,* IV.i.133–4), is sometimes interpreted as an allusion to him.

Lord Chamberlain. A senior official of the royal household, immediately superior to the Master of the Revels,* in charge of all Court entertainments. See Lord Chamberlain's Men.

Lord Chamberlain's Men. A theatre company formed in 1594 under the patronage of Henry Carey, 1st Lord Hunsdon, Lord Chamberlain from 1585 till his death in 1596. Shakespeare may have been an original member; he was prominent within it by March 1595, and remained with it as shareholder and playwright for the rest of his career.

In its early years, the company performed mainly at the Theatre,* then at the Curtain. It was known as Hunsdon's Men between July 1596 and March 1597, when the second Lord Hunsdon was appointed Lord Chamberlain. By 1599 it occupied the Globe Theatre,* and for the next ten years was the leading London company, with unusually stable membership, and with Richard Burbage* as its principal actor.

In 1603, when James I* succeeded Elizabeth,* he gave the company a royal patent, and it became the King's Men. From 1603 to 1616 it played an average of twelve performances a year at Court. James supplied nine members, including Shakespeare, with four-and-a-half yards of red cloth each to make liveries to wear in his coronation procession.

In late 1608 the company bought the Blackfriars Theatre,* and probably started using it as their winter house in 1609. The Globe burned down in 1613, and was rebuilt the following year. The company continued to be successful till the closing of the theatres, in 1642.

Lords' Room. The gallery above the stage in some Elizabethan theatres, apparently used sometimes for spectators, sometimes as an acting area.

Lost Years, Shakespeare's. Nothing is known of Shakespeare between the birth of his twins in 1585 and Robert Greene's* reference to him in London in 1592. There are many legends such as John Aubrey's* report that he was 'a schoolmaster in the country', and there has been much speculation. Considering how much he had written by 1598, it seems likely that he began to write some years before 1592.

Love Betrayed. See *Twelfth Night*.

Love in a Forest. See *As You Like It*.

Lover's Complaint, A. A poem published in the first edition of Shakespeare's Sonnets★ (1609) and there stated to be his; its authenticity is doubted.

Love's Labour's Lost. Shakespeare's early comedy was first printed in quarto,★ in 1598, probably from his manuscript. It was reprinted in the First Folio,★ in 1623. The text includes several passages in both revised and unrevised form, but the revisions may have been made at the time of composition rather than later. Some editions print both forms, rather confusingly. The play's date is uncertain, but probably not later than 1594. No direct source is known, though the three Lords have the same names as commanders in the contemporary French civil wars, and there are other topical allusions, some of them no longer explicable. The play may have been written for a private audience, but it was performed in the public theatres. It appears to have been played at Court at Christmas 1597 and early in 1605.

An unperformed adaptation, *The Students*, was published in 1762, but the play was not revived till 1839, when Madame Vestris★ put it on at Covent Garden.★ Samuel Phelps★ gave it at Sadler's Wells★ in 1857, but only for nine performances.

Paul Scofield as Don Armado in Peter Brook's Stratford-upon-Avon production, 1946–7

Despite a number of revivals, and although Granville-Barker's★ *Preface* of 1930 had drawn attention to its theatrical qualities, the play had little success till Peter Brook★ directed it at Stratford-upon-Avon in 1946 and 1947. Hugh Hunt directed a successful production with the Old Vic★ Company in 1949, with Michael Redgrave★ as Berowne, and there have been subsequent revivals at Stratford-upon-Avon,

London, and elsewhere. The play's simplicity of setting makes it suitable for open-air performance, and it has often been given in the Open-Air Theatre, Regent's Park.*

Love's Labour's Lost is about artificiality of behaviour, and its language, too, is often full of artifice. This makes it difficult to read. But its design is eminently theatrical, and its disturbingly original final episodes can be profoundly moving in performance.

Love's Labour's Won. Listed by Francis Meres* among Shakespeare's plays, and also in a bookseller's list of 1603, discovered in 1953. It may be an alternative title for another play – perhaps *The Taming of the Shrew** (not otherwise listed by Meres), though the bookseller has 'taming of a shrew' in his list – or a lost play.

Love's Martyr. The volume of poems in which 'The Phoenix and the Turtle'* first appeared, in 1601; the title poem is by Robert Chester (c. 1566–1640).

Lucian (c. 120–180). Greek writer of satirical dialogues, one of which influenced *Timon of Athens.**

Lucy, Sir Thomas (1532–1600). Landowner of Charlecote, near Stratford-upon-Avon. Late seventeenth-century gossip first recorded by Richard Davies* said that Shakespeare was prosecuted for stealing deer from his grounds, wrote a satirical ballad in revenge, was prosecuted again, and had to leave Stratford-upon-Avon, later caricaturing Lucy in *The Merry Wives of Windsor,** I.i.

Lyceum Theatre. London theatre best known for the tenancy of Sir Henry Irving* from 1878 to 1902, during which he staged and, with Ellen Terry,* appeared in many Shakespeare productions.

Lyly, John (c. 1554–1606). English writer and dramatist; his prose romances *Euphues, or the Anatomy of Wit* (1579) and *Euphues and his England* (1580), written in a highly elaborate and artificial style, were fashionable and influential for over a decade. His comedies, written for Court performance by boys' companies, mostly between 1584 and 1590, developed prose as a dramatic instrument and influenced Shakespeare.

M

Macbeth. Shakespeare's tragedy was first printed in the First Folio* (1623), and is usually dated c. 1606. Freely based on Holinshed's* *Chronicles*, it is Shakespeare's shortest tragedy, and some scholars believe the surviving text to be an abbreviation prepared for a special performance, possibly at Court. The authenticity of the Hecate scenes (III.v, IV.i) has often been doubted. These include the first lines of two songs found also in Thomas Middleton's* play *The Witch*, and Middleton has been proposed as the author of the scenes, but the question is disputed. The passage describing Edward the Confessor's touching for the King's Evil (IV.iii) may be a compliment to King James I,* the patron of Shakespeare's company, who himself carried out this practice. James traced his ancestors back to Banquo and had a special interest in witchcraft, about which he wrote a book, *Demonology* (1597).

Apparent allusions to early performances appear in *The Puritan** (c. 1606), perhaps by Middleton, and in Beaumont's* *Knight of the Burning Pestle* (c. 1607); Simon Forman* saw *Macbeth* in 1611.

Macbeth was soon revived after the Restoration, usually, perhaps always, in an adaptation by William Davenant* which gives a balletic quality to the witches, who sing, dance, and fly; increases the importance of Lady Macduff (partly, no doubt, because actresses were now taking the female roles); modernizes the language and brings it into greater conformity with contemporary ideas of decorum; and adds explicit moralization. Thomas Betterton* and his wife excelled in the leading roles. The witches were normally played by men until well into the nineteenth century, and occasionally afterwards.

James Quin* played Macbeth frequently between 1717 and 1751. David Garrick's* revival in 1744 restored much of Shakespeare's play, but still omitted the Porter and the murder of Lady Macduff's children and retained the singing and dancing witches, as well as adding a new dying speech for Macbeth. Garrick and Mrs Pritchard* excelled as Macbeth and Lady Macbeth. Charles Macklin* introduced Scottish costume in 1773. J. P. Kemble* played Macbeth frequently from 1788 to 1817, often with Sarah Siddons* as the greatest of all Lady Macbeths. Edmund Kean* was a more dynamic Macbeth from 1814.

W. C. Macready* first played the role in 1820, improving on

Macbeth and Banquo with the witches (I.iii), a painting by Henry Fuseli for Boydell's Shakespeare Gallery, engraved by James Caldwall

Kemble's text, and Samuel Phelps,★ in his production of 1847, abandoned Davenant's revisions, which however were reintroduced by Charles Kean★ at the Princess's in a spectacular production of 1857. Henry Irving,★ who at the Lyceum★ in 1888 had Ellen Terry★ as Lady Macbeth, was not greatly admired as Macbeth, though he also produced the play in 1875 and 1895. Barry Jackson★ produced a modern-dress version in 1928. John Gielgud★ first played Macbeth in 1930, and Laurence Olivier★ in 1937, both at the Old Vic.★ Gielgud played it again in 1942, and Olivier, at Stratford-upon-Avon, in 1955.

Though it has a reputation in the theatre for bringing bad luck, *Macbeth* has been one of Shakespeare's most successful plays. It has been directed on film by, among others, Orson Welles★ (1949) and Roman Polanski★ (1971). There are operatic versions by Verdi★ (1847, revised 1865) and Bloch★ (1910).

McKellen, Ian. English actor; his Shakespeare roles include Richard II (Prospect Players, 1968–70), Hamlet (Prospect Players, 1971), Edgar (Actors' Company, 1973), and Romeo, Leontes, and Macbeth (Stratford-upon-Avon, 1976). See also *Sir Thomas More*.

Macklin, Charles (1699–1797). Irish actor and dramatist, best known for his interpretation of Shylock first seen in 1741, described as 'the Jew that Shakespeare drew', and played seriously instead of comically, as had been customary. He last played the role in 1789, when he was about ninety. In 1754 he gave the first series of public lectures on Shakespeare.

Macready, William Charles (1793–1873). English actor, manager of Covent Garden Theatre★ 1837–9, and of Drury Lane,★ 1841–3. He played most of the leading tragic roles, and helped in

Charles Macklin as Shylock, from Bell's edition of Shakespeare (engraved 1775)

the restoration of Shakespeare's text in place of the traditional adaptations. In 1838 he restored *King Lear*★ in place of Tate's★ version. He retired in 1851. His revealing personal diaries have been published, and there is a good biography by Alan S. Downer (*The Eminent Tragedian: William Charles Macready*, 1966).

Maddermarket Theatre. A sixteenth-century house in Norwich which Nugent Monck,★ under the influence of William Poel,★ converted into an Elizabethan-style theatre in 1921. All Shakespeare's plays have been performed there, by amateur companies.

Malone, Edmond (1741–1812). Irish scholar, a pioneer in the study

W. C. Macready as Macbeth: an engraving by T. Sherratt of a painting by H. Tracey

of the chronology of Shakespeare's plays, author of an important *History of the Stage* (1780), first editor of the Sonnets,★ editor of the *Works* (1790). When he died he was working on a revised edition, completed by James Boswell the younger, published in 1821 and known as the *Third Variorum* or *Boswell's Malone*. He exposed the forgeries of William Ireland.★

Manningham, John (d. 1622). An English lawyer and diarist. On 13 March 1602 he recorded an anecdote: 'Upon a time when Burbage played Richard III there was a citizen grew so far in liking with him that before she went from the play she appointed him to come that night unto her by the name of Richard the Third. Shakespeare, overhearing their conclusion, went before, was entertained, and at his game ere Burbage came. Then message being brought that Richard the Third was at the door, Shakespeare caused return to be made that William the Conqueror was before Richard the Third. Shakespeare's name William.'

On 2 Feb. 1602(?) Manningham saw *Twelfth Night*★ at the Middle Temple★: 'At our feast we had a play called *Twelfth Night, or What You Will*, much like *The Comedy of Errors*, or *Menaechmi* in Plautus, but most like and near to that in Italian called *Inganni*. A good practice in it to make the steward believe his lady widow was in love with him, by counterfeiting a letter as from his lady in general terms, telling him what she liked best in him, and prescribing his gesture in smiling, his apparel, etc., and then when he came to practise making him believe they took him to be mad.'

Manuscripts, Shakespeare's. No Shakespeare manuscripts are known except for the signatures★ and the three pages of *Sir Thomas More*★ believed to be in his hand.

Marina. See *Pericles*.

Marlowe, Christopher (1564–93). English poet and playwright, leading dramatist of the Admiral's Men.★ Born in the same year as Shakespeare, he seems to have developed earlier. His best plays are *Tamburlaine* (in two parts), *Dr. Faustus*, and *Edward II*. Their dating is uncertain, as is that of Shakespeare's early plays, so it is difficult to be sure which influenced the other. *Tamburlaine* (c. 1587), at least, probably predates any Shakespeare play.

Marlowe's narrative poem *Hero and Leander* is of the same kind as Shakespeare's *Venus and Adonis*.★ It is the only contemporary work from which Shakespeare quotes directly and consciously (as distinct from works which are used as sources). This is in *As You Like It*,★ when Phebe says:

> Dead shepherd, now I find thy saw of might:
> 'Who ever lov'd that lov'd not at first sight?' (III.v.80–81)

Marlowe Society. A Cambridge University dramatic society, founded in 1908. Under George Rylands,* and the auspices of the British Council, past and present members, many of whom have become leading actors, along with professional players, have recorded complete texts of all Shakespeare's works.

Marriage, Shakespeare's. On 27 November 1582, a special licence was issued by the Bishop of Worcester for the marriage of 'Willelmum Shaxpere et Annam Whateley de Temple Grafton.' On the following day Fulk Sandells and John Richardson, friends of the bride's family, entered into a bond of £40 exempting the Bishop and his officers from liability if the marriage of 'William Shagspere . . . and Anne Hathwey of Stratford', which was to take place 'with once asking of the bannes of matrimony', should prove invalid.

This procedure was normal. Banns were forbidden between 2 December and 13 January. Shakespeare's could have been read on 30 November, and he could have married at any time after that. Anne's pregnancy explains why he would not have wished to wait till the banns could have been asked three times.

The licence presents a problem in naming 'Annam Whateley de Temple Grafton.' We know from other evidence that Shakespeare's bride was Anne Hathaway.* Errors in names are not uncommon in the registers; and Anne Hathaway may have been living at Temple Grafton, which is three-and-a-half miles west of Shottery. It is not known where the marriage took place; there is a late-recorded tradition that it was at Luddington, a small village near Stratford-upon-Avon.

Martin, Frank (1890–1974). The Swiss composer wrote an opera, *Der Sturm* (1956), based on *The Tempest.**

Mary Arden's House. A fine, timber-framed farm-house in Wilmcote, three miles from Stratford-upon-Avon, said by John Jordan* to have belonged to Shakespeare's mother's family. It was acquired in 1930 by the Shakespeare Birthplace Trust,* and is maintained as a showplace.

Masque. A form of entertainment, in its early stages, during the fourteenth century, related to 'mumming': friends with masks, musicians, and torches would unexpectedly visit a house, dancing, sometimes presenting gifts, and inviting spectators to join in the dance. Later, spectacular elements were elaborated, resulting in courtly entertainments of great formality, with speeches and allegorical shows or 'devices'.

Mary Arden's House

The masque reached its height at James I's★ court in the work of Inigo Jones, who devised and designed them, and Ben Jonson,★ who wrote them. Only at this period did literary and dramatic elements become of real importance. Shakespeare did not write independent masques, but there are masques and masque-like entertainments in a number of his plays, including *Love's Labour's Lost,*★ *Romeo and Juliet,*★ *Much Ado About Nothing,*★ *Timon of Athens,*★ and *Henry VIII.*★ The less developed stages of the form usually suited his dramatic purposes better than the more highly developed, to which however Prospero's masque in *The Tempest*★ is closer.

Massed entries. See Crane, Ralph.

Master of the Revels. A Court official, under the Lord Chamberlain,★ with responsibility for the Court Revels, which traditionally lasted from All Saints' Day (1 November) to the beginning of Lent, with performances of masques and plays centring on the twelve days of Christmas. Plays performed in public theatres were often given at Court, and in the later sixteenth century the Master became the official licenser and censor of plays, at first for performance, and, from 1607, for printing.

Measure for Measure. Shakespeare's comedy, first printed in the First Folio★ (1623), was performed at Court on 26 December 1604, and is usually dated in that year. It is based on George Whetstone's★ two-part play *Promos and Cassandra* (1578). William Davenant's★ adaptation, *The Law Against Lovers*, in which Angelo repents and marries Isabella, and which introduces Benedick from *Much Ado About Nothing*,★ was performed at Lincoln's Inn Fields★ in 1662. Charles Gildon's★ *Measure for Measure, or Beauty the Best Advocate* was played during the 1699/1700 season at the same theatre, with Thomas Betterton★ as Angelo; it omitted most of the comedy and added Purcell's★ opera *Dido and Aeneas*. Shakespeare's play was performed at Drury Lane★ in 1738, when James Quin★ played the Duke, as he did in 1742, and later at

Covent Garden.★ Susannah Cibber was admired as Isabella, a role which Sarah Siddons★ first played at Bath in 1779. She often acted with her brother, John Philip Kemble,★ as the Duke. Samuel Phelps★ played the Duke in his revival at Sadler's Wells★ in 1846.

The play dwindled in popularity in the later part of the nineteenth century, and in the early years of this century there were objections to its performance on grounds of obscenity. William Poel★ produced it in London in 1893 and in Manchester and Stratford-upon-Avon in 1908. Tyrone Guthrie★ produced it several times, as at the Old Vic★ in 1933 with Charles Laughton as Angelo, Flora Robson as Isabella, and James Mason

Claudio and Isabella: a painting by W. Holman Hunt (1827–1910)

as Claudio. Mason played Angelo for Guthrie at Stratford, Ontario★ in 1954. Peter Brook's★ Stratford-upon-Avon production of 1950 had John Gielgud★ as a moving Angelo. Judi Dench★ was Isabella at Stratford-upon-Avon in 1962, and John Barton★ directed the play there in 1970.

Measure for Measure's critical reputation has fluctuated. Its profound examination of moral issues distinguishes it from most of Shakespeare's other comedies, and, along with *All's Well that Ends Well*★ and *Troilus and Cressida,*★ it is often set apart from them as a 'problem play'.★ The conflict between Isabella and Angelo has great theatrical power and the play rarely fails to excite and disturb audiences.

Mechanicals. (i.e. labouring men), term given to Bottom and his fellows in *A Midsummer Night's Dream.*★

Memorial Theatre, Stratford-upon-Avon. See Royal Shakespeare Theatre.

Menaechmi. See Plautus.

Mendelssohn, Felix (1809–47). German composer whose overture to *A Midsummer Night's Dream*★ was written in 1826, when he was seventeen. The remainder of his score, perhaps the finest sequence of incidental music ever written for a Shakespeare play, appeared in 1843.

Merchant of Venice, The. Shakespeare's comedy, entered on the Stationers' Register★ on 22 July 1598, was first printed in 1600 in an exceptionally good text. A reprint of 1619 was falsely dated 1600 (see Jaggard, William). The First Folio★ text (1623) was based on a corrected copy of the First Quarto.★ The main plot is based on a tale in a compilation by Ser Giovanni Fiorentino called *Il Pecorone.* Both the casket story and the pound-of-flesh story were well-known. Shakespeare may have been influenced by a lost play, *The Jew,* known from an allusion of 1579, and he must have known Marlowe's★ play *The Jew of Malta. The Merchant of Venice* is usually dated 1594–5, partly on the strength of a supposed allusion to the execution in June 1594 of Roderigo Lopez.★

Court performances on 10 and 12 February 1605 are recorded. An adaptation, *The Jew of Venice,* by George Granville, later Lord Lansdowne, was acted in 1701, with Thomas Betterton★ as Bassanio. Shylock was played for broad comedy. This adaptation was frequently revived. Shakespeare's play was restored at Drury Lane★ in 1741, with Charles Macklin★ as a serious Shylock. He continued to play the role for almost fifty years. The play became popular, often with musical interpolations. J. P. Kemble★ first played Shylock in 1784, and continued in it for twenty years, often with Sarah Siddons★ as Portia.

Edmund Kean★ made a triumphant London début as Shylock, acclaimed by William Hazlitt,★ at Drury Lane in 1814, wearing a black wig instead of the traditional red one. His son Charles★ put on a spectacular production at the Princess's in 1858. Ellen Terry★ had a great success as Portia in the Bancrofts' beautifully designed production at the Prince of Wales' Theatre in 1875. She continued in the role in Henry Irving's★ Lyceum★ production of 1879. Irving played Shylock, one of his greatest roles, with nobility and pathos. At this time, the fifth act was sometimes entirely omitted. Donald

'Shylock': a watercolour sketch by Sir David Wilkie (1785–1841)

Wolfit★ was a distinguished Shylock during the 1940s, and Laurence Olivier★ played the role in Jonathan Miller's★ National Theatre★ production in 1970.

Though the relative importance of the play's varied elements has often caused critical and theatrical problems, it has had great appeal for both its romantic and its dramatic qualities, and Shylock, for all the uncertainties about his interpretation, has been recognized as one of Shakespeare's great characters.

Meres, Francis. English author of a book called *Palladis Tamia: Wit's Treasury*, printed in 1598. Its chief importance lies in a list of plays by Shakespeare, which for some of them is the only objective evidence as to their date. The passage runs: 'As Plautus and Seneca are accounted the best for comedy and tragedy among the Latins, so Shakespeare among the English is the most excellent in both kinds for the stage; for comedy, witness his *Gentlemen of Verona*, his *Errors*, his *Love Labour's Lost*, his *Love Labour's Won*, his *Midsummer's Night Dream*, and his *Merchant of Venice*; for tragedy, his *Richard II*, *Richard III*, *Henry IV*, *King John*, *Titus Andronicus*, and his *Romeo and Juliet*.' The reference to *Love Labour's Won*★ creates a puzzle.

Meres makes other allusions to Shakespeare, some simply in lists of writers; the two most interesting are 'As the soul of Euphorbus was thought to live in Pythagoras, so the sweet witty soul of Ovid lives in mellifluous and honey-tongued Shakespeare, witness his *Venus and Adonis*, his *Lucrece*, his sugared sonnets among his private friends, etc.'; and 'As Epius Stolo said, that the Muses would speak with Plautus' tongue, if they would speak Latin, so I say that the Muses would speak with Shakespeare's fine-filed phrase if they would speak English.'

Francis Meres's praise of Shakespeare, 1598

Wits Common-Wealth. 282

among his priuate friends,&c.

As *Plautus* and *Seneca* are accounted the best for Comedy and Tragedy among the Latines: so *Shakespeare* among y͂ English is the most excellent in both kinds for the stage; for Comedy, witnes his *G͂etlem͂e of Verona,* his *Errors,* his *Loue labors lost,* his *Loue labours wonne,* his *Midsummers night dreame,* & his *Merchant of Venice*: for Tragedy his *Richard the 2. Richard the 3. Henry the 4. King Iohn, Titus Andronicus* and his *Romeo* and *Iuliet.*

As *Epius Stolo* said, that the Muses would speake with *Plautus* tongue, if they would speak Latin: so I say that the Muses would speak with *Shakespeares* fine filed phrase, if they would speake English.

As *Musæus,* who wrote the loue of *Hero* and *Leander,* had two excellent schollers, *Thamaras* & *Hercules*: so hath he in England two excellent Poets, imitators of him in the same argument and subiect, *Christopher Marlow,* and *George Chapman.*

As *Ouid* saith of his worke;

Iamiq; opus exegi, quod nec Iouis ira, nec ignis,
Nec poterit ferrum, nec edax abolere vetustas.

And as *Horace* saith of his; *Exegi monumentũ ære perennius; Regaliq; situ pyramidũ altius; Quod non imber edax; Non Aquilo impotens possit diruere; aut innumerabilis*

O o 2. *annorum*

III

Mermaid Tavern, The. In Bread Street, Cheapside, London. The story that Shakespeare joined in convivial meetings there with other poets may be no more than a romantic legend, but the host, William Johnson, was a trustee in Shakespeare's purchase of the Blackfriars Gatehouse.★

Merry Conceits of Bottom the Weaver, The. See *A Midsummer Night's Dream*.

Merry Wives of Windsor, The. Shakespeare's comedy was entered in the Stationers' Register★ on 18 January 1602 and published in that year in a bad quarto.★ A better text appeared in the First Folio★ (1623). A passage in Act V printed only in the Folio and alluding to the ceremony of the feast of the Knights of the Garter has obvious topical reference. It has been argued that the play was written for the Garter ceremony of 23 April 1597, when the patron of Shakespeare's company, Lord Hunsdon (see Lord Chamberlain's Men, and Mompelgard, Frederick, Count of) was installed, and later revised for public performance about 1601, and that the Folio text is that of the first performance, and the quarto based on that of the revision. The difficulty with the theory is that the play uses several characters who are also in one or more of Shakespeare's later history plays, that *2 Henry IV*★ and *Henry V*★ were probably not written by 23 April 1597, and that some critics feel it unlikely that Shakespeare transferred characters from the comedy to the history plays rather than the other way around. G. R. Hibbard, in the New Penguin edition, suggests that the play incorporates part of a short entertainment written for the 1597 ceremony.

A legend that the play was written rapidly because Queen Elizabeth★ expressed the desire to see Falstaff★ in love was first recorded by John Dennis.★ No definite source is known, though the plot uses traditional elements. The play contains proportionally more prose in relation to verse than any other by Shakespeare, and it is his only comedy to have what is essentially (in spite of Falstaff's historical origins) a contemporary English setting.

Court performances are recorded in 1604 and 1638. Pepys★ saw it three times between 1660 and 1667, with little pleasure. John Dennis's★ adaptation, *The Comical Gallant*, was played at Drury Lane★ in 1702, but the original play was reinstated within a few years, and was popular. James Quin★ (from 1720) and John Henderson (from 1777) were specially successful as Falstaff.

A musical adaptation by Frederick Reynolds,★ the music arranged by Henry Bishop,★ was played at Drury Lane in 1824, and some of the music was included in later revivals up to Charles Kean's★ production at the Princess's in 1851. Samuel Phelps★ was a good Falstaff in 1874. Beerbohm Tree★ played the role several times, in 1902 with Madge Kendal and Ellen Terry★ as Mistress Ford and Mistress Page.

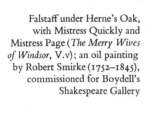

Falstaff under Herne's Oak, with Mistress Quickly and Mistress Page (*The Merry Wives of Windsor*, V.v); an oil painting by Robert Smirke (1752–1845), commissioned for Boydell's Shakespeare Gallery

There have been numerous London and Stratford-upon-Avon productions during the twentieth century. Ian Richardson★ was a brilliant Ford in Terry Hands's Stratford-upon-Avon production (1968, etc.), with Brewster Mason as a dignified Falstaff. The play has also been popular in America, with James Hackett★as a successful Falstaff for nearly forty years, from 1832 in London, 1838 in New York. He had a highly moral view of the character. Michael Langham's production at Stratford, Ontario★ in 1956 had Douglas Campbell as Falstaff.

The Merry Wives of Windsor has been much less successful with critics than with audiences, and its Falstaff has suffered by comparison with the presentation of the character in *1* and *2 Henry IV.*★ The play forms the basis of Nicolai's★ opera *The Merry Wives of Windsor*, Verdi's★ *Falstaff*, and Vaughan Williams's★ *Sir John in Love*. Artists have often illustrated it, especially the episodes of Falstaff and the buck-basket and Falstaff at Herne's Oak.

Middle Temple. An Inn of Court★ in which John Manningham★ saw a performance of *Twelfth Night*★ on 2 February 1602. Donald Wolfit★ and his company gave the play in a special performance there in 1951.

The hall of the Middle Temple, where John Manningham saw *Twelfth Night* in 1602

Middleton, Thomas (c. 1570–1627). English dramatist; of his many plays, the one most closely related to Shakespeare, in a way that is not fully understood, is *The Witch*, because it includes the full texts of two songs mentioned in the stage directions to the scenes in *Macbeth*★ involving Hecate, which are suspected of being interpolations by Middleton.

Midsummer Night's Dream, A. Shakespeare's comedy was first printed in quarto★ in 1600, probably from his manuscript. The edition was reprinted in 1619, falsely dated 1600 (see Jaggard, William). The play was printed again in the First Folio★ (1623), from a copy of the 1619 edition which seems to have been marked up from a theatre prompt★ book. It was mentioned by Francis Meres★ in 1598. It is usually dated about 1594 because the bad weather of that year is thought to be reflected in Titania's lines at II.i.81–117, though there is no certainty that these are topical. Nor is there any external evidence for the theory that the play was written for a wedding; the title-page of the first quarto says that it had been 'sundry times publicly acted'. Shakespeare invented the plot, with help from Chaucer's 'Knight's Tale', Ovid's★ *Metamorphoses*, and English folk lore.

Puck: a painting by Sir Joshua Reynolds engraved by Luigi Schiavonetti

The only recorded early performance was at Court in 1604, as *A Play of Robin Goodfellow*. A droll,★ *The Merry Conceits of Bottom the Weaver*, based on the mechanicals' scenes, was printed in 1661. In 1662, Pepys★ found *A Midsummer Night's Dream* 'the most insipid ridiculous play that ever I saw in my life'. Thomas Betterton★ produced a spectacular operatic adaptation, *The Fairy Queen*, with music by Henry Purcell,★ in 1692, and musical adaptations during the eighteenth century included Richard Leveridge's★ *Comic Masque of Pyramus and Thisbe* (1716), revised by J. F. Lampe★ as *Pyramus and Thisbe* in 1745. Charles Johnson grafted the play-within-the-play into *As You Like It*★ to make *Love in a Forest* (1723).

The clowns are omitted from the musical version, sometimes attributed to Garrick,★ *The Fairies* (1755), which introduced many additional songs (see Smith, J. C.); George Colman★ abbreviated it as *A Fairy Tale* (1763). J. P. Kemble★ gave Frederick Reynolds's★ musical version at Covent Garden★ in 1816, provoking an indignant attack by William Hazlitt,★ concluding that 'Poetry and the stage do not agree together'.

Mendelssohn's★ famous overture, written in 1826, was used by Madame Vestris★ in the first successful production of Shakespeare's original play since the Restoration, given at Covent Garden in 1840. Even better was Samuel Phelps's★ production at Sadler's Wells★ in 1853, in which he played Bottom. Charles Kean's,★ at the Princess's in 1856, sacrificed poetry and drama to spectacle. Beerbohm Tree's★ elaborate version of 1900, revived in 1911, at Her Majesty's, represents a culmination of the pictorial method of staging Shakespeare. Granville-Barker's★ controversial Savoy production of 1914 swept away the traditional accretions.

Subsequent productions have included heavily pictorial ones, such as Basil Dean's at Drury Lane★ in 1924, Max Reinhardt's★ in 1927, etc., and Tyrone Guthrie's★ at the Old Vic★ in 1937, and more austere ones such as Harcourt Williams's at the Old Vic in 1929 and 1931 and Peter Brook's★ revolutionary Stratford-upon-Avon one of 1970. The play has frequently been performed in the open air, especially at Regent's Park,★ and has been filmed, notably by Max Reinhardt (1935), turned into a ballet by Frederick Ashton (*The Dream*, 1964), and made into an opera by Benjamin Britten★ (1960). During the twentieth century it has been one of Shakespeare's most popular plays, even though directors have rarely achieved an ideal balance of its varied elements.

Miller, Jonathan (b. 1934). English director; his Shakespeare productions include *King Lear*★ (Nottingham, 1969), *The Merchant of Venice*★ (with Laurence Olivier,★ National,★ 1970), *The Tempest*★ (Mermaid, 1970), *Hamlet*★ (Greenwich, 1974), etc.

Milton, John (1608–74). English poet; his first published poem was his sonnet 'An Epitaph on the Admirable Dramatic Poet, W. Shakespeare', printed anonymously in the Second Folio★ (1632), and retitled 'On Shakespeare, 1630' in his first collected edition of 1645. It was also printed in Shakespeare's *Poems* (1640), and in the Third and Fourth Folios★ (1663–4 and 1685).

Mirror for Magistrates. A collection of nineteen verse 'tragedies' by William Baldwin and others, published in 1559, in each of which the ghost of a dead figure in English history tells his story in the form of a 'complaint'. An edition of 1563 adds eight more lives, and includes an Induction by Thomas Sackville. Later editions adding new material appeared in 1574, 1587, and 1610. The work aims to provide instructive examples ('mirrors') for rulers ('magistrates'). Shakespeare may have been influenced by it in his history plays.

Mirror Scenes. A term given to scenes such as that of the gardeners (III.iv) in *Richard II*★ which may be held to mirror the basic concerns of a play rather than to further its action.

Misery of Civil War, The. See Crowne, John.

Modern-dress productions. In Shakespeare's time, and till the end of the eighteenth century, his plays were regularly performed largely, if not entirely, in costumes of the time. Barry Jackson's★ production of *Cymbeline*,★ in 1923, seems to have been the first revival of this practice, which has continued to be used from time to time, and can be justified mainly by the argument that modern costumes are more meaningful as indications of, e.g., social status than those of the past, which can seem merely like fancy dress.

'Hamlet in Plus-fours': Colin Keith-Johnson in Barry Jackson's production of *Hamlet*, directed by H. K. Ayliff, Kingsway Theatre, London, 1925

Modern spelling. Almost all editions of Shakespeare's plays from the First Folio★ onwards have brought the spelling into conformity with current practice. It is sometimes difficult to distinguish between variant spellings and variant forms, so that e.g. some editors modernize *murther* to *murder*, others retain *murther* on the grounds that it is a different word.

Moiseiwitsch, Tanya (b. 1914). Theatre designer whose work includes *1* and *2 Henry IV*★ at Stratford-upon-Avon, 1951, and many Shakespeare productions at the Festival Theatre, Stratford, Ontario★ (which she helped to design) and elsewhere.

Mompelgard, Frederick, Count of. He visited England in 1592, and had trouble with his post-horses. He became Duke of Württemberg in 1593. He coveted the title of Knight of the Garter, which he claimed Elizabeth★ had offered him. She eventually gave him it in 1597, but omitted to tell him so. The episode appears to be alluded to in *The Merry Wives of Windsor*,★ which may have been written for the Garter ceremony of 1597, at which the Duke was installed in his absence. The play includes a horse-stealing episode, with a reference to 'cosen garmombles' (IV. v.71, quarto text only), which may be a joke on his name, with other possible allusions.

Monck, Nugent (1877–1958). See Maddermarket Theatre.

Montaigne, Michel de (1533–92). French writer of essays, a form which he virtually invented. A translation into English by John Florio★ was published in 1603 and was known to Shakespeare, who drew on it in *The Tempest*★ and possibly elsewhere.

Montemayor, Jorge de (c. 1521–61). See *Diana*.

Monument, Shakespeare's. An effigy in the north wall of the chancel

Shakespeare's monument in Holy Trinity Church, Stratford-upon-Avon

of Holy Trinity Church, Stratford-upon-Avon, made by Gheerart Janssen;★ one of the only two authentic portrayals of Shakespeare. (See Portraits of Shakespeare.) It bears two inscriptions. One is in Latin:

> Iudicio Pylium, Genio Socratem, Arte Maronem:
> Terra tegit, populus maeret, Olympus habet.

i.e. 'In judgement a Nestor, in genius a Socrates, in art a Virgil; the earth covers him, the people mourn him, Olympus has him.'

The other inscription reads:

> Stay, passenger, why goest thou by so fast?
> Read, if thou canst, whom envious death hath placed
> Within this monument: Shakespeare, with whom
> Quick nature died; whose name doth deck this tomb,
> Far more than cost, sith all that he hath writ
> Leaves living art but page to serve his wit.
>
> > Obiit anno domini 1616 Aetatis
> > 53 Die 23 April.

The monument was erected by 1623, during Anne Shakespeare's life-time. It was repaired in 1749. In 1790 the original lead pen was re-placed by a quill, which is renewed annually on 23 April.

More, Sir (St.) Thomas. See *Sir Thomas More*.

Morgan, McNamara (d. 1762). Irish barrister whose adaptation of *The Winter's Tale*★ as *The Sheep-Shearing; or, Florizel and Perdita*, was acted at Covent Garden★ in 1754.

Morgann, Maurice (1726–1802). A British civil servant whose *Essay on the Dramatic Character of Falstaff* (1777) is an early and distinguished example of character criticism.

Morley, Thomas (1557–c. 1603). English musician, author of *A Plain and Easy Introduction to Practical Music* (1597), composer of tunes to which 'It was a Lover and his lass' (*As You Like It*★) and 'O mistress mine' (*Twelfth Night*★) can be sung, though it is not sure whether he wrote the music to the words, or Shakespeare wrote the words to the music.

Motto, Shakespeare's. See Arms, Shakespeare's.

Mountjoy, Christopher. A French Huguenot tire-maker, who lived in London in a house at the corner of Silver and Monkwell Streets, in Cripplegate ward. His daughter, Mary, married his apprentice, Stephen Belott, on 19 November 1604. In 1612 Belott brought a suit against Mountjoy alleging that he had not honoured his financial obligations in relation to the marriage. Shakespeare had lodged in the household, and was called as a witness on 11 May 1612. He is described in the deposition as a 'gentleman' of Stratford-upon-Avon. He said that he had known the parties for ten years, that Belott was 'a very good and industrious servant' and was well treated by the Mountjoys, who had begged Shakespeare 'to move and persuade' Belott to marry their daughter, which he did. Shakespeare could not remember the financial provisions, though the plaintiff and defendant were living in the same house 'and they had amongst themselves many confer-ences about their marriage . . .'. Belott won the suit.

The relevance of this suit to Shakespeare is that it shows he was living with the Mountjoys at some time between 1602 and 1604, and that by 1612 he was living in Stratford-upon-Avon. The deposition also provides one of the few undisputed specimens of his signature.★

Mousetrap, The. Hamlet's name (III.ii.232) for the play-within-the-play with which he hopes to 'catch the conscience of the King'.

Mr W.H. See *Sonnets*.

Mucedorus. An anonymous play published in 1598, frequently reprinted, and in the seventeenth century sometimes attributed to Shakespeare.

Much Ado About Nothing. Shakespeare's comedy was first printed in quarto★ in 1600, probably from the author's manuscript. This edition was reprinted in the First Folio★ (1623). The play was not mentioned by Meres★ in 1598, and is usually dated 1598–1600. It is based on a traditional story which had been told by Ariosto in his *Orlando Furioso* (1516, translated 1591), and by Bandello, translated into French by Belleforest.★ It was played at Court in 1613, and a poem by Leonard Digges★ printed in 1640 suggests that it remained popular. William Davenant★ adapted it as *The Law Against Lovers* (1662), with little success.

The original play was performed in 1721, and there were further revivals in 1739 and 1746, but it did not fully regain its popularity until David Garrick★ first played Benedick, in 1748, after which he revived it regularly until he retired in 1776. His first, and greatest, Beatrice was Mrs Pritchard.★

During the later part of the century Frances Abington and Elizabeth Farren shone as Beatrice. Charles Kemble★ succeeded as Benedick from 1803, and the play's popularity during the nineteenth century culminated in Henry Irving's★ Lyceum★ revival of 1882, in which Ellen Terry★ gave her legendary Beatrice, which she went on playing for a quarter of a century.

Ellen Terry as Beatrice in *Much Ado About Nothing*, Lyceum Theatre, 1882

The most famous twentieth-century production is John Gielgud's★ at Stratford-upon-Avon, first given in 1949, when he did not appear in it, but revived in 1950 with himself as Benedick and Peggy Ashcroft★ as Beatrice, and repeated several times during the 1950s.

Much Ado About Nothing has proved to be one of Shakespeare's most resilient plays. Twentieth-century productions have frequently updated the action. Hugh Hunt directed it in modern dress in 1947, Douglas Seale, at Stratford-upon-Avon in 1958, in costumes of about

1851, Franco Zeffirelli,* at the Old Vic* in 1965 in a farcical version set in late nineteenth-century Sicily, and John Barton* at Stratford-upon-Avon in 1976 in a setting of nineteenth-century British India with Judi Dench* as an unusually serious, and wholly credible, Beatrice. The play was enjoyable in all these varied interpretations. Critics have been troubled by the moral ambiguities of the Hero-Claudio plot, but theatrically the sub-plot characters of Beatrice and Benedick, along with Dogberry and the Watch, have always carried the play to success.

Mulberry tree, Shakespeare's. A mulberry tree in the garden of New Place,* cut down by Francis Gastrell* in 1758, said to have been planted by Shakespeare. The wood was sold to a watchmaker, Thomas Sharpe, who carved many souvenirs from it and swore a deathbed affidavit in 1799 that the tree was indeed planted by Shakespeare, and was the source of all the articles claimed to have been made from it.

Music based on Shakespeare. A great many musical works have been based on, and inspired by, Shakespeare's plays and poems. They include solo songs, part songs, cantatas, operas, incidental music for use in the theatre, concert overtures, symphonic poems, ballet scores, etc. Information about some of this music is given under the names of individual composers.

Music room. An area in the Elizabethan theatre occupied by the musicians; its precise location is unknown.

N

Nash family. Thomas Nash (d. 1587) had two sons, Anthony (d. 1622) and John (d. 1623), to whom Shakespeare left 26s. 8d. each to buy mourning rings. They witnessed some of his legal agreements. Anthony's son Thomas (1593–1647) married Shakespeare's grand-daughter, Elizabeth Hall,* in 1626. As master of New Place* he entertained Queen Henrietta Maria in 1643. He died in 1647, and is buried next to Shakespeare.

Nashe, Thomas (1567–c.1601). English writer whose Preface to Robert Greene's* prose-romance *Menaphon* (1589) includes some enigmatic remarks referring to the *Ur-Hamlet.** His *Pierce Penniless his Supplication to the Devil* (1592) includes a reference to 'brave Talbot' in *1 Henry VI** which assists in the play's dating. Shakespeare appears to have known this and other writings by Nashe, one of the most brilliant stylists of his age.

National Theatre. After many years of effort, the National Theatre company began to operate at the Old Vic★ Theatre under the direction of Laurence Olivier★ in 1963, with his production of *Hamlet.*★ Other Shakespeare productions have included *Othello*★ (1964) and *The Merchant of Venice*★ (1970), both with Olivier. Peter Hall★ took over the directorship in 1973, and directed John Gielgud★ in *The Tempest* (1974) and Albert Finney in *Hamlet* (1975). The theatre's own buildings opened in 1976, and there John Schlesinger has directed Gielgud as Caesar in *Julius Caesar*★ (1977).

New Arden Edition. A one-play-per-volume edition of Shakespeare's works, still in progress. It began to appear in 1951 under the general editorship of Una Ellis-Fermor, who was succeeded in 1958 by Professors Harold F. Brooks and Harold Jenkins, later joined by Professor Brian Morris. It was originally intended as a revision of the Arden★ edition, but developed independently. Each volume has a full scholarly apparatus, including an extended introduction, collations, detailed annotations, reprints of source material, etc.

New Cambridge edition. The series began in 1921 with *The Tempest,*★ and early volumes were edited by J. Dover Wilson★ with introductions by Sir Arthur Quiller-Couch. After the latter's death in 1944 Wilson took complete responsibility, but in later years individual volumes were edited by others. The series concluded with Wilson's edition of the Sonnets,★ published in 1966. Each volume has an Introduction, a freshly edited, modernized text, a Stage History, a Commentary, and a Glossary.

New Penguin edition. A one-volume-per-play edition, established under the General Editorship of T. J. B. Spencer in 1967. Each volume has an extended introduction, a freshly-edited, modernized text, a detailed Commentary, and an Account of the Text.

New Place. A house built opposite the Guild Chapel,★ on the corner of Chapel Street and Chapel Lane in Stratford-upon-Avon, in the late fifteenth century by Sir Hugh Clopton. John Leland, Henry VIII's antiquary, toured England searching for records in cathedrals and monasteries from 1534 to 1542. In an account of his journey published by Thomas Hearne in 1710-12 as *The Itinerary of John Leland* (9 vols.), he describes New Place as 'a pretty house of brick and timber'.

Shakespeare bought it for £60 on 4 May 1597. In documents relating to the sale, it is said to have ten fireplaces, two barns, two gardens, and two orchards. It is believed to have had a frontage of sixty feet and a depth of seventy feet. In 1598 the Stratford-upon-Avon Corporation paid Shakespeare or his father 10d 'for one load of stone'. This may have been left over from repairs to the house.

A late description survives. In 1767, a Richard Grimmitt, who had been born in 1683, remembered that 'in his youth he had been a play-fellow with Edward Clopton Sr., eldest son of Sir John Clopton Kt., and had been often with him in the great house near the Chapel in Stratford, called New Place; that to the best of his remembrance there was a brick wall next the street, with a kind of porch at that end of it next the chapel; when they crossed a small kind of green court before, they entered the house, which was bearing to the left and fronted with brick, with plain windows consisting of common panes of glass set in lead, as at this time.'

This confirms the only visual evidence, a drawing made in 1737 by George Vertue, based on a description from an unknown source. The sketch reproduced here shows 'the outward appearance towards the street'. Vertue explains that 'there was before the House itself . . . a little courtyard, grass growing there – before the real dwelling house, this outside being only a long gallery etc. and for servants.'

New Place remained in Shakespeare's possession till he died. He probably settled his family in the house soon after buying it. By 4 February 1598 he was named as a householder in Chapel Street ward; a survey of grain and malt lists him as owning eighty bushels of malt, a normal supply for household brewing.

In spite of his London commitments, Shakespeare maintained his interest in the property. In 1602, for instance, he bought a cottage on the south side of Chapel Lane. He seems to have lived increasingly in Stratford-upon-Avon from 1611. At his death, the house passed to his daughter, Susanna,* and her husband, Dr John Hall,* and then to their daughter and son-in-law, Elizabeth and Thomas Nash.*

New Place was sold in 1675 to Sir Edward Walker, and passed from him to his daughter and, in 1699, into the Clopton family. It was extensively rebuilt by Sir John Clopton, who settled it on his son, Hugh, in 1702 before it was ready for reoccupation. When Sir Hugh died, it passed to his daughters, who sold it to the Reverend Francis Gastrell* in 1756. He demolished it in 1759.

The site of New Place was acquired by the Shakespeare Birthplace Trust* in 1892. The foundations of the house, and a well which presumably stood in the original courtyard, remain. This site, along with

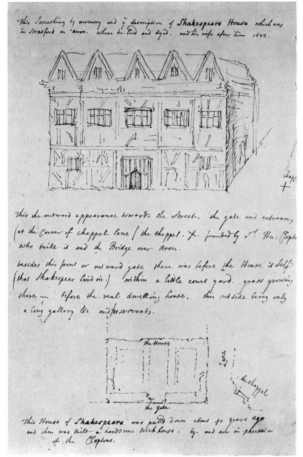

This Something by memory and by description of Shakespeare House which was in Stratford on Avon. where he lived and dyed. and his wife after him 1623.

this the outward appearance towards the Street. the gate and entrance, (at the Corner of chappel lane (the chappel. X. founded by Sr. Hu. Clopton who built it and the Bridge over Avon.

besides this front or outward gate there was before the House it self (that Shakespeer lived in.) within a little court yard. grass growing there — before the real dwelling house. this out side being only a long gallery &c. and for servants.

the House

the chappel

the gate.

This House of Shakespeare was pulld down about 40 years ago and then was built a handsome brick house. by. and now in possession of the Cloptons.

George Vertue's drawing of the frontage of New Place, 1737

a beautifully maintained knot garden and the Great Garden, is open to the public. The house next door, which belonged to Thomas Nash, also belongs to the Trust and is maintained as a museum.

New Shakspere Society. Founded in 1873 by F. J. Furnivall, it reprinted primary materials such as Brooke's *Romeus and Juliet*★ and *The Two Noble Kinsmen*,★ and published scholarly papers read at its meetings. It disbanded in 1894.

New Variorum edition. See Furness, H. H.

New York Shakespeare Festival. Developed from the Shakespeare Workshop founded by Joseph Papp (b. 1921) in 1953. Since 1962 the

Festival has had a permanent home in the open-air Delacorte Theatre in Central Park, New York, where Papp has directed many of the plays, and to which admission is free.

Nicolai, Otto (1810–49). German composer of an opera (1849) based on *The Merry Wives of Windsor*.★

Nicoll, Allardyce (1894–1976). Historian of the drama, founder of *Shakespeare Survey*★ and the Shakespeare Institute.★

North, Sir Thomas (1535?–1601). Translator whose *Lives of the Noble Grecians and Romans* (1579) from Jacques Amyot's French version of Plutarch's★ *Lives* was Shakespeare's main source for his Roman plays.★ Shakespeare often follows its wording closely: T. J. B. Spencer's *Shakespeare's Plutarch* (1964) conveniently reprints North's version of the lives mainly used by Shakespeare, and gives passages directly based on it at the foot of the page.

Nunn, Trevor (b. 1940). Artistic director of the Royal Shakespeare Company★ since 1968; his productions with it include *King Lear*★ and *Much Ado About Nothing*★ (1968), *The Winter's Tale*★ and *Henry VIII*★ (1969), *Hamlet*★ (1970), a season of Roman plays★ (1972), *Macbeth*★ (1974), and *Romeo and Juliet*★ (1976).

Trevor Nunn's production of *Hamlet*, 1970: Hamlet (Alan Howard) before the duel

O

Octavo. A book made of sheets of paper folded three times, producing sixteen pages (eight leaves) from each sheet. In Shakespeare's time, single plays were usually printed in quarto,★ but *The True Tragedy*★ (see 'Contention' Plays) of 1595 is in octavo, as are *The Passionate Pilgrim*★ and numerous reprints of *Venus and Adonis*★ and *The Rape of Lucrece.*★ For ease of reference, as in lists of reprints, octavo volumes are sometimes loosely called quartos.

Oldcastle, Sir John (c. 1375–1417). A Lollard martyr who became Lord Cobham. Shakespeare, following his source play, *The Famous Victories of Henry the Fifth,*★ originally used this name in *Henry IV*★ for Falstaff.★ Probably because of protests by the current Lord Cobham, Shakespeare altered the name before the play was printed, but traces remain, and the Epilogue to *2 Henry IV*★ includes the disclaimer 'Falstaff shall die of a sweat, unless already 'a be kill'd with your hard opinions; for Oldcastle died a martyr and this is not the man.' The Admiral's Men,★ a rival company, then put on a successful two-part play called *The True and Honourable History of the Life of Sir John Oldcastle, the Good Lord Cobham* (acted 1599–1600). The second part is lost, but the first was printed anonymously in 1600, reprinted in 1619 with a mistaken ascription to Shakespeare, and included in the second issue of the Third Folio★ (1664).

Old Vic Theatre. A theatre built in an unfashionable area of London, south of the river, in 1818 as the Royal Coburg, renamed the Victoria in 1833, which gave mainly melodramas till it was taken over in 1880 by Emma Cons, who reopened it as a temperance music-hall, the Royal Victoria Hall and Coffee Tavern. In 1914 her niece, Lilian Baylis,★ established it as a home of Shakespeare. By 1923 all the plays had been presented.

It continued as the main London home of Shakespeare with distinguished performances under directors such as Robert Atkins★ (1919–25), Harcourt Williams (1929–33), and Tyrone Guthrie★ (1933–4, 1936–43), with actors such as Edith Evans,★ Laurence Olivier,★ John Gielgud,★ Ralph Richardson,★ Donald Wolfit,★ Peggy Ashcroft,★ etc. Lilian Baylis died in 1937.

The theatre was damaged in the war, but the Old Vic company continued its work, mainly at the New Theatre, and it reopened in 1950. In 1953 under Michael Benthall it embarked on a plan to pro-

The interior of the old Vic Theatre

duce all Shakespeare's plays in five years, culminating in 1958 with *Henry VIII* with Gielgud and Edith Evans.

The Old Vic company was disbanded in 1963, and from then till 1976 the theatre was used by the National Theatre company.★

Olivier, Lord (Laurence Olivier; b. 1907). One of the greatest English actors and a major figure in the history of the English theatre; Founder Director of the National Theatre★ (1963–73). His Shakespeare roles include Romeo (Old Vic,★ alternating Mercutio, 1935, New York, 1940), Hamlet, Sir Toby Belch, Henry V (Old Vic, 1937), Macbeth (Old Vic and New, 1937, Stratford-upon-Avon, 1955), Iago (Old Vic, 1938), Coriolanus (Old Vic, 1938, Stratford-upon-Avon, 1959), Richard III (New, 1944, etc.), Hotspur, Justice Shallow (New, 1945–6), King Lear (New, 1946), Antony in *Antony and Cleopatra*★ (St James's, 1951), Titus Andronicus (Stratford-upon-Avon, 1955, etc.), Malvolio (Stratford-upon-Avon, 1955), Othello (National Theatre company, 1964, filmed 1965), and Shylock (National Theatre company, 1970). He has also starred in and directed films of *Henry V*★ (1944), *Hamlet*★ (1948), and *Richard III*★ (1955), and has directed a number of Shakespeare's plays on the stage.

Laurence Olivier with Vivien Leigh in *Macbeth*, III.ii, in Glen Byam Shaw's production, Stratford-upon-Avon, 1955

Operas based on Shakespeare's plays. Many operas have been based on Shakespeare; there is an excellent survey by Winton Dean in *Shakespeare in Music*, edited by Phyllis Hartnoll (1964). Information in the present volume is given under the names of individual composers, e.g. Britten, Benjamin; Verdi, Giuseppe.

Oregon Shakespeare Festival. Founded by Angus Bowmer in 1935 in Ashland, Oregon, it presents Shakespeare's plays on a stage based on the dimensions given in the contract for the Fortune Theatre,★ with amateur and semi-professional performers.

Orff, Carl (b. 1895). German composer whose works include incidental music (1939) for *A Midsummer Night's Dream*.★

Othello. Shakespeare's tragedy first appeared in quarto★ in 1622; a somewhat different and longer text appeared in the First Folio★ (1623). The origin and relationship of these two versions of the play is a matter of scholarly debate. The play was given at Court in November 1604, and was probably written in that or the previous year. It is based on a story by Cinthio.★ It was one of Shakespeare's most popular plays throughout the seventeenth and eighteenth centuries, and was played without major revisions. Thomas Betterton,★ James Quin,★ and Spranger Barry★ had particular success as Othello, Charles Macklin★

'The Return of Othello' (*Othello*, II.i) painted in oils by Thomas Stothard (1755–1834) for Boydell's Shakespeare Gallery

and David Garrick★ as Iago. J. P. Kemble★ and Mrs Siddons★ were popular as Othello and Desdemona for twenty years from 1785. Othello was one of the greatest roles of Edmund Kean,★ who played it from 1814 to 1833, when he collapsed during a performance. W. C. Macready,★ a fine Iago, played Othello more frequently though less successfully. Samuel Phelps★ played both roles during most of his long career, scoring particularly as Othello.

The first distinguished negro Othello seems to have been Ira Aldridge, who played the role in England several times between 1826 and 1865. In America, Edwin Forrest★ was the leading Othello during this period. Henry Irving★ failed as Othello but Iago became one of his greatest roles; sometimes he alternated with Edwin Booth★ in both roles. Paul Robeson played Othello with varying success in several productions between 1930 and 1959. Tyrone Guthrie's★ Freudian reading of the play at the Old Vic★ in 1938, with Ralph Richardson★ as Othello and Laurence Olivier★ as Iago, was a failure, though Richardson had succeeded as Iago at the Old Vic in 1932, and Olivier was to give a brilliant, individual interpretation of Othello with the National Theatre company★ in 1964, filmed in 1965.

Othello has been one of Shakespeare's most frequently performed

Ovid

plays. It offers splendid opportunities to its performers, and rarely fails to hold its audiences, though Zeffirelli's* Stratford-upon-Avon production of 1961 was tedious in its over-emphasis on spectacle, and actors have sometimes been over-ambitious in thinking they will succeed in both Othello and Iago. The play has frequently been filmed, e.g. by Orson Welles* (1951) and (in Russian) by Sergei Yutkevitch (1955), and is the basis of one of the greatest of all operas, Verdi's* *Otello*.

Ovid (Publius Ovidius Naso; 43 B.C.–A.D. 18). Roman poet. Shakespeare knew his works well, and used his *Metamorphoses* in both the original and the translation by Arthur Golding.* For *The Rape of Lucrece** he used Ovid's *Fasti*, which had not been translated into English at the time.

O.U.D.S. (Oxford University Dramatic Society). Founded in 1885, it has produced many Shakespeare plays. After the Second World War Nevill Coghill* worked with and supported it.

Oxford, Edward de Vere, 17th Earl of (1550–1604). A courtier and writer who has absurdly been put forward as the author, or part-author, of Shakespeare's plays. The theory was first advanced by J. T. Looney in his '*Shakespeare' Identified in Edward de Vere the Seventeenth Earl of Oxford* in 1920, and has had other adherents including Percy Allen who, in *Talks with Elizabethans Revealing the Mystery of 'William Shakespeare'* (1947), communicated the outcome of his psychic conversations with Oxford, Bacon,* and Shakespeare.

P

Painter, William. See Boccaccio, Giovanni.

Palladis Tamia. See Meres, Francis.

Pandosto. See Greene, Robert.

Papal Tyranny in the Reign of King John. See Cibber, Colley, and *King John*.

Papp, Joseph. See New York Shakespeare Festival.

'Parnassus' Plays. Three anonymous satirical plays – *The Pilgrimage to Parnassus*, and *The Return from Parnassus*, Parts I and II – acted at St John's College, Cambridge, probably at Christmas 1598, 1599, and 1601. They are about student life, and contain interesting allusions to Shakespeare and his theatre. A love-sick young courtier quotes part of

130

Venus and Adonis★ and exclaims 'O sweet Master Shakespeare! I'll have his picture in my study at the Court!... Let this duncified world esteem of Spenser and Chaucer, I'll worship sweet Master Shakespeare, and to honour him will lay his *Venus and Adonis* under my pillow.'

A character suggests that Shakespeare should try 'a graver subject ... Without love's foolish lazy languishment.' Actors at the Globe remark 'Few of the university men pen plays well; they smell too much of that writer Ovid ... Why, here's our fellow Shakespeare puts them all down, ay and Ben Jonson, too. O, that Ben Jonson is a pestilent fellow, he brought up Horace giving the poets a pill, but our fellow Shakespeare hath given him a purge that made him beray his credit.' And Richard Burbage★ auditions a student for the role of Richard III.

Pasco, Richard (b. 1926). English actor, whose Shakespeare roles include Pericles (Birmingham Repertory Theatre, 1954), Henry V, and Berowne (Bristol Old Vic, 1964), Hamlet (Bristol Old Vic, 1965, 1967), and, with the Royal Shakespeare Company,★ Buckingham in *Henry VIII*★ (1969), Orsino (1970), Richard II and Bolingbroke (alternating with Ian Richardson,★ 1973–4), Timon (1980), etc.

Passionate Pilgrim, The. Only two sheets of the first edition of this collection of poems, probably published in 1599, survive. The second

Richard Pasco as Richard II and Ian Richardson as Bolingbroke in John Barton's production of *Richard II*, Stratford-upon-Avon, 1973–4

edition, certainly of that year, was published by William Jaggard★ as by William Shakespeare. The twenty poems include corrupt versions of Shakespeare's sonnets★ 138 and 144, and three extracts from his *Love's Labour's Lost.*★

Some of the remaining poems are known to be by other poets, and none of them can be confidently attributed to Shakespeare. An edition of 1612 added nine poems by Thomas Heywood.★ In an Epistle to his *Apology for Actors*, also of 1612, he protested against the 'manifest injury' done to him by printing his poems 'in a less volume, under the name of another, which may put the world in opinion I might steal them from him . . . But as I must acknowledge my lines not worthy his patronage under whom he hath published them, so the author I know much offended with Master Jaggard that, altogether unknown to him, presumed to make so bold with his name.' Probably as a result, the original titlepage of the 1612 edition was replaced with one that did not mention Shakespeare's name.

Pastoralism. A literary and dramatic mode deriving from classical literature, including the poems of Theocritus and Virgil, which celebrates the country life of humble folk, especially shepherds and shepherdesses. Common features of it are an opposition between courtly sophistication and rustic innocence, praise of the simple life regulated by the seasons, and nostalgia for a lost Golden Age.

Shakespeare frequently uses these and related conventions, always in a sophisticated and critical manner. His most obviously pastoral works are *As You Like It*★ and *The Winter's Tale.*★

Patent Theatres. At the Restoration in 1660, Charles II granted patents to Thomas Killigrew★ and Sir William Davenant,★ giving them the exclusive right to manage theatres at which plays were performed. The theatres which their companies, and their successors', occupied were the patent theatres. The major patent theatres were Drury Lane,★ from 1663, and Covent Garden,★ from 1732. From 1766, the Haymarket Theatre★ had a royal patent during the summer months. The monopoly created by these patents was much resented and abused, and they were finally abolished in 1843.

Pattern of Painful Adventures, The. See Twine, Laurence.

Pavier, Thomas. See Jaggard, William.

Payne, Ben Iden (1881–1976). English actor and director, Director of the Shakespeare Memorial Theatre,★ Stratford-upon-Avon, 1935–42; he produced many of Shakespeare's plays in Stratford-upon-Avon and elsewhere, including the University of Texas, etc.

Peacham, Henry. See Longleat Manuscript.

Peele, George (1556–96). Playwright, one of the 'University Wits'.★ He was active during Shakespeare's early years in the theatre, and has often been proposed as a possible part-author of *1 Henry VI*★ and *Titus Andronicus*.★

Pelican Shakespeare. A paper-back edition, one play per volume, under the general editorship of Alfred Harbage, with short introductions, and notes on the page. It appeared from 1956 to 1967, with a collected volume in 1969.

Pembroke, Earls of. See Herbert, William and Philip.

Pepys, Samuel (1633–1703). The great English diarist recorded and commented on many visits to Shakespeare plays and adaptations from 1660 to 1669. His library includes a manuscript setting of Hamlet's 'To be or not to be', possibly made for him by his music teacher, Cesare Morelli.

Pericles. This play was first printed in quarto★ in 1609. It was not included in the First Folio★ (1623), but appeared in the second issue (1664) of the Third Folio.★ The text is corrupt, and the original play may not have been written entirely by Shakespeare. It was entered in the Stationers' Register★ on 20 May 1608, and was probably written shortly before then. It is based on the traditional tale of Apollonius of Tyre★ as told by John Gower★ in his *Confessio Amantis* (1385–93). Gower appears as the narrator. The story was also told by Laurence Twine★ in *The Pattern of Painful Adventures*, entered in 1576, and printed firstly without date, and secondly in 1607. In 1608 appeared a prose tale, *The Painful Adventures of Pericles, Prince of Tyre*, by George Wilkins,★ described as 'The True History of the Play of Pericles, as it was lately presented by the worthy and ancient poet, John Gower.' This appears to be based on the original play, as well as on Twine, and can sometimes be used to correct the corrupt text.

The play was popular in its own times. The quarto was reprinted five times by 1635. Several early performances are recorded, and Ben Jonson,★ in his 'Ode to Himself' (1629), enviously remarked that 'No doubt some mouldy tale/Like *Pericles* . . . may keep up the play-club

We cannot tell why *Pericles* was omitted from the Folio: perhaps because no authentic text was available. The first two acts of the surviving version are generally felt to be much inferior to the later three. It should be remembered that edited versions necessarily tidy up the original text.

Pericles was the first Shakespeare play to be given after 1642, in 1660

and 1661, with Thomas Betterton★ as Pericles. Since then it has been comparatively unsuccessful, no doubt largely because the authentic text was not available. A radical adaptation by George Lillo, *Marina*, was played at Covent Garden★ in 1738. Samuel Phelps's★ Sadler's Wells★ version of 1854 had spectacular scenery. John Coleman made drastic alterations in his unsuccessful Stratford-upon-Avon production of 1900.

Thaisa is recovered from the sea: a frontispiece from Nicholas Rowe's edition of Shakespeare, 1709

Pericles has had greater theatrical success in the twentieth century. Robert Atkins★ produced an unexpurgated version at the Old Vic★ in 1921, and also at the Open-Air Theatre, Regent's Park★ in 1939. Nugent Monck,★ who had directed it at the Maddermarket, Norwich,★ brought it to Stratford-upon-Avon in 1947, omitting the first act, with Paul Scofield★ as Pericles. Richard Pasco★ led the cast in Douglas Seale's Birmingham production of 1954. Tony Richardson directed the play at Stratford-upon-Avon in 1958, and Terry Hands in 1969, with Ian Richardson★ as Pericles. The Prospect Players gave it in 1973, set entirely in a male brothel.

Phelps, Samuel (1804–78). English actor, and manager from 1844 to 1862 of Sadler's Wells Theatre,★ London, where he presented and acted in all but six of Shakespeare's plays with great good taste and distinction. He had a concern for the overall values of each play exceptional in his time, and frequently restored the original text in favour of traditional revisions and rearrangements.

His *Pericles*★ (1854) was the first since the Restoration, his *Antony and Cleopatra*★ (1849) the first for a century. His own best performances included Lear, Othello, and Bottom. His last appearance was as Cardinal Wolsey, in the year of his death.

Phelps as Hamlet: a painting by N. J. Crowley (1819–57)

Phillips, Augustine (d. 1605). An actor, one of the original Lord Chamberlain's Men★ (Shakespeare's company) from their formation in 1594; named among the list of the Principal Actors in the First Folio★ of Shakespeare's plays. His will, proven in 1605, is a source of information about the company. His bequests included 'a thirty shillings piece in gold' to Shakespeare.

Phillips, Robin (b. 1942). English actor and director, appointed Artistic Director of the Stratford Festival, Ontario,★ in 1974.

Phoenix and the Turtle, The. Shakespeare's poem was first published, without title but ascribed to him, as one of a group of commendatory poems appended to Robert Chester's *Love's Martyr, or Rosalind's Complaint* (1601). It is a sixty-seven line elegy. The first twenty lines call on the birds to mourn; then comes an anthem for the phoenix and the turtle-dove; and the poem ends with a 'threnos', or lament for the dead, composed by Reason. It probably has irrecoverable allegorical significance.

'Pied Bull' quarto. The first edition of *King Lear*,★ published by Nathaniel Butter 'at the sign of the Pied Bull' in 1608. This name distinguishes it from William Jaggard's★ reprint of 1619, falsely dated 1608.

Pirated texts. See Bad quartos.

Plague. Outbreaks of plague frequently caused the City of London authorities to enforce the theatres to close to reduce the danger of infection. At these times theatre companies usually toured the provinces. During Shakespeare's career there were severe outbreaks in 1592–4, 1603, and 1609.

Planché, James Robinson (1796–1880). English dramatist, antiquary, historian of costume, authority on heraldry; his *History of British Costume* (1834) has been much used by theatre designers, and his work with Charles Kemble★ on a production of *King John*★ in 1823 was influential as the first to set one of Shakespeare's plays in the costumes of the period of the action.

A playbill for the production of *King John*, in which the first consistent attempt was made to set one of Shakespeare's histories in 'the Habit of the Period'

He was associated with Madame Vestris★ in her important revivals of *Love's Labour's Lost*★ and *A Midsummer Night's Dream*★ (for which he prepared the texts), and also worked with Benjamin Webster on a remarkable production of *The Taming of the Shrew*★ in Elizabethan style in 1844 and 1846.

Platter, Thomas. Swiss doctor who visited London in 1599 and wrote, in German, an account of his travels which includes reference to a visit to a tragedy about Julius Caesar, probably Shakespeare's, at the Globe,★ and a description of the Curtain Theatre.

Plautus, Titus Maccius (c. 254–184 B.C.). Roman dramatist, author of more than twenty surviving comedies based on Greek originals. They were much studied in schools in the sixteenth century, and were sometimes acted, exerting an influence on the development of English comedy. His *Menaechmi* is the main source of *The Comedy of Errors,*★ to which his *Amphitruo* also contributed. His influence can be detected in other plays by Shakespeare, and in *Hamlet*★ Polonius speaks of the actors for whom 'Seneca cannot be too heavy nor Plautus too light' (II.ii.395–7).

Play-within-a-play. This dramatic convention, popular in Elizabethan times, was a favourite with Shakespeare, who used it with great subtlety. It occurs in his work in varied forms, most prominently in *Love's Labour's Lost,*★ *The Taming of the Shrew,*★ *A Midsummer Night's Dream,*★ *Hamlet,*★ and *The Tempest.*★

Plutarch (c. 50–130). Greek biographer. See North, Sir Thomas.

Poel, William (1852–1934). Actor and producer, founder (1894) of the Elizabethan Stage Society,★ with which he produced many of Shakespeare's plays in conditions approximating to those of the

A scene from William Poel's production of the first quarto text of *Hamlet*, St George's Hall, London, 1881

Elizabethan theatre. His first production in this style was in 1881, of the First Quarto* of *Hamlet*.*

He was an eccentric, and far more of a visual than a textual purist, with strong ideas about verse-speaking. His theories about the desirable balance of voices sometimes led him to cast women in such surprising roles as Thersites.

His work constituted a powerful reaction against the nineteenth-century 'spectacular' tradition in Shakespeare production, and has been highly influential. His actors included Nugent Monck (see Maddermarket Theatre), Harley Granville-Barker,* and Robert Speaight, author of *William Poel and the Elizabethan Revival* (1954). Edith Evans* played Cressida for him in 1912, in the first professional English stage performance of *Troilus and Cressida*.*

Poems. Shakespeare's principal independently printed poems are *Venus and Adonis** (1593), *The Rape of Lucrece** (1594), 'The Phoenix and the Turtle'* (1601), the Sonnets* (1609), and (less certainly by Shakespeare) *The Passionate Pilgrim** (1599) and *A Lover's Complaint** (printed along with the Sonnets in 1609).

Polanski, Roman. See *Macbeth*.

Pope, Alexander (1688–1744). English poet, the second editor of Shakespeare (1725). His main contribution is in the division of the scenes, and he is the first editor to consult the early quartos,* though he emended freely on grounds of taste. He included only the plays in the First Folio.* He distinguishes 'Some of the most shining passages ... by commas in the margin', while 'suspected passages, which are excessively bad' (such as the Porter episode in *Macbeth**) 'are degraded to the bottom of the page'.

Portraits of Shakespeare. The only two portraits with strong claims to authenticity are the Droeshout* engraving and the bust on the monument.* Many paintings have been claimed as portraits of Shakespeare; some are genuine paintings of the time faked to resemble the authentic portraits; some are forgeries; others are genuine portraits of the time of unknown sitters. The subject is treated by David Piper in 'O Sweet Mr. Shakespeare: I'll have his picture' (National Portrait Gallery, 1964). See also: Chandos portrait; Chesterfield portrait; Flower portrait; Grafton portrait; Kesselstadt death mask; Soest portrait; Scheemakers, Peter.

Princess's Theatre, London. See Kean, Charles.

Pritchard, (Mrs) Hannah (1711–68). English actress who frequently performed with David Garrick,* and was specially distinguished as Lady Macbeth, Gertrude, and Queen Katherine.

Private theatres. Roofed and enclosed theatres of Shakespeare's time which were smaller and had higher admission prices than the public theatres, but were nevertheless open to the public. They were originally occupied by boy actors.★ The main one during Shakespeare's career was the second Blackfriars,★ used by the Children of the Chapel from 1600 to 1608, and by his company, the King's Men,★ from 1609 to 1642.

Problem Plays. A term first applied to Shakespeare by F. S. Boas in 1896 to describe *Hamlet*,★ *All's Well that Ends Well*,★ *Troilus and Cressida*,★ and *Measure for Measure*.★ Since then *Hamlet*★ has not always been included.

Profanity Act. See Censorship.

Prokofiev, Serge (1891–1953). The Russian composer wrote incidental music (unpublished) for *Hamlet*★ in 1937, and an important full-length score for a ballet based on *Romeo and Juliet*★ (first performed in 1938).

Prologue. See Chorus.

Promos and Cassandra. See Whetstone, George.

Prompt-book. The 'book', or copy, of a play used during performance by the prompter, and marked with cuts, cues for music, and other indications for performance. The early texts of some of Shakespeare's plays appear to have been printed from prompt copies rather than from the manuscript as it left the author's hands.

Two pages from a prompt book of *Hamlet* (IV.iv) used by David Garrick

Pronunciation. There are many differences between the pronunciation of Shakespeare's time and modern standard pronunciation, some of them preserved in dialects. The standard study is Helge Kökeritz's *Shakespeare's Pronunciation* (1953).

Punctuation. Elizabethan punctuation was different from, and freer than, modern. In setting up type, compositors seem to have felt at liberty to alter the punctuation of their manuscripts. The result is that we cannot speak with certainty of Shakespeare's practice.

Purcell, Henry (1659–95). The great composer's music associated with Shakespeare includes a score for *The Fairy Queen*,★ one (whose authenticity has been questioned) for a 1695 revival of Thomas Shadwell's revision of Dryden★ and Davenant's★ version of *The Tempest*,★ and incidental music (1694) for Shadwell's★ *The History of Timon of Athens, the Man-Hater*, based on Shakespeare. Purcell's opera *Dido and Aeneas* was interpolated between the acts of Charles Gildon's★ version of *Measure for Measure*★ (published in 1700). His only settings of Shakespeare's words are for the Shadwell libretto: 'Come unto these yellow sands', sung by Ariel and chorus, and 'Full fathom five', sung by the non-Shakespearian Milcha, with chorus.

Puritan, The, or The Puritan Widow. An anonymous play of about 1606, attributed in the eighteenth century to Shakespeare, but now thought to be by Thomas Middleton.★ It includes a probable allusion to *Macbeth*★: 'Instead of a jester, we'll ha' the ghost i' the white sheet sit at upper end o' the table' (IV.iii.89–91). See Apocryphal Plays.

Q

Quarto. A book made from sheets folded twice, making eight pages (four leaves) for each sheet. Most of the early editions of Shakespeare were in quarto.

Quayle, Anthony (b. 1913). English actor and producer. He directed the Shakespeare Memorial Theatre,★ Stratford-upon-Avon, from 1948 to 1952, and, with Glen Byam Shaw,★ from 1952 to 1956. He played Falstaff (1951), Bottom (1954), Aaron (1955), and other roles.

Queen Mab Speech. In *Romeo and Juliet*,★ Mercutio's speech (I.iv. 53–103) in which he talks of Queen Mab, 'the fairies' midwife'.

Quilter, Roger (1877–1953). The English composer wrote several well known settings of Shakespeare lyrics, including his 'Three

Shakespeare Songs' ('Come away, death', 'O mistress mine', and 'Blow, blow, thou winter wind'), of 1906.

Quin, James (1693–1766). English actor who played many Shakespeare roles, from 1734 to 1751 mostly at Covent Garden,★ rivalling David Garrick★ at Drury Lane.★ His style was formal and declamatory, quite unlike the more volatile Garrick. His most famous role was Falstaff.★ Tobias Smollett writes of him in his novel *Humphrey Clinker* (1771).

Quiney, Richard (d. 1602). Father of Thomas.★ As an alderman of Stratford-upon-Avon (which had been hit by bad weather and two

Quin as Falstaff, a mezzotint by James McArdell (1729?–65)

severe fires), he regularly visited London for negotiations with the Privy Council on behalf of the Corporation. His correspondence on these occasions includes references to Shakespeare and also the only known letter addressed to Shakespeare. On 24 January 1598, Abraham Sturley, also a member of the Corporation, wrote to Quiney from Stratford-upon-Avon suggesting that, as Shakespeare was considering buying some land 'at Shottery or near about us', it would be worth asking him 'to deal in the matter of our tithes'. On another visit he became short of money, and wrote to Shakespeare asking for the loan of the large sum of £30:

'Loving countryman, I am bold of you as of a friend, craving your help with £30 upon Mr. Bushell's and my security, or Mr. Mytton's with me. Mr. Rosswell is not come to London as yet, and I have especial cause. You shall friend me much in helping me out of all the debts I owe in London, I thank God, and much quiet my mind which would not be indebted. I am now towards the Court in hope of answer for the dispatch of my business. You shall neither lose credit nor money by me, the Lord willing, and now but persuade yourself so as I hope and you shall not need to fear but with all hearty thankfulness I will hold my time and content your friend and if we bargain farther you shall be the paymaster yourself. My time bids me hasten

to an end, and so I commit this [to] your care and hope of your help.
I fear I shall not be back this night from the Court. Haste. The Lord
be with you and with us all. Amen. From the Bell in Carter Lane the
25 October 1598. Yours in all kindness Ryc. Quyney.'

The address is 'H [aste] to my loving good friend and countryman
Mr. Wm. Shakespeare deliver these', and there is a seal.

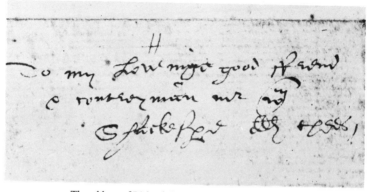

The address of Richard Quiney's letter to Shakespeare

This letter seems not to have been sent, as it was found among
Quiney's papers. A few days afterwards, on 30 October, his father
wrote in terms which suggest that Richard was still negotiating with
Shakespeare, perhaps for the land mentioned by Sturley: 'if you bargain with Mr. Sha. or receive money therefor, bring your money
home if you may . . .'. The implication is that Shakespeare was in
London. A letter of 4 November from Sturley acknowledges one
from Quiney importing 'that our countryman Mr. Wm. Shak. would
procure us money, which I will like of as I shall hear when, and where,
and how . . .'.

Eventually Quiney's negotiations were successful: the Queen agreed
to relieve 'this town twice afflicted and almost wasted by fire', and
Quiney's London expenses were borne by the Exchequer.

Quiney, Thomas. Husband of Shakespeare's daughter Judith.★

R

Rape of Lucrece, The. Shakespeare's narrative poem was first published in 1594, probably from his own manuscript, by Richard Field,★

from Stratford-upon-Avon, who had also printed *Venus and Adonis*★ the previous year. Like the earlier poem, it bears a dedication to Henry Wriothesley,★ 3rd Earl of Southampton. It is written in rhyme royal (seven-line stanzas, rhyming a b a b b c c) and has 1855 lines. It was reprinted seven times by 1640.

Shakespeare's dedication
of *The Rape of Lucrece*
(1594)

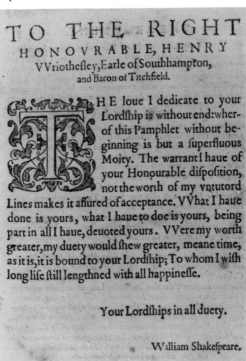

TO THE RIGHT
HONOVRABLE, HENRY
VVriothesley, Earle of Southhampton,
and Baron of Titchfield.

HE loue I dedicate to your Lordſhip is without end:wherof this Pamphlet without beginning is but a ſuperfluous Moity. The warrant I haue of your Honourable diſpoſition, not the worth of my vntutord Lines makes it aſſured of acceptance. VVhat I haue done is yours, what I haue to doe is yours, being part in all I haue, deuoted yours. VVere my worth greater, my duety would ſhew greater, meane time, as it is, it is bound to your Lordſhip; To whom I wiſh long life ſtill lengthned with all happineſſe.

Your Lordſhips in all duety.

William Shakeſpeare.

A 2

In *The Rape of Lucrece*, as in *Venus and Adonis*,★ Shakespeare was following the fashion for the Ovidian narrative poem. Its elaborate style and discursive structure form barriers to the modern reader, yet its rhetoric is often powerful, and the portrayal of Tarquin's inner turmoil, the result of an irresistible yet self-destructive urge, adumbrates a dominant theme of Shakespeare's major tragedies, notably *Macbeth*.★

Ravenscroft, Edward (c. 1640–97). English dramatist; he adapted *Titus Andronicus*★ in 1678. In the Address to the printed text (1687), he claims to 'have been told by some anciently conversant with the stage that it was not originally his [Shakespeare's], but brought by a private author to be acted, and he only gave some master touches to one or two of the principal parts or characters; this I am apt to believe, because 'tis the most incorrect and indigested piece in all his works; it seems rather a heap of rubbish than a structure.' This is the first suggestion that *Titus Andronicus* is not entirely by Shakespeare.

Recurrent Imagery. See Imagery.

Redgrave, Sir Michael (b. 1908). English actor whose Shakespeare roles include Orlando (Old Vic,★ with Edith Evans,★ 1936, etc.), Macbeth (Aldwych, 1947), Berowne and Hamlet (Old Vic, 1949–50), Richard II and Hotspur (Stratford-upon-Avon, 1951), Shylock, King Lear, and Antony (Stratford-upon-Avon, 1953), Benedick and Hamlet (Stratford-upon-Avon, 1958), and Claudius (National Theatre company, 1963).

Reed, Isaac (1742–1807). English scholar. He revised George Steevens's★ edition of Shakespeare in 1785, and assisted Steevens with his edition of 1793. In 1803 he produced an extensively revised edition of this, known as the First Variorum.★

Rehan, Ada (1860–1916). Irish-born American actress, who played from 1879 to 1899 with Augustin Daly's★ company, often in London. Her most famous Shakespearian roles were Kate, in *The Taming of the Shrew,*★ and Rosalind, in *As You Like It.*★

Regent's Park, London, Open-Air Theatre. Founded in 1933 in an enclosure in the park by Sidney Carroll, and run by Robert Atkins★ from 1933 to 1943 and 1946 to 1960. Many Shakespeare performances have been given there in the summer months.

Reinhardt, Max (1873–1943). Austrian director of spectacular productions of several Shakespeare plays and of a film (1935) of *A Midsummer Night's Dream.*★

Religion, Shakespeare's. The records of Shakespeare's baptism,★ marriage,★ and burial, show that he was, as the law required, a conforming member of the Church of England. His works show considerable familiarity with the Bible,★ the Book of Common Prayer, and the Homilies.

Richard Davies,★ late in the seventeenth century, wrote that Shakespeare 'died a papist'. He cites no evidence. There is some reason to suppose that Shakespeare's father had Catholic sympathies (see Spiritual Testament, John Shakespeare's), and his daughter Susanna★ was fined for recusancy, though she later married a staunch Protestant with Puritan leanings.

Reported texts. See Bad Quartos.

A scene from Max Reinhardt's film of *A Midsummer Night's Dream*, 1935

Reynolds, Frederick (1764–1841). A prolific English dramatist who adapted a number of Shakespeare's comedies in musical versions for Covent Garden Theatre.★ They were *A Midsummer Night's Dream*★ (1819), *Twelfth Night*★ (1820), *The Two Gentlemen of Verona*★ (1821), *The Tempest*★ (1821), *The Merry Wives of Windsor*★ (1824), and *The Taming of the Shrew*★ (1828). The composer Sir Henry Bishop★ collaborated with him.

Rhyme Royal. A stanza of seven iambic pentameters, rhyming a b a b b c c, used by Shakespeare in *The Rape of Lucrece*,★ and in *A Lover's Complaint*.★

Richard II. Shakespeare's history play was first published in quarto★ in 1597. Richard's abdication (IV.i.154–318) was omitted, doubtless because of the contemporary political situation, in this and the two subsequent reprints of the quarto (both in 1598). After the succession issue had been resolved, the episode was considered less contentious, and it appeared in the fourth quarto, of 1608, advertised as having 'new additions of the Parliament scene, and the deposing of King Richard; as it hath been lately acted by the King's Majesty's servants, at the Globe.' The First Folio★ text (1623) includes a better version of the deposition scene based probably on a prompt book.

The date of the play is uncertain, but is unlikely to be later than

1595. It is based mainly on Holinshed,★ and possibly also on Samuel Daniel's★ *First Four Books of the Civil Wars* (1595). It is the first play in Shakespeare's second tetralogy based on English history. Written entirely in verse, it is stylistically very different from the other three. The first recorded performance is one specially commissioned by the Earl of Essex's★ supporters on 7 February 1601 as a gesture of support for his rebellion the following day. The players argued that it was 'so old and so long out of use' that they would have 'small or no company at it', but performed it nevertheless. A court case ensued, but the company was exonerated. An improbable performance on a ship captained by William Keeling★ is recorded in 1607. It was also given at the Globe★ on 12 June 1631.

Nahum Tate's★ adaptation, as *The Sicilian Usurper*, appears to have been played twice only, in 1681. Lewis Theobald's★ adaptation appeared at Lincoln's Inn Fields★ in 1719, with some success. Shakespeare's play was given at Covent Garden★ in 1738, with revivals in the two following seasons. It was neglected until Edmund Kean★ played in a version by Richard Wroughton at Drury Lane★ in 1815, revived from time to time till 1828. W. C. Macready★ came closer to Shakespeare in his performances. The most successful nineteenth-century production was Charles Kean's★ at the Princess's in 1857,

King Richard II: he was the first King of England to sit for his portrait. This one of about 1388 is by an unknown artist

which had eighty-five performances. It was scenically spectacular, archaeologically respectable, and textually short. F. R. Benson★ was a distinguished Richard at Stratford-upon-Avon and elsewhere at the turn of the century; C. E. Montague's review of his performance in the *Manchester Guardian* has become a classic of theatre criticism, often anthologized. Beerbohm Tree's★ spectacular version at His Majesty's in 1903 included a new version of the pageant of Bolingbroke's entry into London which Charles Kean had introduced, and also a coronation for Henry IV. Granville-Barker★ had played Richard in 1899 in a performance in Elizabethan style directed by William Poel.* John Gielgud,* perhaps the greatest exponent of the role in the twentieth century, played it first at the Old Vic* in 1929–30, and also at the Queen's in 1937. Maurice Evans was successful as Richard in both England and America from 1934. Distinguished post-war perform- ances include Michael Redgrave's* at Stratford-upon-Avon (1951), John Neville's at the Old Vic* (1954, etc.), and the Royal Shake- speare Company* production by John Barton* (1973–4) in which Richard Pasco* and Ian Richardson* alternated as Richard and Bolingbroke.

Richard II is an uneven play, and the scenes of Aumerle's rebellion against Bolingbroke have frequently embarrassed actors and directors, but the role of Richard himself offers unequalled opportunities to actors who can command pathos and speak verse.

Richard III. The fourth play in Shakespeare's first historical tetralogy was entered in the Stationers'* Register on 20 October 1597 and printed the same year. It was probably written soon after *3 Henry VI,** in 1592 or 1593, and is based mainly on Holinshed's* *Chronicles*. There are contemporary allusions to Burbage's* success as Richard, and the play's popularity is also demonstrated by the five reprints of the first edition before it reappeared in the First Folio* (1623). The only specific early performance to be recorded was at Court on 16 Novem- ber 1633.

In 1700, Colley Cibber's* radical adaptation appeared, with himself as Richard. It is much abbreviated and reshaped, includes material from several of Shakespeare's other history plays, omits Queen Margaret and other important characters, and adds many lines written by Cibber. A theatrically effective melodrama, it held the stage for close on two centuries and provided a leading role in which many actors triumphed. Cibber played Richard till 1733, with a final performance in 1739. James Quin* succeeded him in 1734.

David Garrick* made his sensational London début in the role at Goodman's Fields on 19 October 1741, and continued to play it till 1776. J. P. Kemble* played Richard from 1783, and in 1811 at Drury. Lane* restored some of Shakespeare's lines. G. F. Cooke* was famous in the role during the same period, and Edmund Kean* undertook it for his second role at Drury Lane, with enormous success, eloquently recorded in Hazlitt's* reviews. W. C. Macready* first played Richard in London in 1819, and in 1821, at Covent Garden,* unsuccessfully

Richard III

King Richard III:
the earliest known portrait

attempted more restorations of Shakespeare. Charles Kean★ played regularly in Cibber's version, notably in a spectacular production at the Princess's in 1854.

Samuel Phelps★ put on a version of Shakespeare's play at Sadler's Wells★ in 1845, but reverted to Cibber in 1861. Henry Irving★ restored Shakespeare, heavily truncated, at the Lyceum★ in 1877, and after this Cibber's influence has gradually faded, though it was felt even in Laurence Olivier's★ film (1955). Geneviève Ward played the restored role of Queen Margaret with great success from 1896 to 1921. F. R. Benson,★ Baliol Holloway and Robert Atkins★ all succeeded as Richard.

Laurence Olivier's brilliant performances were given for the Old Vic★ in 1944–5 and 1948–9, and for his film version he had John Gielgud★ as Clarence and Ralph Richardson★ as Buckingham; Margaret was omitted, but Jane Shore was introduced as a non-speaking role. Ian Holm played Richard in Peter Hall's★ Stratford-upon-Avon production, as part of *The Wars of the Roses,*★ in 1963, etc., with Peggy Ashcroft★ as Margaret. The play has been very successful in America, mainly in Cibber's version; Edwin Booth★ restored Shakespeare in 1877, but John Barrymore used Cibber in 1920.

In its integration of overall structure and linguistic detail *Richard III* represents a great advance over Shakespeare's earlier histories. Theatrically it still suffers under the influence of Cibber's adaptation; it awaits a director who will fully realize its own individual qualities, which are inextricably linked with those of the earlier plays of the tetralogy.

Richardson, Ian (b. 1934). British actor; he played Hamlet at the Birmingham Repertory Theatre in 1959, and went to Stratford-upon-Avon in 1960. His roles with the Royal Shakespeare Company* include Oberon (1962), Antipholus of Ephesus (1962, etc.), Ford (1964, etc.), Coriolanus and Bertram (1967), Pericles (1969), Angelo and Prospero (1970), Richard II and Bolingbroke (alternately with Richard Pasco,* 1973–4), Berowne (1973), and Iachimo (1974).

Richardson, Sir Ralph (b. 1902). English actor who has played many Shakespeare roles, most notably Bottom (Old Vic,* 1937) and Falstaff (Old Vic, 1945).

Riche, Barnabe (c. 1540–1617). British soldier and writer; his *Riche his Farewell to Military Profession* (1581) includes *Apollonius and Silla*, translated from Belleforest's* version of Bandello, which is the main source of *Twelfth Night.**

Rival Poet, The. The poet referred to in Sonnets* 78–83, 85, and 86, who at one time and another has been speculatively identified with most poets of Shakespeare's time.

Rivals, The. See *The Two Noble Kinsmen.*

Riverside edition. A one-volume edition of Shakespeare's works published in 1974, edited by G. Blakemore Evans and others, with introductions to the individual works and much ancillary material.

Roman Plays, Shakespeare's. *Titus Andronicus,* *Julius Caesar,* *Antony and Cleopatra,* and *Coriolanus.* *Cymbeline* also makes some use of Roman history.

Romances. Many of Shakespeare's plays use motifs common in romance literature, such as separation, wanderings, reunion, reconciliation, and forgiveness, but the term is usually confined to his last four tragi-comedies, *Pericles,* *Cymbeline,* *The Winter's Tale,* and *The Tempest,* sometimes with the addition of *The Two Noble Kinsmen,* as in them these elements occur in the greatest concentration. These plays are also known as the Last Plays.

Romantic Comedies. A term sometimes used to distinguish *The Merchant of Venice,* *Much Ado About Nothing,* *As You Like It,* and *Twelfth Night* from the Early Comedies* and 'Problem Comedies',* though it may also be applied to a wider range of plays.

Romeo and Juliet. Shakespeare's early tragedy is based on a long poem by Arthur Brooke, *The Tragical History of Romeus and Juliet* (1562), and there are numerous other versions of the story. The play was first printed, in a bad quarto,* in 1597, as 'An excellent conceited tragedy of Romeo and Juliet, as it hath been often (with great applause) played publicly by the Right Honourable the Lord of Hunsdon his servants.' The second quarto, of 1599, declares itself to be 'newly corrected, augmented, and amended', and has about 700 more lines than the first.

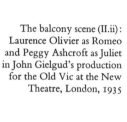

The balcony scene (II.ii): Laurence Olivier as Romeo and Peggy Ashcroft as Juliet in John Gielgud's production for the Old Vic at the New Theatre, London, 1935

Romeo and Juliet has been variously dated from 1591 to 1596. Over the centuries it has been one of Shakespeare's most successful plays. It was acted in 1662, soon after the reopening of the theatres. Thomas Otway borrowed from it for *The History and Fall of Caius Marius* (1679), which ousted Shakespeare's play till 1744, when Theophilus Cibber★ revived an adaptation of it, retaining from Otway Juliet's awakening before Romeo's death for a last farewell. David Garrick's★ adaptation of 1748 also included his own final duologue for the lovers as well as a dirge for Juliet, with music by Thomas Arne.★ His adaptation seems to have been more popular than any other Shakespeare play on the London stage during the second half of the eighteenth century. The reawakening scene was abandoned in major productions during the 1840s. The play has continued to be popular, and has been frequently filmed, e.g. by Franco Zeffirelli★ (1968). It has inspired numerous other works, such as operas by Bellini★ (1830) and Gounod★ (1867), Berlioz's★ dramatic symphony (1839), Tchaikovsky's★ fantasy-overture (1869–80), and Prokofiev's★ full-length ballet (1938).

Romeus and Juliet, The Tragical History of (1562). A long poem by Arthur Brooke★ (d. 1563), on which Shakespeare based *Romeo and Juliet*.★

Rosalynde. A prose romance by Thomas Lodge★ (c. 1557–1625), printed in 1590; the main source of *As You Like It*.★

Rose Theatre. See Admiral's Men.

Rosencrantz and Guildenstern. A clever burlesque of *Hamlet* by W. S. Gilbert★ first published in 1874 in the magazine *Fun*, with reference to Irving's★ performances; acted 1891; revived some years later.

Rossini, Gioacchino (1792–1868). The Italian composer's *Otello* (1816) is the first opera based on Shakespeare's play.

Rowe, Nicholas (1674–1718). English dramatist. He prepared the first edited text of Shakespeare, published in six volumes in 1709. It preserves some of the corruptions of the Fourth Folio,★ on which it is based, and includes the non-Shakespearian plays added to the Third Folio,★ but Rowe consulted some of the quartos,★ too, and restored passages not found in the Folios, such as Hamlet's 'How all occasions . . .' (IV.iv). He provided lists of *Dramatis Personae*, divided the plays into acts and scenes, indicated locations of scenes,★ and added stage directions.★

His edition, commissioned by the publisher Jacob Tonson, has forty-five illustrative engravings. It is prefaced by the first formal

Frontispiece to *Richard III* in Nicholas Rowe's edition (1709)

biography, deriving largely from information provided by Thomas Betterton,★ and using much traditional material.

Royal Shakespeare Theatre. The present building in Stratford-upon-Avon originated in the one opened as the Shakespeare Memorial

Theatre in 1879, in which festival performances were given for short periods each year, most notably by F. R. Benson's★ company from 1886 to 1919. It was built under the sponsorship of the Flower★ family, who have continued to take an active part in its administration.

The Shakespeare Memorial Theatre (opened 1879), in 1895

In 1919 W. Bridges-Adams★ took over the artistic direction of the festival. The theatre was incorporated under royal charter as a non-profit making organization in 1925. The next year, the building burned down. The present one was opened in 1932. B. Iden Payne★ was director from 1935–42, Milton Rosmer in 1943, Robert Atkins★ from 1944–5, Barry Jackson★ from 1946–8, Anthony Quayle★ from 1948–52, Anthony Quayle and Glen Byam Shaw,★ 1952–6, and Glen Byam Shaw, 1956–9. Peter Hall,★ who became Director in 1960, secured support from the Arts Council, organized the company on a semi-permanent basis, and acquired the Aldwych Theatre as a London home for it.

The theatre became the Royal Shakespeare Theatre in 1961, and Michel Saint-Denis and Peter Brook★ became co-directors of the company. In 1968 Trevor Nunn★ was appointed Artistic Director, and increased the development of the company as the major British performers of Shakespeare's plays, with occasional productions of

Shakespeare's contemporaries at Stratford-upon-Avon, performances of plays of all periods at the Aldwych, extensive touring operations at home and abroad, experimental productions in studio theatres, and the prospect of a permanent London home in the Barbican.

Russell, Thomas (1570–1634). A friend of Shakespeare's, who left him £5 and asked him to be an overseer of his will. He seems also to have been a friend of Henry Willoughby, the assumed author of *Willobie his Avisa.*★ He was the stepfather of Leonard Digges.★

Rutland, Francis Manners, 6th Earl of (1578–1632). On 31 March 1613, his steward recorded a payment 'to Mr. Shakespeare in gold about my lord's impresa, 44s.; to Richard Burbage for painting and making it, in gold, 44s.' An 'impresa' was a painted paper or pasteboard shield with emblems or mottoes. Apparently Shakespeare had devised this one. The occasion was the tilt on King James I's★ Accession Day, 24 March. Shakespeare portrays such a tilt in *Pericles,*★ II.ii.

Rylands, George (b. 1902). English scholar and critic, for many years Fellow of King's College, Cambridge. He directed many of Shakespeare's plays for the Marlowe Society,★ and has exercised a strong influence on twentieth-century productions of Shakespeare. He compiled an anthology of passages from Shakespeare, 'The Ages of Man', which formed the basis of a successful series of recitals by Sir John Gielgud.★ He directed the recording of uncut versions of all Shakespeare's plays by the Marlowe Society,★ along with professional players.

Rymer, Thomas (1641–1713). English historiographer and critic, an adherent of neoclassicism, whose *Short View of Tragedy* (1693) includes a notorious attack on *Othello*★: 'the tragical part is plainly none other than a bloody farce, without salt or savour'.

S

Sadler, Hamnet (or Hamlet; d. 1624). Baker of Stratford-upon-Avon. His wife (d. 1614) was called Judith. Shakespeare's twins may have been named after them. Hamnet witnessed Shakespeare's will in 1616, and was left 26s. 8d. to buy a mourning ring.

Sadler's Wells Theatre. Performances were given in a 'Musick House' on this site in Islington, London, during the early eighteenth century, and a theatre was built there in 1765. It housed the important Shakespeare productions of Samuel Phelps★ from 1844 to 1862. The building deteriorated, and became partly derelict. Lilian Baylis★ rebuilt it, and in 1931 it became an additional home for the Old Vic★ company. From 1934 it was used primarily as a home for opera and ballet.

Salvini, Tommaso (1829–1916). Italian tragedian, most famous as Othello (which he played in English as well as Italian); also a distinguished Hamlet, Macbeth, Iago, and Lear.

Sauny the Scot. See *Taming of the Shrew, The.*

Saxo Grammaticus (c. 1150–1206). The Danish author of *Gesta Danorum*, or *Historia Danica*, first printed in 1514, from which Belleforest★ translated the story of Hamlet.

Scheemakers, Peter (1691–1770). Flemish sculptor of the statue of Shakespeare erected in Westminster Abbey by public subscription in 1740, based on the Chandos portrait.★ It was frequently copied and imitated, often in porcelain.

Schlegel, August Wilhelm von (1767–1845). German scholar; the translation of Shakespeare's plays begun by him and completed by Ludwig Tieck★ has acquired classic status. His 1808 lectures *On Dramatic Art and Literature* propound a Romantic view of Shakespeare related to that of Coleridge,★ whom he may have influenced.

School of Night. A phrase in *Love's Labour's Lost* (IV.iii.250–1) which has been taken to allude to a supposed intellectual circle centring on Sir Walter Raleigh.

Schubert, Franz (1797–1828). The great Austrian composer wrote music for German translations of three lyrics by Shakespeare: 'Come, thou monarch of the vine' (*Antony and Cleopatra★*), 'Hark, hark the lark' (*Cymbeline★*), and 'Who is Sylvia?' (*The Two Gentlemen of Verona★*). The two last are among his most popular songs.

Schücking, Levin Ludwig (1878–1964). German critic, author of *Character Problems in Shakespeare's Plays* (1919), etc., and editor, with Walther Ebisch, of *A Shakespeare Bibliography* (1931, Supplement, 1937).

Scofield, Paul (b. 1922). English actor whose notable Shakespeare roles include Don Armado, Lucio, and Mercutio (Stratford-upon-Avon, 1946–7), the Bastard in *King John,★* Hamlet, and the Clown in *The Winter's Tale★* (Stratford-upon-Avon, 1948), Pericles (Rudolf Steiner Hall, 1950), Richard II (Lyric, Hammersmith, 1952–3), Hamlet (Phoenix, etc., 1955), Coriolanus (Stratford, Ontario,★ 1961), King Lear (Stratford-upon-Avon, 1962–3), Timon of Athens (Stratford-upon-Avon, 1965), Macbeth (Stratford-upon-Avon, 1967), and Prospero (Leeds, etc., 1974–5). He also played King Lear in Peter Brook's★ film (1970).

Paul Scofield as King Lear
in Peter Brook's production,
Stratford-upon-Avon (1962)

Scoloker, Anthony. Known only as the author of *Diaphantus, or the Passions of Love*, 1604, which includes a reference to 'friendly Shakespeare's tragedies, where the comedian rides when the tragedian stands on tip-toe: faith it should please all, like Prince Hamlet.' There is also a description of Hamlet: 'Puts off his clothes, his shirt he only wears,/Much like mad Hamlet; thus as passion tears.'

Second-best bed, Shakespeare's. See Hathaway, Anne.

Second Folio. See Folio.

Secretary hand. The normal handwriting of Shakespeare's time, used in, e.g., his signatures.★

See If You Like It, or, *'Tis all a Mistake.* See *Comedy of Errors, The.*

Seneca, Lucius Annaeus (c. 4 BC–AD 65). Roman philosopher and dramatist. His nine verse tragedies, possibly intended to be declaimed rather than acted, and formally structured, have sensationally bloody themes. They were known in England, were all translated by 1581, and exerted a powerful influence over native playwrights. Shakespeare's most Senecan plays are *Titus Andronicus,*★ *Richard III,*★ and *Julius Caesar*★; in *Hamlet*★ (II.ii.395–7), Polonius comments that 'Seneca cannot be too heavy, nor Plautus too light' for the players. Seneca's essays also were influential.

Shadwell, Thomas (c. 1642–92). English dramatist who in 1674 prepared an operatic version of the Dryden★-Davenant★ adaptation of

The Tempest.★ The original music was by a variety of composers. That written for a revival of 1695 has been generally, though not certainly, attributed to Henry Purcell.★

Shadwell also adapted *Timon of Athens*★ as *The History of Timon of Athens, the Man-Hater*, in 1678. Both works were successful, the latter holding the stage till the middle of the eighteenth century.

Shakespeare, Anne. Sister of William,★ baptized 1571, buried 1579. See also Hathaway, Anne.

Shakespeare, Edmund. Brother of William,★ baptized 1580, probably the 'player' buried in St Saviour's, Southwark, in 1607 'with a forenoon knell of the great bell' which cost twenty shillings.

Shakespeare, Gilbert. Brother of William★, baptized 1566; he appears to have worked in London as a haberdasher, and to have been a bachelor; he was buried in Stratford-upon-Avon on 3 February 1612.

Shakespeare, Hamnet. Only son of William,★ twin of Judith,★ baptized 2 February, 1585; buried 11 August 1596.

Shakespeare, Joan. (a) Sister of William,★ baptized 15 September 1558; died young. (b) Another sister, also Joan, baptized 15 April 1569; married a hatter, William Hart; had four children; lived in the Birthplace in Henley Street, and by her brother William's will received '£20 and all my wearing apparel ... and ... the house with the appurtenances in Stratford wherein she dwelleth for her natural life under the yearly rent of 12d.' Her husband was buried one week before William Shakespeare.

Joan continued to live as a widow in Henley Street, and was buried on 4 November 1646. Their daughter, Mary, lived only from 1603 to 1607. Shakespeare left £5 to each of their three sons, William (1600–39), who died unmarried; Thomas (1605, died before 1670), who married, and succeeded his mother in the Birthplace; and Michael (1608–18).

The Birthplace★ belonged to Susanna Hall, whose daughter Elizabeth★ left it and the adjoining Henley Street house to Thomas's two sons, Thomas (b. 1634) and George (1636–1702). George's descendants occupied the Birthplace till 1806, when it was sold to Thomas Court. Descendants of the Harts are the closest surviving relatives of Shakespeare.

Shakespeare, John (d. 1601). Father of William,★ husband of Mary (Arden★), described in Stratford-upon-Avon records as a glover; also dealt in wool. He became a prominent and prosperous townsman, and was elected alderman in 1565 and bailiff in 1568. After about 1576 he seems to have fallen on hard times; he stopped attending council meetings, and was replaced as alderman in 1586. He fell into debt and stopped going to church, perhaps for fear of arrest. He died in September 1601. See also Spiritual Testament, John Shakespeare's.

Shakespeare, Judith (1585–1662). Daughter of William,* twin of Hamnet*; baptized 2 February 1585; married a vintner, Thomas Quiney,* 10 February 1616. On 26 March, her husband was prosecuted for fornication with Margaret Wheeler, who had died that month along with her baby by Quiney. He confessed, and was sentenced to perform public penance; but this penalty was remitted. This event seems to have caused Shakespeare to alter his will.*

Judith and Thomas had three sons, Shakespeare, who died in infancy, and Richard and Thomas, who both died in 1639, aged twenty-one and nineteen. Their father lived till at least 1655. Judith died in 1662, aged seventy-seven, and was buried in Stratford-upon-Avon.

Shakespeare, Margaret (1562–3). Sister of William*; baptized 2 December 1562; buried 30 April 1563.

Shakespeare, Richard (1574–1613). Brother of William*; baptized 11 March 1574; buried 4 February 1613.

Shakespeare, Susanna (1583–1649). Daughter of William*; baptized 26 May 1583. Her name occurs in a recusant list of 1606 for failing to receive communion on Easter Sunday, which implies that she was suspected of having Catholic sympathies. She married John Hall* on 5 June 1607. Their daughter, Elizabeth,* was baptized on 21 February 1608. On 15 July 1615 she sued John Lane for slanderously saying that she 'had the running of the reins and had been naught with Ralph Smith at [?and] John Palmer.' For thus accusing her of having venereal disease and of committing adultery, Lane was excommunicated. She and her husband were the executors of Shakespeare's will,* and she inherited New Place* and most of his other lands and property. Hall died in 1635. Susanna continued to live at New Place with her daughter and son-in-law, Elizabeth and Thomas Nash.* She died on 11 July 1649 and was buried next to her husband in the chancel of

Holy Trinity Church.* Her gravestone is inscribed:

> Witty above her sex, but that's not all;
> Wise to salvation was good Mistress Hall.
> Something of Shakespeare was in that, but this
> Wholly of him with whom she's now in bliss.
> Then, passenger, hast ne'er a tear
>   To weep with her that wept with all?
> That wept, yet set herself to cheer
>   Them up with comforts cordial.
> Her love shall live, her mercy spread,
> When thou hast ne'er a tear to shed.

Shakespeare, William (1564–1616). The principal entries relating directly to his life and career are: Apocryphal Plays; Arms, Shakespeare's; Authorship; Baptism, Shakespeare's; Birthday, Shakespeare's; Birthplace, Shakespeare's; Blackfriars Gatehouse; Chronology; Crabtree, Shakespeare's; Dark Lady of the Sonnets; Dedications; Epitaph, Shakespeare's; Folio, the First; Grammar School, Stratford-upon-Avon; Hathaway, Anne; Lost Years, Shakespeare's; Marriage, Shakespeare's; Monument, Shakespeare's; New Place; Portraits of Shakespeare; Religion, Shakespeare's; Signatures, Shakespeare's; Tithes; Welcombe enclosures; Will, Shakespeare's. There is a separate entry for each of his works.

Shakespeare, William, as actor. Shakespeare's name heads the list of 'the principal actors in all these plays' in the First Folio* and of the 'principal comedians' in the 1616 Folio reprint of Ben Jonson's* *Every Man in his Humour*, acted in 1598. He is also listed among the 'principal tragedians' in Jonson's *Sejanus*, acted in 1603. We cannot certainly name any parts as his. John Davies,* in enigmatic lines, wrote 'Hadst thou not played some kingly parts in sport . . .' Rowe's* enquiries yielded only the report 'that the top of his performance was the Ghost in his own *Hamlet*'. George Steevens,* in 1778, published a legend that he played Adam in *As You Like It*.* Phrases in Sonnets* 110 and 111 suggest distaste for a life which makes him 'a motley to the view' and for 'public means which public manners breeds'.

Shakespeare Apocrypha, The. See Apocryphal plays.

Shakespeare Association. Founded in 1916 by Sir Israel Gollancz, the Association held regular meetings, and published papers, monographs, facsimiles of rare texts, and a series of facsimiles* of Shakespeare quartos which is still in progress, though the Association is no longer active.

Shakespeare Association of America. A scholarly society founded in 1923. Its first organ was the *Shakespeare Association Bulletin*, founded in 1924, developed in 1950 into *Shakespeare Quarterly*.★

Shakespeare Bibliothek, Munich. A library and research centre for postgraduate study of Shakespeare and the English Renaissance of the University of Munich, founded by W. H. Clemen★ in 1964. It is open to visiting scholars, and is especially rich in materials concerning Shakespeare in Germany.

Shakespeare Birthplace Trust. Formed in 1847 when the Birthplace was bought for the nation, the Trust administers the Shakespeare properties in Stratford-upon-Avon and its neighbourhood, and also arranges cultural and educational activities. The Shakespeare Centre in Henley Street houses its offices and the Nuffield Library, which incorporates the Trust's collection of books and archives, as well as the library of the Royal Shakespeare Theatre.★ The Trust has been directed since 1945 by Dr Levi Fox.

Shakespeare Centre. See Shakespeare Birthplace Trust.

Shakespeare Conference. See Shakespeare Institute.

Shakespeare Gallery. See Boydell's Shakespeare Gallery.

Shakespeare Gesellschaft. The German Shakespeare Society founded at Weimar in 1865. It publishes the *Shakespeare Jahrbuch*. In 1964 it divided into East and West. The West German branch is based in Bochum, the East German in Weimar.

Shakespeare Institute. Allardyce Nicoll★ founded the Institute in 1951 as a graduate centre of the English Department of the University of Birmingham, specializing in the study of Shakespeare and his contemporaries. It was originally housed in Mason Croft, Stratford-upon-Avon, formerly home of the novelist Marie Corelli. Professor T. J. B. Spencer took over as director in 1961.

The Institute is now housed in Birmingham, where it has an extensive library of books and microfilms, though it retains the use of Mason Croft, where the biennial Shakespeare Conference is held. The Conference, whose membership is by invitation, has a close connection with the annual *Shakespeare Survey*,★ also founded by Allardyce Nicoll.

Shakespeare Memorial Library, Birmingham. Founded in 1864, destroyed by fire in 1879, but soon restored, it is part of the Birmingham Central Reference Library, and has an important collection of printed and other materials.

Shakespeare Memorial Theatre. See Royal Shakespeare Theatre.

Shakespeare Newsletter. An occasional publication founded in 1951 and edited by Louis Marder. It includes news items, reviews, digests of books and articles, bibliographies, etc.

Shakespeare Quarterly. Official publication of the Shakespeare Association of America,★ first published in 1950, succeeding the *Shakespeare Association Bulletin*; it includes an annual bibliography, articles and notes, and reviews of books and performances.

Shakespeare Society. A scholarly organization founded in London in 1840 by J. P. Collier★ and others which published much original material. Collier's forgeries resulted in its disbandment in 1853.

Shakespeare Studies. An annual American volume of scholarly and critical articles and reviews, founded in 1965 and edited by J. Leeds Barroll and others.

Shakespeare Survey. A British annual publication, founded in 1948 by Allardyce Nicoll★ who edited it till he was succeeded by Kenneth Muir in 1966. Each volume has a specific theme, and includes critical and scholarly articles along with surveys of current Shakespeare studies. Alternate volumes have included a selection of papers given at the previous year's Shakespeare Conference.

Shakespeare's birthday. See Birthday, Shakespeare's.

Sharpham, Edward (1576–1608). Dramatist. His *The Fleir* (c. 1605) has Shakespearian echoes and includes what appears to be a reference to stage business in early performances of *A Midsummer Night's Dream*:★ 'Faith, like Thisbe in the play, 'a has almost killed himself with the scabbard.'

Shaw, George Bernard (1856–1950). The great dramatist's many writings concerned with Shakespeare include many brilliant reviews contributed to the *Saturday Review* between 1895 and 1898; a short play, *The Dark Lady of the Sonnets* (1910), which is a piece of propaganda for a National Theatre★; a substitute Act V for *Cymbeline*★ (*Cymbeline Refinished*, 1945); and a puppet play, *Shakes versus Shav* (1949). They are collected by Edwin Wilson as *Shaw on Shakespeare* (1961, etc.).

Shaw, Glen Byam (b. 1904). Actor and director, co-director with Anthony Quayle★ of the Shakespeare Memorial Theatre,★ Stratford-upon-Avon, 1952–6; Director, 1956–9.

Sheep-Shearing, The. See Morgan, McNamara.

Shostakovitch, Dmitri (1906–75). The Russian composer wrote the musical scores for Grigori Kozintsev's★ films of *Hamlet*★ (1964) and *King Lear*★ (1971). His opera *Katerina Ismailova* (1934), also known as

Lady Macbeth of Mtensk, is not based on Shakespeare.

Shottery. See Hathaway, Anne.

Sibelius, Jean (1865–1957). The Finnish composer wrote incidental music for *The Tempest*★ in 1926. He also has an impressive setting of 'Come away, death' (*Twelfth Night*★).

Sicilian Usurper, The. See Tate, Nahum.

Siddons, Mrs Sarah (1755–1831). The great tragic actress was the sister of John Philip and Charles Kemble.★ Her most famous part was Lady Macbeth; she was also remarkable as Desdemona, Ophelia, Volumnia, Constance, Queen Katherine, Rosalind and Hermione.

Sidney, Sir Philip (1554–86). See *Arcadia*.

Signatures, Shakespeare's. The six undisputed signatures are on a de-position in the Belott-Mountjoy★ suit (11 May 1612), on a convey-

Mrs Siddons as Lady Macbeth: a painting by G. H. Harlow engraved by C. Rolls

ance of the Blackfriars Gatehouse★ (10 March 1613), on the mortgage of the Blackfriars Gatehouse (11 March 1613), and on the three sheets of the will★ (25 March 1616). There are many forgeries, and a few

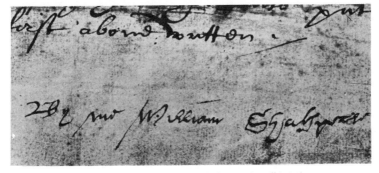

One of the three signatures on Shakespeare's will (1616)

other signatures that may be genuine, including one in a copy of Florio's★ translation of Montaigne★ in the British Library, and one in William Lambarde's *Archaionomia* (1568) in the Folger★ Library.

Signet Shakespeare. An American paper-back edition of Shakespeare's works, one play per volume, under the general editorship of Sylvan Barnet, with introductions, notes on the page, and selected criticism. It was published from 1963 to 1968, and in collected form in 1972.

Sir John Oldcastle. See Oldcastle, Sir John.

Sir Thomas More. A play written for the Admiral's Men,★ surviving in an incomplete scribal transcript submitted to Sir Edmund Tilney, Master of the Revels,★ perhaps about 1593, perhaps about 1601, who required revisions, which were supplied in five different hands. One of these, known as Hand D, is believed by many to be Shakespeare's. If so, it is his only surviving literary manuscript. It is a scene of three pages depicting More, as Sheriff of London, pacifying apprentices in a May-day rebellion against foreigners. Studies of handwriting, spelling, style, and thought have supported

Sir Thomas More: an early anonymous copy of Holbein's portrait

the attribution to Shakespeare. The revisions did not satisfy the censor. The play's first known professional performance was at Nottingham in 1964, with Ian McKellen★ as More.

Sisson, C. J. (1885–1966). Scholar and critic, especially expert in the handwriting of Shakespeare's time. His edition of Shakespeare was published in 1954, and is supplemented by *New Readings in Shakespeare* (2 vols., 1956), discussions of individual textual problems.

Smetana, Bedrich (1824–84). The Czech composer wrote a symphonic poem, 'Richard III' (1858).

Smith, John Christopher (1712–95). An English composer of German origin who wrote the music for musical versions of *A Midsummer Night's Dream*★ (*The Fairies*, 1755) and *The Tempest*★ (1756), both at Drury Lane.★

Smock Alley Theatre. A theatre in Dublin established during the Restoration. A copy of the Third Folio★ used by the company as a promptbook shows that at least fourteen of Shakespeare's plays were performed there during the late seventeenth century. During the eighteenth century, many leading English actors performed there.

Soest portrait of Shakespeare.
A painting by the Dutch artist Gerard Soest, who settled in London in 1656 and died in 1681. The figure is dressed in a late seventeenth-century conception of early seventeenth-century costume. David Piper (see Portraits of Shakespeare) says that it 'may well reflect a tradition in living memory, early in the second half of the seventeenth century, of the poet's appearance'. It, or a copy probably by the artist, now hangs in the Shakespeare Centre,★ Stratford-upon-Avon.

The Soest portrait

Soliloquy. Shakespeare often uses the convention by which characters address themselves or the audience, sometimes while alone, sometimes as an aside while other characters are present.

Sonnets. One hundred and fifty-four sonnets were published in 1609 as *Shakespeare's Sonnets never before imprinted* in a volume bearing a dedication by the publisher, Thomas Thorpe,★ to 'Mr W.H.' Two of the sonnets, Nos. 138 and 144, had already been printed, in inferior texts, in 1599, in *The Passionate Pilgrim.*★ Most of the sonnets were reprinted in 1640 by John Benson.★

Their date of composition is unknown. Francis Meres★ referred in 1598 to Shakespeare's 'sugared sonnets among his private friends'. Sonnet cycles had an extraordinary vogue during the 1590s. Otherwise, conjectures are based on stylistic evidence, including parallels with the plays; on possible topical allusions (especially in No. 107, known as the 'dating sonnet', though the event referred to has been variously identified); and on theories about the persons and events which form the subject matter of the sonnets. Most scholars assign them to 1592–8, though for different reasons.

Thomas Thorpe's
dedication of the
Sonnets (1609)

TO.THE.ONLIE.BEGETTER.OF.
THESE.INSVING.SONNETS.
Mʳ.W.H. ALL.HAPPINESSE.
AND.THAT.ETERNITIE.
PROMISED.

BY.

OVR.EVER-LIVING.POET.

WISHETH.

THE.WELL-WISHING.
ADVENTVRER.IN.
SETTING.
FORTH.

T. T.

All the sonnets but three are in the 'Shakespearian' form, having three quatrains of ten-syllabled lines followed by a couplet, and rhyming abab cdcd efef gg. The exceptions are No. 99, which has an additional, introductory line; No. 126, which has only twelve lines and is entirely in couplets; and No. 145, which is in octosyllabics.

The first one hundred and twenty-six sonnets are addressed mainly to a young man. The first seventeen implore him to marry and beget children. In Nos. 40 to 42, the friend steals the poet's mistress. In Nos. 78 to 86, a rival poet★ wins the affection of the friend, who appears also to be the writer's patron. Nos. 127 to 152 are addressed mainly to the writer's mistress, a dark woman. Nos. 153 and 154 are versions of a Greek epigram, and are sometimes believed not to be by Shakespeare.

There are differing opinions about whether the sonnets are autobiographical. 'With this key,' wrote Wordsworth, 'Shakespeare unlocked his heart.' 'If so,' retorted Browning, 'the less Shakespeare he.' Though they portray or allude to related situations, they do not tell a coherent story. The order in which they are printed is not necessarily the order of their composition. Many attempts have been made to rearrange them into a more logical sequence, but none has achieved general acceptance.

Many identifications have been offered of the poet's friend and his mistress. The poem *Willobie his Avisa*★ has been thought to have some connection with the story behind the sonnets. The friend has often, though not always, been supposed to be the dedicatee, 'Mr W.H.', described by Thorpe as 'the only begetter of these ensuing sonnets'.

The two favourite candidates have been Henry Wriothesley,* 3rd Earl of Southampton (though he was not 'Mr.', and the initials are reversed), and William Herbert,* 3rd Earl of Pembroke (whose rank is also a problem). Nominations for the 'rival poet' and the black woman (or 'dark lady'*) have come, gone, and come again: none has had more than temporary acceptance.

To read all the sonnets consecutively is difficult. Shakespeare's varied handling of the form requires the reader to make constant adjustments of response. Some of the poems are intellectually contorted, introspective, and enigmatic. Others are among the most confident and lyrical love poems in English.

Sources of Shakespeare's Works. Most of Shakespeare's plays, like those of his contemporaries, are based on history, or on other stories that had already been told. Bernard Shaw* referred mischievously to Shakespeare's 'gift of telling a story (provided someone else told it to him first)'. But Shakespeare almost always transformed his inherited material.

The entries on individual works name their major sources. Geoffrey Bullough's *Narrative and Dramatic Sources of Shakespeare* (8 vols., 1957–75) reprints the major sources with valuable critical essays on Shakespeare's use of them in each work.

Southampton, Earl of. See Wriothesley, Henry.

Spevack, Marvin. Compiler of *A Complete and Systematic Concordance to the Works of Shakespeare* (6 vols., 1968–70). It is keyed to the Riverside edition.* Vols. I–III list all uses of all words in the text, without context, and also give separate character concordances to each play. Vols. IV–VI list the words alphabetically for the works as a whole, and give context. Supplementary volumes appeared in 1975: Vol. VII is a concordance to stage-directions and speech-prefixes, and Vol. VIII to the 'bad' quartos,* etc. *The Harvard Concordance to Shakespeare* (1973) is a single-volume work based on Vols. IV–VI.

'Spiritual Testament', John Shakespeare's. A booklet containing a handwritten Catholic protestation of faith by John Shakespeare* in fourteen articles discovered in the rafters of his house in Henley Street, Stratford-upon-Avon, in 1757. John Jordan* submitted a transcript of all of it except the first leaf (which by then was missing) for publication in *The Gentleman's Magazine* in 1784, but it was rejected. Malone* studied the original and printed it in his 'Historical Account of the English Stage' in his 1790 edition of Shakespeare's works, along with a transcript of the missing first page which Jordan was somehow able to supply. By this time, Malone was beginning to lose faith in the document's authenticity.

The original booklet is now lost, and we depend for our knowledge of it on Malone's printed transcript. For a long time Jordan was suspected of having forged the entire document, but about 1923 a Spanish version of the same basic statement, a 'Last Will of the Soul, made in health for the Christian to secure himself from the temptations of the Devil at the hour of death' and drawn up by Carlo Borromeo, who died in 1585, was discovered in the British Museum. It is known that British Jesuit missionaries, including Edmund Campion, visited Borromeo in 1580 and disseminated thousands of copies of the document on their return to England.

In 1966 an early printed English translation was acquired by the Folger★ Library, which proves that the document as printed by Malone was genuine, except for the first page, as to which Malone's suspicions of Jordan are justified.

The loss of the original document leaves several questions unanswered, but it does seem that at some point in his life Shakespeare's father subscribed to the Catholic faith.

Sprague, Arthur Colby (b. 1895). American scholar who has been highly influential in the study of the stage history of Shakespeare, and the critical application of its results. His main books are *Shakespeare and the Actors* (1944), *Shakespearian Players and Performances* (1953), and *Shakespeare's Histories: Plays for the Stage* (1964).

Spurgeon, Caroline (1869–1941). See Imagery.

Stage directions. The stage directions in the early editions of Shakespeare's plays are a mixture of those that he wrote himself and, in editions printed from manuscripts which had passed through the theatre (see prompt-book), of modifications of these by theatre personnel concerned with the practical needs of performance. Sometimes these can be distinguished on the basis of hypotheses about the manuscript from which the play was printed. Directions tend to be sparse, as the scripts were for performance, not for reading, and Shakespeare must usually have been at hand to amplify them orally when necessary.

Most modern editors vary the directions and add to them, in differing degrees according to the aims of the edition.

Stanford, Sir Charles Villiers (1852–1924). Irish composer of an opera based on *Much Ado About Nothing*,★ with that title, performed at Covent Garden★ in 1901.

Stationers' Register. In Shakespeare's time, printing and publication were the monopoly of the Stationers' Company. Members who wished to publish a book were required to enter its title in a register, and to pay a fee, which gave them a copyright in it. Not all bothered to do so, but the register is a valuable source of information, especially about the date of works not printed immediately on registration. For example, the earliest record of *Troilus and Cressida*★ is an entry of 7 February 1603, though it was not printed till 1609.

Steevens, George (1736–1800). English scholar who published an edition of twenty of Shakespeare's plays in 1766, a complete edition, based on Dr Johnson's★ but with additional notes by himself, in 1773 (revised 1778, revised again by Isaac Reed,★ 1785), and his final edition, as an answer to Malone's,★ in 1793. He realized the value to an editor of the quartos,★ and had an exceptional knowledge of Elizabethan literature.

He enjoyed both the friendship and the enmity of many literary figures of his time, including David Garrick,★ who lent him quartos of Shakespeare's plays from his library, and Dr Johnson. In his 1793 edition, he provided obscene notes to bawdy passages, attributing them to two worthy clergymen with whom he had quarrelled.

Stoll, Elmer Edgar (1874–1959). American critic who reacted against A. C. Bradley★ and insisted that study of Shakespeare's plays should be based on the dramatic conventions of the time at which they were written. His best-known book is *Art and Artifice in Shakespeare* (1933).

Strachey, Lytton (1880–1932). English man of letters whose essay on 'Shakespeare's Final Period' (1904) attacks the sentimental view of Shakespeare's late plays.

Stratford, Ontario. The festival here began in 1953, with two plays directed by Tyrone Guthrie★ on an open stage incorporating Elizabethan features and designed by Tanya Moiseiwitsch★ which has influenced the design of many subsequent theatres. At first it was covered by a tent; the permanent building was opened in 1957. It has continued to present Shakespeare's plays, with modifications to the stage and the use of additional auditoria, often with great success.

Strauss, Richard (1864–1949). The German composer wrote a tone poem, *Macbeth* (1888), and also set three of Ophelia's songs.

Students, The. See *Love's Labour's Lost*.

Sullivan, Sir Arthur (1842–1900). W. S. Gilbert's great collaborator made his first success with incidental music for *The Tempest* (1861); he composed settings for several Shakespeare songs, of which 'Orpheus

Stratford, Ontario: the Festival Theatre

with his Lute' is the best known, and, later, incidental music for *The Merchant of Venice*★ (1871), *Henry VIII*★ (1877), and *Macbeth*★ (1888).

Supposes. A play published in 1573, translated by George Gascoigne★ from Ariosto's *I Suppositi*, the first extant English play written entirely in prose, used by Shakespeare for the Bianca plot of *The Taming of the Shrew*.★

Swan Theatre. Built on the Bankside, London, about 1595; drawn by de Witt★; the Lord Chamberlain's Men★ probably played in it in 1596; it had 'fallen to decay' by 1632.

T

Taming of a Shrew, The. An anonymous play, registered and published in 1594, generally believed to be a bad quarto★ of *The Taming of the Shrew*★ or of an earlier play from which both derive.

Taming of the Shrew, The. Shakespeare's comedy, written probably in the early 1590s, was first printed in the First Folio★ (1623). A play printed as *The Taming of a Shrew*★ in 1594, once believed to be Shakespeare's source, is now generally regarded as a bad quarto.★ It includes a continuation and conclusion of the Christopher Sly episodes omitted from the Folio which may derive from a Shakespearian original, and are sometimes performed and included in editions. Shakespeare's plot of Bianca and her suitors derives from *Supposes*,★ translated by George Gascoigne★ from Ariosto's *I Suppositi*.

For long after the Restoration, performances were normally in adaptation, such as John Lacy's *Sauny the Scot* (1667), Christopher Bullock's *The Cobbler of Preston*

Ada Rehan as Kate in *The Taming of the Shrew*, painted by Eliot Gregory (1854–1915)

(1716), Charles Johnson's of the same title and date, and, above all, David Garrick's★ *Catherine and Petruchio*,★ of 1754, which held the stage until late in the nineteenth century. The first revival of Shakespeare's play was in 1844, under the auspices of Benjamin Webster and J. R. Planché,★ in a production which, uniquely for its time, attempted to revive Elizabethan staging methods. Samuel Phelps★ played both the original play and Garrick's adaptation. Augustin Daly's★ production of 1887 shortened and rearranged Shakespeare's text and had Ada Rehan★ as a splendid Kate; it was given in both America and England.

Many later productions, and Franco Zeffirelli's★ film (1967), have treated the play as an uproarious farce, but among those which have shown that it can be both amusing and touching when played in its own terms was John Barton★ and Peter Hall's★ at Stratford-upon-Avon in 1960, with Peter O'Toole and Peggy Ashcroft★ as Petruchio and Kate, replaced in a revival with almost equal success by Derek Godfrey and Vanessa Redgrave.

Tarlton, Richard (d. 1588). Comic actor, a favourite of Queen

Elizabeth;* sometimes sentimentally identified with Yorick in *Hamlet*.*

Tate, Nahum (1652–1715). Irish poet and playwright, librettist of Purcell's* opera *Dido and Aeneas*, author of *While shepherds watched their flocks by night*; Poet Laureate, 1692. He adapted *Richard II*★ in 1680; this was rapidly suppressed on political grounds; Tate revised it again as *The Sicilian Usurper*, without success. In 1681 he adapted *Coriolanus*,★ as *The Ingratitude of a Commonwealth*, also unsuccessfully. But his version of *King Lear*,★ 1681, which omits the Fool, introduces a love affair between Edgar and Cordelia, and finally commits Lear, Gloucester, and Kent to peaceful retirement, succeeded in supplanting Shakespeare's play from the stage, and went on being played, with modifications and restorations, until W. C. Macready* returned to Shakespeare's text in 1838.

Susannah Cibber in Tate's adaptation of *King Lear*, a mezzotint after Peter van Bleeck: Cordelia, with her companion, Arante, is saved by Edgar from an attack by ruffians

Tchaikovsky, Peter Ilyich (1840–93). The great Russian composer wrote a symphonic fantasy on *The Tempest*★ (1873), a fantasy overture on *Hamlet*★ (1888), incidental music to the same play (1891), and a fantasy overture on *Romeo and Juliet*★ (1869, revised 1870, final version, 1880).

Tempest, The. Shakespeare's tragi-comedy was first printed in the First Folio* (1623), where it is well printed, with divisions into acts and scenes. It was played at Court on 1 November 1611, and was probably written not long before. No source for the plot is known, though Shakespeare appears to have used accounts of the wreck of a ship called the *Sea-Venture* which sailed for Virginia in June 1609 and was wrecked on the coast of Bermuda. The storm in Shakespeare's play seems to be based on a letter of William Strachey describing the wreck which was written on 15 July 1610 and circulated in manuscript, though it was not published till 1625. Other books, such as Florio's★ translation of Montaigne★ and Golding's★ of Ovid,★ influenced individual passages of the play, sometimes quite closely.

The Tempest was performed as part of the festivities for the marriage of James I's★ daughter, Princess Elizabeth, to the Elector Palatine during the winter of 1612/13. An adaptation by William Davenant★ and John Dryden★ was played at the Duke's Theatre, Lincoln's Inn Fields,★ in 1667. Miranda is matched by a young man, Hippolito, who

Miss Priscilla Horton (1818–95) as Ariel, which she played in W. C. Macready's production of 1838: an oil painting by Daniel Maclise (1806–1870)

has never seen a woman, and she is given a younger sister, Dorinda. Caliban has a sister, Sycorax, and Ariel a female sprite, Milcha. Thomas Shadwell's★ operatic version of this play was given at the Dorset Garden Theatre★ in 1674, in a spectacular production; music for a revival of 1695 is attributed to Henry Purcell.★

David Garrick★ presented an operatic version of the Dryden-Davenant text, with music by J. C. Smith,★ at Drury Lane★ in 1756, but restored Shakespeare's play in the following year. J. P. Kemble★

gave a modified version of the adaptation at Drury Lane from 1789, and did more to purify the text in his Covent Garden★ version of 1806, in which he played Prospero. A musical version by Frederick Reynolds,★ the music arranged by Henry Bishop,★ appeared at Covent Garden in 1821, with W. C. Macready★ (to his regret) as Prospero. Macready played Shakespeare's text at the same theatre in 1838, as did Samuel Phelps★ at Sadler's Wells★ in 1847, etc. Charles Kean's★ spectacular revival at the Princess's in 1857 was severely shortened. Beerbohm Tree's★ revival at the Haymarket★ in 1904 also emphasized spectacle, and centred on Caliban, Tree's own role. John Gielgud★ played Prospero at the Old Vic★ in 1930 and 1940, at Stratford-upon-Avon in Peter Brook's★ production of 1957, and at the National Theatre★ in 1974.

The Tempest uses plot-elements which relate it to the other 'Last Plays',★ or late romances, but it focuses on the end of the story and concentrates romance material into a neo-classical framework which relates it to one of Shakespeare's earliest plays, *The Comedy of Errors.*★ The play has sometimes been regarded as his farewell to his art, but both Prospero and the whole play are multi-faceted in ways that make it infinitely suggestive. It has inspired other works of art, including an opera by Frank Martin★ (1956), a fantasia by Berlioz,★ a symphonic fantasy by Tchaikovsky,★ a sequence of poems, *The Sea and the Mirror*, by W. H. Auden, and many paintings.

Temple Garden Scene. *1 Henry VI*, II.iv, invented by Shakespeare, in which Richard Plantagenet invites his supporters to pluck white roses, while the supporters of his opponent, the Earl of Somerset, pluck red roses. The Earl of Warwick prophesies that

> this brawl today,
> Grown to this faction in the Temple Garden,
> Shall send between the Red Rose and the White
> A thousand souls to death and deadly night! (ll. 124–7)

Terence (Publius Terentius Afer, c. 185–159 BC). Roman dramatist who, like Plautus,★ imitated Greek comedies, and whose plays were known and studied in Elizabethan England, providing models for contemporary dramaturgy. He probably exerted a direct influence on Shakespeare.

Terry, Dame Ellen (1848–1928). English actress, best known for her performances with Henry Irving★; mother of Gordon Craig.★ Her principal Shakespeare roles were Beatrice, Ophelia, Portia, Desdemona, Juliet, Viola, Lady Macbeth, Imogen, Queen Katherine, and Volumnia.

Her correspondence with Bernard Shaw★ (published in 1931) and her delightful autobiography, *The Story of My Life* (1908), are full of insights into the theatre of her time.

Theatre, The. Built by James Burbage★ in 1576 in Shoreditch, London; the first English theatre; pulled down from 28 December 1598 by Burbage's sons and others after disagreements with the landlord, Giles Allen. The timber was ferried across the river to Bankside and used to build the Globe.★

Theobald, Lewis (1688–1744). (Pronounced 'Tibbald'), writer, translator, and dramatist. In 1726 he published *Shakespeare Restored*,

Ellen Terry as Juliet in Henry Irving's production at the Lyceum Theatre, London, 1882

an attack on Alexander Pope's★ edition of 1725. Pope responded by making him the hero of the original *Dunciad* (1728):

> There hapless Shakespeare, yet of Theobald sore,
> Wished he had blotted for himself before.

But *Shakespeare Restored* includes the most famous of all Shakespeare emendations – in the description of Falstaff's★ death, 'a babbl'd of green fields' for 'a Table of greene fields' (*Henry V*,★ II.iii.19–20).

In 1733 he published his complete edition which includes many emendations that have since been regularly accepted; he is regarded now as the first of Shakespeare's major editors.

In 1719 he presented an adaptation of *Richard II*★ which had some success; and in 1727 he prepared for the stage *The Double Falsehood* (see *Cardenio*).

Theophany. Appearance of a god, as of Jupiter in *Cymbeline*,★ V.iv.

Third Folio. See Folio.

Thomas, Ambroise (1811–96). The French composer wrote an opera (1868) based on *Hamlet*.★

Thomas, Lord Cromwell. An anonymous play registered in the

Stationers' Register★ in 1602, published in that year as 'by W.S.', and included in the second issue of the Third Folio,★ but no longer ascribed to Shakespeare.

Thomas of Woodstock. See *Woodstock*.

Thomson, James. See *Coriolanus*.

Thorndike, Dame Sybil (1882–1976). English actress. She played many Shakespeare roles with Ben Greet's★ company in America from 1904 to 1907 and at the Old Vic★ from 1914 to 1918. Later Shakespeare roles included Lady Macbeth (Paris, 1921, Prince's, 1926, etc.), Queen Katherine (Empire, 1925), Volumnia (with Laurence Olivier,★ Old Vic, 1938), and Constance (Old Vic, 1941). She was married to Sir Lewis Casson.★

Thorpe, Thomas. Publisher of Shakespeare's Sonnets★ in 1609, and author of the dedication to Mr W.H.

Throne of Blood. A Japanese film (*Kumonoso-jo*) based on *Macbeth*,★ directed by Akira Kurosawas, and made in 1957.

Tieck, Johann Ludwig (1773–1853). German writer and Shakespeare critic who completed Schlegel's★ translation of the works.

Tillyard, E. M. W. (1889–1962). English scholar who wrote *The Elizabethan World Picture* (1943), a useful exposition of some aspects of Renaissance thought, *Shakespeare's History Plays* (1944), an influential study, and other books on Shakespeare's plays.

Timon of Athens. Shakespeare's tragedy was first printed in the First Folio★ (1623) in a text generally believed to have been printed from Shakespeare's incompleted manuscript. Its date is uncertain, but in style and content it seems related to *King Lear*★ and the later plays, and it is usually dated about 1607–8. Editors have to make decisions on textual discrepancies and inconsistencies, and a still greater degree of tinkering is necessary to prepare the text for performance.

Thomas Shadwell's★ adaptation, as *The History of Timon of Athens, the Man-Hater*, was successfully acted in 1678; Henry Purcell★ wrote music for it in 1694. It was frequently revived till the middle of the eighteenth century. Richard Cumberland's adaptation was played at Drury Lane★ in 1771–2, and in Dublin, with J. P. Kemble,★ in 1783. Another, unpublished version, apparently by Thomas Hull, who acted Flavius, was given at Covent Garden★ in 1786.

George Lamb presented Shakespeare's play with omissions and with some material from Cumberland in the last scene at Drury Lane in 1816. Edmund Kean's★ performance as Timon is the subject of a fine review by Leigh Hunt. Samuel Phelps★ successfully produced a carefully prepared version of Shakespeare's text (omitting the Fool) at Sadler's Wells★ in 1851 and 1856, playing Timon himself. More recent Timons have included F. R. Benson★ (Stratford-upon-Avon, 1892), Robert Atkins★ (Old Vic,★ 1922), and Wilfred Walter (Stratford-upon-Avon, 1928). Barry Jackson★ presented a modern-dress version in Birmingham in 1947, Tyrone Guthrie★ directed the play at the Old Vic in 1952, and Michael Benthall★ directed Ralph Richardson★ in an abbreviated text at the same theatre in 1956. John Schlesinger produced an authentic text, with some rearrangements, at Stratford-upon-Avon, in 1965, with Paul Scofield★ as a memorable Timon. There have been few

Edmund Kean as Timon of Athens, which he played in 1816: a drawing by George Cruikshank engraved by J. Alais

performances in America, but it was played in a successful modern-dress production at Stratford, Ontario★ in 1963.

Unless anyone accepts the challenge of making a satisfactory acting version, *Timon of Athens* will not be a popular play, but the nature of the text gives it great fascination for the student of Shakespeare's working methods, and some of its episodes are fine in their own right.

Tithes. In 1605, Shakespeare paid £440 for a half-interest in the lease of certain tithes in the Stratford-upon-Avon area. His interest brought him £60 a year, above his yearly rents of £5 and £17. Shakespeare's friend Anthony Nash★ collected the tithes for him. In 1611 Shakespeare joined two other leaseholders in a chancery court suit to protect their rights.

Titus Andronicus. Shakespeare's early tragedy was first printed in 1594 in a quarto★ of which the only known copy was discovered in Sweden in 1904. It was reprinted in 1600 and 1611. The 1611 quarto was reprinted in the First Folio,★ with the addition of the whole of III.ii, which presumably came from a manuscript, and a few other lines.

The date of the play's composition is problematical; it may be as early as 1589. Francis Meres* included it in his list of Shakespeare's plays in 1598, but scholars have often been reluctant to believe that Shakespeare wrote all of it, a doubt first fostered in 1687 by Edward Ravenscroft.* Sources of the play have been suggested in Ovid's* *Metamorphoses*, Seneca's* *Thyestes* and *Troades*, and a chapbook which survives only in an eighteenth-century version, discovered in 1936.

Henslowe* recorded performances of a 'Tittus and Vespaccia' in 1592 and a 'Titus & Ondronicus' in 1594. Either of these may or may not have been Shakespeare's play. It appears to have been popular in Shakespeare's time. An early drawing related to it is in the Longleat Manuscript.*

A version by Edward Ravenscroft was played in 1678, and was revived several times till 1725. No further performances are known until 1839, when an adaptation by one N. H. Bannister was given in Philadelphia. It re-appeared in London in 1852, when a negro actor, Ira Aldridge, played Aaron, apparently in Ravenscroft's adaptation.

Anthony Quayle as Aaron in Peter Brook's production of *Titus Andronicus*, Stratford-upon-Avon, 1955

Shakespeare's play was given at the Old Vic* in 1923, when the last act aroused laughter. Peter Brook's* historic production was given at Stratford-upon-Avon in 1955, with Laurence Olivier* as an immensely moving Titus. Later productions have included Trevor Nunn's,* also at Stratford-upon-Avon, in 1972.

If Shakespeare was ever 'of an age', it was in *Titus Andronicus*, but, given tactful handling, the play's scenes of suffering can still be powerful.

Tolstoy, Count Leo (1828–1910). The great Russian novelist's essay *Shakespeare and the Drama* (1906) is an uncomprehending attack on *King Lear*.*

Tom O'Bedlam. A term used for an inmate of the lunatic asylum, Bedlam Hospital, London, the role adopted by Edgar in *King Lear*.*

Topical allusions. There are a few clear topical allusions in Shakespeare's plays (see, e.g., Essex, Earl of; Marlowe, Christopher; boy actors). Unexplained passages in some plays, especially *Love's Labour's Lost,*★ probably held topical significance for their first audiences, and many attempts have been made to show that Shakespeare bodied forth contemporary events, personalities, and issues under the guise of history or fiction (see, e.g., Lopez, Roderigo; James I).

Tragedies, Shakespeare's. The First Folio★ distinguishes eleven plays as tragedies: in order of printing *Coriolanus,*★ *Titus Andronicus,*★ *Romeo and Juliet,*★ *Timon of Athens,*★ *Julius Caesar,*★ *Macbeth,*★ *Hamlet,*★ *King Lear,*★ *Othello,*★ *Antony and Cleopatra,*★ and *Cymbeline.*★ The last is now classed as a comedy, or romance.

Troilus and Cressida,★ now classed as a comedy or problem play,★ was to have been grouped among the tragedies, but was withdrawn and placed between the histories★ and tragedies.

Four of Shakespeare's histories, *3 Henry VI,*★ *King John,*★ *Richard II,*★ and *Richard III,*★ have strongly tragic characteristics, including the death of the protagonist.

Tree, Sir Herbert Beerbohm (1853–1917). English actor and theatre manager who controlled the Haymarket Theatre★ from 1887 to 1897, when he moved to Her Majesty's (later His Majesty's). He produced and acted in many lavish and spectacular versions of Shakespeare's plays in the tradition of Charles Kean★ and Henry Irving.★

Troilus and Cressida. Shakespeare's play was entered in the Stationers' Register★ on 7 February 1603 'as it is acted by my Lord Chamberlain's Men'. This appears to be a blocking entry,★ and the first quarto★ did not appear till 1609. Its original title-page described it as having been 'acted by the King's Majesty's Servants at the Globe'. During the printing this title was replaced by a 'cancel',★ which omits the reference to performance. This issue also adds an epistle according to which this is 'a new play, never staled with the stage, never clapper-clawed with the palms of the vulgar, and yet passing full of the palm comical'. There is no satisfactory explanation of this discrepancy.

The text printed in the Folio★ (1623) includes the Prologue and about forty-five lines not printed in the quarto. On both title-pages of the quarto, the play is called a history (a word which then had no more specific meaning than 'story'). The Epistle clearly classes it as a comedy. There is evidence that it was to have been included among the tragedies in the Folio, but that its printing there had to be delayed for copyright reasons, with the result that it was finally placed between the histories and the tragedies. The printing difficulties are reflected in the fact that it is not listed in the 'Catalogue' of plays at the beginning of the volume.

The classification of the play is still disputed; it can be regarded as a comedy, a history, a tragedy, or a satire. It is often classed among the problem plays.★ It is usually assumed to have been written not very long before its entry in the Stationers' Register. Its difficult style has given rise to the theory that it was intended for a specialized audience, perhaps at one of the Inns of Court.★ The most important source is Homer's *Iliad*, mainly in George Chapman's★ translation, along with William Caxton's *Recuyell of the Histories of Troy* (1475) and John Lydgate's *Troybook* (c. 1412–20).

Shakespeare also probably knew other treatments of the Troy story, including Chaucer's *Troilus and Criseyde*.

The play seems to have been performed in Dublin during the Restoration period, and Dryden's★ radical adaptation, *Troilus and Cressida, or Truth Found Too Late*, first performed at Dorset Garden★ in 1679, held the stage until 1734. It includes a powerful quarrel scene between Troilus and Hector. J. P. Kemble★ made an unperformed adaptation, but the first recorded performance in modern times was at Munich in 1898. In England, an unsuccessful costume-reading in

Hermione Gingold as Cassandra in William Poel's production at Stratford-upon-Avon, 1913

1907 was followed by William Poel's★ production of an abbreviated text with the Elizabethan Stage Society in 1912, with a remarkable cast including Edith Evans★ as Cressida, Esmé Percy as Troilus, and Hermione Gingold as Cassandra. The production was repeated at Stratford-upon-Avon in 1913.

Since then the play has grown in popularity, especially in University productions. It was first performed at the Old Vic★ in 1923. B. Iden Payne★ directed it at Stratford-upon-Avon in 1936, with Donald Wolfit★ as Ulysses, and in 1938 came a modern-dress★ version, directed by Michael MacOwan, at the Westminster. The play gained

in significance because of the political climate. Tyrone Guthrie★ directed another modern-dress production at the Old Vic in 1956. Peter
Hall★ and John Barton★ directed it at Stratford-upon-Avon in 1960,
with Dorothy Tutin★ as Cressida and Max Adrian as Pandarus, and
John Barton also directed it there in 1968 and 1976.

Troilus and Cressida is perhaps Shakespeare's most pessimistic play, a
profound examination of human values, especially in relation to love
and war, in the light of eternity. It does not seek popular appeal, but
has found receptive audiences for the first time in the twentieth
century.

Troublesome Reign of John, King of England, The. An anonymous play published in two parts in 1591, strongly anti-Catholic in
tone, used by Shakespeare as a source for *King John.*★

True Tragedy of Richard Duke of York, The. See 'Contention'
plays.

Tutin, Dorothy (b. 1930). English actress whose Shakespeare roles
include Juliet (1958, 1961), Viola (1958, 1960), Ophelia (1958), Portia
(1960), Cressida (1960, etc.), Desdemona (1961), and Rosalind

Dorothy Tutin as Cressida in the
production of *Troilus and Cressida* by
Peter Hall and John Barton,
Stratford-upon-Avon, 1960

(1967–8), at Stratford upon-Avon as well as Lady Macbeth (Guildford, etc., 1976) and Cleopatra (Prospect Players, 1977).

Twelfth Night. Shakespeare's comedy was first printed in the First
Folio★ (1623). It is based mainly on the tale of Apollonius and Silla in
Barnabe Riche's★ *Farewell to Military Profession* (1581).

Francis Meres★ does not mention it, and internal references suggest
that it was written about 1601. John Manningham★ saw a performance at the Middle Temple★ on 2 February 1602. Court performances

Twelfth Night: Lila de Nobili's set for the opening scene in Peter Hall's production, Stratford-upon-Avon, 1958

are recorded in 1618 and 1623, and Leonard Digges★ alluded to the play's popularity in lines printed in 1640. Pepys★ saw Thomas Betterton★ play Sir Toby Belch in 1661 at Lincoln's Inn Fields.★ He did not admire the play. A distant adaptation by Charles Burnaby, *Love Betrayed*, was published in 1703. Shakespeare's play was revived at Drury Lane★ in 1741, with Charles Macklin★ as Malvolio, and continued to be played regularly both there and at Covent Garden.★ Frederick Reynolds's★ musical version, with music by Henry Bishop,★ appeared at Covent Garden in 1820, and was successful for some years.

Shakespeare's play was revived at the Haymarket★ in 1846 for Charlotte Cushman★ (as Viola) and her sister Susan (as Olivia). Samuel Phelps★ produced it at Sadler's Wells★ in 1848, playing Malvolio, and again in 1857. Kate Terry played both Viola and Sebastian at the Olympic in 1865. Henry Irving★ was Malvolio in his Lyceum★ production of 1884, with Ellen Terry★ as Viola. Ada Rehan★ was admired as Viola in an adaptation produced by Augustin Daly★ in 1893 (New York) and 1894 (London). William Poel's★ several productions with the Elizabethan Stage Society included one at the Middle Temple in 1897. His methods contrasted with those of Beerbohm Tree★ at His Majesty's in 1901.

Harley Granville-Barker's* revolutionary production was given at the Savoy in 1912. There have been many productions at the Old Vic* and Stratford-upon-Avon. At the Old Vic, Edith Evans* was Viola in 1932; Laurence Olivier* played Toby Belch in 1937, for a Tyrone Guthrie* production in which Viola and Sebastian were again, regrettably, doubled; and Peggy Ashcroft* played Viola for Hugh Hunt in 1950. At Stratford-upon-Avon, Vivien Leigh played Viola, and Laurence Olivier Malvolio, in John Gielgud's* production of 1955; Peter Hall* (1958 and 1960) had Dorothy Tutin* as Viola; John Barton* (1969, etc.) directed a beautifully balanced production with Judi Dench* as Viola and Donald Sinden as Malvolio.

Twelfth Night, unquestionably one of the greatest of Shakespeare's comedies, has delighted critics and audiences alike. It contains many excellent acting roles, and different directors have varied the emphases, stressing sometimes the merry, sometimes the melancholy aspects, but the play has rarely failed to please audiences all over the world.

Twine, Laurence (fl. 1576). Writer and translator whose *The Pattern of Painful Adventures,* registered in 1576, provided Shakespeare with a source for *Pericles.** An edition of 1607 may have drawn Shakespeare's attention to the subject. The book also had a direct influence on George Wilkins's* *The Painful Adventures of Pericles Prince of Tyre* (1608).

Twins, The. See *Comedy of Errors, The.*

Two Gentlemen of Verona, The. Shakespeare's early comedy was first printed in the First Folio* (1623), probably from a transcript of a prompt-book.* It is the first of his plays mentioned by Francis Meres* in 1598, and may be judged on stylistic grounds to be one of his earliest plays. It is based on part of Montemayor's *Diana,** perhaps indirectly.

The first recorded performance was at Drury Lane* in 1762, in an adaptation by Benjamin Victor. Shakespeare's play was given at Covent Garden* in 1784. J. P. Kemble* played a revised version, based partly on Victor, at Covent Garden in 1808, with little success. A spectacular musical version by Frederick Reynolds* was given at Covent Garden in 1821. Later nineteenth-century productions by W. C. Macready,* Samuel Phelps,* Charles Kean,* and Augustin Daly* had little success.

Harley Granville-Barker* directed it at the Court Theatre in 1904, and there have been a number of other twentieth-century productions, including ones by Bridges-Adams* (Stratford-upon-Avon, 1925),

B. Iden Payne* (Stratford-upon-Avon, 1938), Denis Carey (Bristol Old Vic, 1951), Michael Langham (Old Vic,* 1956), Peter Hall* (Stratford-upon-Avon, 1960), and Robin Phillips* (Stratford-upon-Avon, 1970; Stratford, Ontario,* 1975).

The play has never had great success, but it contains lyrical verse of great beauty, and Launce is the first in the line of Shakespeare's great clowns. Launce's dog, Crab, is perhaps the most effective non-speaking role in the canon. The song 'Who is Silvia' has had independent popularity, especially in Schubert's* setting.

Launce and his dog, Crab: a water-colour drawing by Richard Westall (1765–1836)

Two Noble Kinsmen, The. This romance was first printed in 1634 as 'by the memorable worthies of their time, Mr John Fletcher, and Mr William Shakespeare, Gent.'. This attribution is now accepted by most scholars, and the scenes generally ascribed to Shakespeare are I.i–iii, III.i, and all of Act V except Scene ii. The play includes a dance identical with one in Beaumont's* *Masque of the Inner Temple and Gray's Inn*, performed in 1613, and is usually believed to have been written in the same year. The major source is Chaucer's *Knight's Tale*.

William Davenant's* adaptation, *The Rivals*, was successfully played from 1664–7. The original play was first revived at the Old Vic* in 1928, and has been occasionally played since then. It offers opportunities for spectacle, and has some impressive verse in Shakespeare's late style along with some touching and amusing episodes.

U

University Wits. A term applied to the main university-educated playwrights of the 1580s, Robert Greene,* Christopher Marlowe,* and Thomas Nashe,* all of Cambridge, and John Lyly,* George Peele,* and Thomas Lodge,* of Oxford.

Upper level. See Lords' Room.

Upstart Crow. See Greene, Robert.

Ur-Hamlet. Title given to a lost play on the basis of allusions by Thomas Nashe,★ Thomas Lodge,★ Philip Henslowe,★ and others. It has sometimes been supposed to be by Thomas Kyd,★ but the evidence is questionable. Its relationship to Shakespeare's play is unknown.

V

Variorum editions. Properly editions 'cum notis variorum', i.e. with notes by various people. The First Variorum is the fifth reprint of George Steevens's★ edition, edited by Isaac Reed★ in 1803, which reprints much material by Johnson,★ Malone,★ and others. The Second Variorum (1813) is a reprint of this. The Third Variorum is known as the Boswell-Malone Variorum (1821; see Malone), and includes Prefaces from most of the eighteenth-century editions. It is the first to include the Poems. The New Variorum edition (see H. H. Furness) is often loosely referred to as 'the Variorum'.

Vaughan Williams, Ralph (1872–1958). The great English composer wrote music for F. R. Benson's★ Stratford-upon-Avon productions of *Richard II*,★ *2 Henry IV*,★ and *Richard III*★ in 1913. His opera *Sir John in Love* (1929) is based on *The Merry Wives of Windsor*★; the cantata *In Windsor Forest* (1929) is based on the opera. The 'Serenade to Music' (1938) sets lines from the last act of *The Merchant of Venice*.★ It was originally written for sixteen specified solo singers and orchestra for the jubilee of the conductor, Sir Henry Wood, but is also heard in a purely orchestral version. Vaughan Williams also wrote settings of Shakespeare as solo songs and part-songs.

Venus and Adonis. Shakespeare's narrative poem was first published in 1593, probably from his own manuscript, perhaps under his supervision, by Richard Field,★ who also came from Stratford-upon-Avon. It has a dedication to

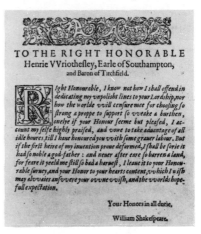

The dedication to *Venus and Adonis*, from the only surviving copy of the first edition, in the Bodleian Library, Oxford

183

Henry Wriothesley,★ 3rd Earl of Southampton, which refers to it as 'the first heir of my invention'. This presumably means that it was Shakespeare's first published work, or his first poem. It is written in a six-line stanza, rhyming a b a b c c, and has 1194 lines.

Venus and Adonis is an early example of the Ovidian narrative poem popular in the 1590s. Its highly wrought style, resembling that of *Love's Labour's Lost,*★ creates difficulties for the modern reader; but it is a brilliant example of its kind, displaying a wit and elegance that link it with Shakespeare's early comedies.

Verdi, Giuseppe (1813–1901). The great Italian composer wrote three operas based on Shakespeare's plays: *Macbeth* (1847, revised 1865), and his two final masterpieces, *Otello* (1887) and *Falstaff* (1893), based mainly on *The Merry Wives of Windsor.*★

Vertue, George. See New Place.

Vestris, (Madame) Elizabeth (1797–1856). English singer, actress, and theatre manageress, whose main importance in relation to Shakespeare is the revival of *Love's Labour's Lost*★ for the first time since the Restoration, at Covent Garden★ in 1839, under the joint management of herself and her husband, Charles Mathews, and the production of the first unadapted (though abbreviated) version of *A Midsummer Night's Dream,*★ also at Covent Garden, in 1840. Her artistic adviser in these enterprises was J. R. Planché.★

Villages, the Shakespeare. John Jordan★ (1746–1809) related a story based on that of Shakespeare's Crabtree★ adding that Shakespeare refused to return to Bidford to renew the drinking contest, saying he had drunk with

The playbill for Madame Vestris's production of *A Midsummer Night's Dream* at Covent Garden, 16 November 1840

Piping Pebworth, dancing Marston,
Haunted Hillborough, hungry Grafton,
Dadging Exhall, papist Wixford,
Beggarly Broom, and drunken Bidford.

These are all villages close to Stratford-upon-Avon.

Vocabulary, Shakespeare's. Spevack's★ *Concordance* lists 29,066 different words in Shakespeare's works, and 884,647 words altogether.

Voltaire (François-Marie Arouet; 1694–1778). The French philosopher helped to spread knowledge of Shakespeare's plays in Europe, but often experienced difficulty in reconciling his admiration for Shakespeare with his own neo-classical literary principles.

Vortigern. See Ireland, William Henry.

W

W.H., Mr. See Sonnets.

Wagner, Richard (1813–1883). The great German composer's early opera, *Das Liebesverbot* (1836), is based on Shakespeare's *Measure for Measure.*★

Walton, Sir William (b. 1902). The English composer wrote distinguished incidental music for Laurence Olivier's★ films of *Henry V*★ (1944), *Hamlet*★ (1948), and *Richard III*★ (1955). He also wrote the music for a film of *As You Like It*★ (1936), and for John Gielgud's★ stage production of *Macbeth*★ (1942).

Warburton, William (1698–1779). Clergyman and scholar who edited Shakespeare's works in eight volumes in 1747, basing his text on Pope's,★ whose literary executor and editor he was. Some of his own emendations have been influential.

Ward, John (1629–81). Vicar of Stratford-upon-Avon, 1662–81. His notebooks include a few facts about Shakespeare and some legends, including 'Shakespeare, Drayton, and Ben Jonson had a merry meeting, and it seems drank too hard, for Shakespeare died of a fever there contracted'.

Warlock, Peter (Philip Heseltine; 1894–1930). The English composer wrote popular settings of several lyrics by Shakespeare.

Wars of the Roses, The. John Barton's★ adaptation of *1, 2,* and *3 Henry VI*★ and *Richard III,*★ acted at Stratford-upon-Avon in 1963 in three parts, as *Henry VI*, *Edward IV*, and *Richard III*. It was also televised.

Webster, John (1580?–1634?). English dramatist; the Epistle to his play *The White Devil* (1612) includes a reference to 'the right happy and copious industry of Master Shakespeare, Master Dekker, and Master Heywood'.

Weever, John (1576–1632). English poet, author of a sonnet in praise of Shakespeare published in 1599, and of lines referring to *Julius Caesar*★ published in 1601.

Weird Sisters. The normal form of reference in *Macbeth*★ to the characters usually known now as the three witches.

Welcombe enclosures. In 1614 proceedings were instigated to enclose land at Welcombe, within the parish of Stratford-upon-Avon, in which Shakespeare had an interest in the tithes.★ He and his cousin, Thomas Greene, were to be compensated for any loss. The Stratford-upon-Avon Corporation opposed the scheme. The conflict dragged on for several years. A number of Greene's notes about it have survived. Shakespeare's attitude is uncertain. He may have favoured the scheme, as is suggested in Edward Bond's play *Bingo* (1973).

Welles, Orson (b. 1915). American actor and director; his Shakespeare roles include Mercutio (1933), Hamlet (1934), Brutus (1938, in his own modern-dress production), and Falstaff★ (in adaptation, 1939). His first London appearance was as Othello in his own production (1951). He played King Lear in his own production in New York (1956), and Falstaff in his adaptation, *Chimes at Midnight*, in Dublin (1960); this was filmed in 1966. He also filmed *Macbeth*★ (1949) and *Othello*★ (1951).

Whateley, Ann. See Marriage, Shakespeare's.

Wheeler, Margaret. See Shakespeare, Judith.

Whetstone, George (1554?–1587?). English author whose two-part play *Promos and Cassandra* (1578) is a principal source for *Measure for Measure*.★ Whetstone retold the story in prose in his *Heptameron of Civil Discourses* (1582), which Shakespeare may also have known.

Whiter, the Rev. Walter (1758–1832). English philologist whose *Specimen of a Commentary on Shakespeare* (1794) anticipates imagery★ studies of the twentieth century. It was almost entirely neglected for a century and a half, but was reprinted, with Whiter's own revisions, edited by Alan Over and Mary Bell, in 1967.

Wilkins, George (fl. 1603–8). A writer of whom little is known. His work includes *The Painful Adventures of Pericles Prince of Tyre* (1608), a prose tale based partly on Shakespeare's *Pericles*,★ and also on Laurence Twine's★ *The Pattern of Painful Adventures*. Wilkins is sometimes supposed to have had a hand in *Pericles*, too.

Will, Shakespeare's. Shakespeare's will was drawn up for him by Francis Collins★ in January 1616, and was revised on 25 March. The principal bequest was of New Place,★ the Henley Street property, the property in Old Stratford, the Blackfriars Gatehouse,★ and all his other property to his daughter Judith,★ and suggests lack of confidence in her husband, Thomas Quiney, whom she married on 2 February. She receives £150, the interest on a further £150 if she is still alive and married three years later, and a silver-gilt bowl. Shakespeare's granddaughter, Elizabeth Hall,★ received the rest of his plate. To his sister, Joan Hart,★ Shakespeare left the house in Henley Street at an annual rent of 12d., and his clothes. Other bequests are £5 to her three sons, £5 to Thomas Russell,★ £13 6s. 8d. to Francis Collins,★ 26s. 8d. each to Hamnet Sadler,★ Anthony Nash,★ and John Nash, neighbours of Shakespeare, to buy mourning rings; the same to John Heminges,★ Richard Burbage,★ and Thomas Condell★ for the same purpose; his sword to Thomas Russell★; £1 to his godson, William Walker; £10 to the poor of Stratford-upon-Avon; and his second-best bed to his wife (see Hathaway, Anne). The will bears three of Shakespeare's six authenticated signatures.★

Willobie his Avisa. A poem by Henry Willobie (born about 1575), printed in 1594. Commendatory verses include the first literary reference to Shakespeare by name:

> Yet Tarquin plucked his glistering grape,
> And Shakespeare paints poor Lucrece' rape.

The poem tells how Avisa, an inn-keeper's wife, rejected many suitors, including 'Henrico Willobego', who confided his love to 'his familiar friend, W.S.', recently recovered from a similar passion. W.S. 'in viewing afar off the course of this loving comedy . . . determined to see whether it would sort to a happier end for this new actor than it did for the old player.' Willobie was related by marriage to Shakespeare's friend, Thomas Russell.★ It is possible that Shakespeare is the Mr W.S. of the deliberately enigmatic poem.

Willow Song. A song with traditional words and music sung by Desdemona (*Othello*,★ IV.iii).

Wilmcote. A village two-and-a-half miles north-west of Stratford-upon-Avon; Shakespeare's grandfather, Robert Arden, bequeathed two estates there, Asbyes, to Shakespeare's mother, Mary Arden.★ See Mary Arden's House.

Wilson, John (1595–1674). Musician who became Professor of Music at Oxford in 1656 and a Gentleman of the Chapel Royal in 1662. His *Cheerful Airs or Ballads* (1660) includes settings of 'Take, O take those lips away' (*Measure for Measure*★) and 'Lawn as white as driven snow' (*Winter's Tale*★). He may be the 'Jack Wilson' referred to in a stage direction (II.i) in the Folio★ text of *Much Ado About Nothing*,★ apparently a performer of the singing role of Balthazar.

Wilson, John Dover (1881–1969). English scholar and critic. His writings include *The Essential Shakespeare*, described as a 'biographical adventure' (1932), *The Manuscript of Shakespeare's 'Hamlet' and the Problems of its Transmission* (1934), *What Happens in 'Hamlet'* (1935), *The Fortunes of Falstaff* (1953), *Shakespeare's Happy Comedies* (1962), and an autobiography, *Milestones on the Dover Road* (1969).

He was the General Editor, along with (initially) Sir A. T. Quiller-Couch, of the New Cambridge edition★ of Shakespeare, which began with *The Tempest*★ in 1921 and was completed with the Sonnets★ in 1966.

Winter's Tale, The. Shakespeare's tragi-comedy was first printed in the First Folio★ (1623). Simon Forman★ saw it at the Globe★ on 15 May 1611, and a Court performance on 5 November of that year is recorded. The dance of satyrs in IV. iv seems to derive from Jonson's★ masque *Oberon*, performed on 1 January 1611, and the composition of the play is usually ascribed to that year. It is based mainly on Robert Greene's★ prose tale *Pandosto*, printed in 1588.

The play seems to have been popular in its own time; seven Court performances are recorded before 1640. It was not played again until 1741, when it was given at both Goodman's Fields and Covent Garden.★ Later eighteenth-century

Charles Kean as Leontes and the young Ellen Terry as Mamillius in *The Winter's Tale* at the Princess's Theatre, London, 1856: an early example of theatrical photography

performances were usually in severely abbreviated versions, of which David Garrick's,★ as *Florizel and Perdita*★ (1756), was the most successful. It concentrates on the last two acts, reflecting disapproval of the wide time-span of the original play.

John Philip Kemble★ used a much fuller text at Drury Lane★ in 1802, when he played Leontes, with Sarah Siddons★ as Hermione. W. C. Macready★ played Leontes frequently from 1815 to 1843; at Covent Garden in 1837 he had Helena Faucit★ as his Hermione. Samuel Phelps★ presented the play successfully at Sadler's Wells★ in 1845, and Charles Kean★ put on a spectacular version at the Princess's in 1856, with great success. Mary Anderson doubled Hermione and Perdita in 1887, also in an abbreviation.

Beerbohm Tree★ directed Ellen Terry★ as Hermione at His Majesty's in 1906. Harley Granville-Barker's★ historic Savoy production of 1912, using an almost complete text, was not a popular success. There have been numerous Old Vic★ and Stratford-upon-Avon productions. Peter Brook★ directed it at the Phoenix in 1951, with John Gielgud★ as Leontes, Diana Wynyard as Hermione, and Flora Robson as Paulina. In Trevor Nunn's★ Stratford-upon-Avon production of 1969, Judi Dench★ doubled Hermione and Perdita.

Formerly criticized for improbability and structural irregularity, *The Winter's Tale* has risen in critical esteem during the twentieth century, and is now recognized as one of Shakespeare's richest poetic dramas, wide-ranging, powerful in psychological suggestiveness, varied in comic effect, tempering romance with astringency, poetically resonant, having some of the qualities of myth, yet also profoundly human.

Wolfit, Sir Donald (1902–68). English actor-manager. He played many Shakespeare roles, including Hamlet at Stratford-upon-Avon in 1936. In 1937 he formed his own Shakespearian company with which he played Hamlet, Macbeth, Shylock, and Malvolio. The company toured widely in the provinces and overseas, and gave occasional London seasons.

Wolfit's other Shakespeare roles included Petruchio, Othello, Iago, Benedick, Falstaff, Richard III, Bottom, Iachimo, and King Lear, the role in which he was most admired. He gave his last Shakespeare performances in 1953, except for recital programmes.

Woodstock. An anonymous play of uncertain date, surviving only in manuscript, dealing with the early part of the reign of Richard II and the murder of his uncle, Thomas of Woodstock, Duke of Gloucester. Shakespeare may have known the play, and it has even been suggested that he designed *Richard II*★ as a sequel to it.

World Shakespeare Congress. A meeting with this title, at which scholarly papers were delivered, was held in Vancouver in 1971, under the auspices of Simon Fraser University. From it developed the International Shakespeare Association,★ with responsibility for organizing future Congresses.

Wotton, Sir Henry (1568–1639). Poet, diplomat, translator; in a letter of 2 July 1613, to his nephew, Sir Edmund Bacon, he gave an account of the burning down of the Globe Theatre★ on 29 June during a performance (which he did not attend) of *Henry VIII.*★ It reads: 'The King's players had a new play, called *All is True*, representing some principal pieces of the reign of Henry VIII, which was set forth with many extraordinary circumstances of pomp and majesty, even to the matting of the stage, the Knights of the Order with their Georges and Garters, the guards with their embroidered coats, and the like, sufficient in truth within a while to make greatness very familiar, if not ridiculous. Now, King Henry making a masque at the Cardinal Wolsey's house, and certain chambers being shot off at his entry, some of the paper, or other stuff, wherewith one of them was stopped, did light on the thatch, where being thought at first but an idle smoke, and their eyes more attentive to the show, it kindled inwardly, and ran round like a train, consuming within less than an hour the whole house to the very grounds.

'This was the fatal period of that virtuous fabric, wherein yet nothing did perish but wood and straw, and a few forsaken cloaks; only one man had his breeches set on fire, that would perhaps have broiled him, if he had not by the benefit of a provident wit put it out with bottle ale.'

Wriothesley, Henry, 3rd Earl of Southampton (1573–1624). Shakespeare's patron, recipient of

The Earl of Southampton at the age of twenty: a miniature by Nicholas Hilliard

his only two dedications, those to *Venus and Adonis*★ (1593), and *The Rape of Lucrece*★ (1594). He encouraged other writers, such as Florio★ and Nashe.★ Rowe★ records a legend that he gave Shakespeare £1000. He has often been identified with the Mr W.H. to whom Thomas Thorpe★ dedicated Shakespeare's Sonnets.★ A performance of *Love's Labour's Lost*★ was arranged for Queen Anne at his London home in January 1605.

Y

Yorkshire Tragedy, A. A domestic tragedy published in 1608 and ascribed to Shakespeare both in the Stationers' Register★ and on the title-page. It was reprinted in 1619. It was not included in the First Folio★ (1623), but appears in the second issue of the Third Folio★ (1664). It is based on a contemporary murder case. Shakespeare's authorship is not accepted.

Z

Zeffirelli, Franco (b. 1923). Stage and film director and opera producer; he directed *Romeo and Juliet*★ at the Old Vic★ in 1960, and a film of the same play in 1968; his production of *Othello*★ at Stratford-upon-Avon in 1961, with John Gielgud★ as Othello, was visually splendid but less successful dramatically. His film of *The Taming of the Shrew*★ (1967) starred Richard Burton and Elizabeth Taylor.

THE CHARACTERS
OF SHAKESPEARE'S PLAYS
A Selective Finding List

Aaron, a Moor, loved by Tamora, *Titus Andronicus*
Abbess (Aemilia), *Comedy of Errors*
Abergavenny, George Neville, Lord, *Henry VIII*
Abhorson, an executioner, *Measure for Measure*
Abraham, Montague's servant, *Romeo and Juliet*
Achilles, Greek warrior, *Troilus and Cressida*
Adam, an old servant, *As You Like It*
Adam, a servant, *Taming of the Shrew*
Adrian, a Volscian, *Coriolanus*
Adrian, attendant on Alonso, *Tempest*
Adriana, wife of Antipholus of Ephesus, *Comedy of Errors*
Aegeon, a merchant of Syracuse, *Comedy of Errors*
Aemilia, an Abbess, *Comedy of Errors*
Aemilius, a Roman nobleman, *Titus Andronicus*
Aeneas, Trojan commander, *Troilus and Cressida*
Agamemnon, Greek commander, *Troilus and Cressida*
Agrippa, friend of Octavius, *Antony and Cleopatra*
Aguecheek, Sir Andrew, suitor of Olivia, *Twelfth Night*
Ajax, Greek commander, *Troilus and Cressida*
Alarbus, Tamora's eldest son, *Titus Andronicus*
Albany, Duke of, Goneril's husband, *King Lear*
Alcibiades, Athenian captain, *Timon of Athens*
Alençon, Duke of, *1 Henry VI*
Alexander, Cressida's servant, *Troilus and Cressida*
Alexas, a eunuch, *Antony and Cleopatra*
Alice, a waiting-woman, *Henry V*
Aliena, name taken by Celia, *As You Like It*
Alonso, King of Naples, *Tempest*
Amiens, a lord, *As You Like It*

Andromache, Hector's wife, *Troilus and Cressida*
Andronicus, Marcus, Titus's brother, *Titus Andronicus*
Angelo, a goldsmith, *Comedy of Errors*
Angelo, the Duke's deputy, *Measure for Measure*
Angus, a nobleman, *Macbeth*
Anne, Lady (Neville), wife of Richard III, *Richard III*
Antenor, Trojan warrior, *Troilus and Cressida*
Antigonus, Paulina's husband, *Winter's Tale*
Antiochus, King of Antioch, *Pericles*
Antipholus of Ephesus, and of Syracuse, twins, *Comedy of Errors*
Antonio, a merchant, *Merchant of Venice*
Antonio, Leonato's brother, *Much Ado About Nothing*
Antonio, Prospero's brother, *Tempest*
Antonio, a sea-captain, *Twelfth Night*
Antonio, Proteus's father, *Two Gentlemen of Verona*
Antony, a servant, *Romeo and Juliet*
Antony, Mark, *Julius Caesar* and *Antony and Cleopatra*
Apemantus, a cynic, *Timon of Athens*
Apothecary, *Romeo and Juliet*
Archidamus, Bohemian lord, *Winter's Tale*
Ariel, a spirit, *Tempest*
Armado, Don Adriano de, a Spaniard, *Love's Labour's Lost*
Arragon, Prince of, *Merchant of Venice*
Artemidorus, *Julius Caesar*
Arthur, Duke of Britaine (Prince), *King John*
Arviragus, Cymbeline's son, known as Cadwal, *Cymbeline*
Audrey, wooed by Touchstone, *As You Like It*
Aufidius, Tullus, Volscian leader, *Coriolanus*
Aumerle, Duke of, later Duke of York, *Richard II*, *Henry V*
Autolycus, a rogue, *Winter's Tale*
Auvergne, Countess of, *1 Henry VI*
Bagot, favourite of Richard, *Richard II*
Balthasar, Portia's servant, *Merchant of Venice*
Balthasar, Don Pedro's attendant, *Much Ado About Nothing*
Balthasar, Romeo's servant, *Romeo and Juliet*
Balthazar, a merchant, *Comedy of Errors*
Banquo, Scottish nobleman, *Macbeth*
Baptista Minola, father of Katherina and Bianca, *Taming of the Shrew*
Bardolph, Lieutenant (or Corporal), *Merry Wives of Windsor*, *1* and *2 Henry IV*, *Henry V*

Bardolph, Lord, *2 Henry IV*
Barnadine, a prisoner, *Measure for Measure*
Barnardo, a sentry, *Hamlet*
Barthol'mew, a page, *Taming of the Shrew*
Bassanio, Portia's suitor, *Merchant of Venice*
Basset, a Lancastrian, *1 Henry VI*
Bassianus, Saturninus's brother, *Titus Andronicus*
Bates, John, a soldier, *Henry V*
Beatrice, Leonato's niece, *Much Ado About Nothing*
Beaufort, Henry, Bishop of Winchester (later Cardinal), *1* and *2 Henry VI*
Bedford, Duke of, *see* John (of Lancaster)
Belarius, known as Morgan, *Cymbeline*
Belch, Sir Toby, *Twelfth Night*
Benedick, a lord of Padua, *Much Ado About Nothing*
Benvolio, friend of Romeo, *Romeo and Juliet*
Berkeley, a gentleman, *Richard III*
Berkeley, Earl, *Richard II*
Berowne, in love with Rosaline, *Love's Labour's Lost*
Bertram, Count of Rousillon, *All's Well that Ends Well*
Bevis, George, follower of Jack Cade, *2 Henry VI*
Bianca, a courtesan, *Othello*
Bianca Minola, Katherina's sister, *Taming of the Shrew*
Bigot, Lord, *King John*
Biondello, Lucentio's servant, *Taming of the Shrew*
Biron, *see* Berowne
Blanch of Spain, Lady, *King John*
Blount, Sir James, *Richard III*
Blunt, Sir John, *2 Henry IV*
Blunt, Sir Walter, *1 Henry IV*
Boleyn, Anne, *Henry VIII*
Bolingbroke, Henry, Duke of Hereford, later Henry IV, *Richard II*, *1* and *2 Henry IV*
Bolingbroke, Roger, a sorcerer, *2 Henry VI*
Bona, Lady, the French Queen's sister, *3 Henry VI*
Borachio, follower of Don John, *Much Ado About Nothing*
Bottom, Nick, a weaver, *Midsummer Night's Dream*
Boult, servant in a brothel, *Pericles*
Bourbon, Admiral, *3 Henry VI*
Bourbon, John, Duke of, *Henry V*

Bourchier, Cardinal, Archbishop of Canterbury, *Richard III*
Boyet, a lord, *Love's Labour's Lost*
Brabantio, Desdemona's father, *Othello*
Brakenbury, Sir Robert, Lieutenant of the Tower, *Richard III*
Brandon, Charles, *see* Suffolk, Duke of
Brandon, Sir William, *Richard III*
Brandon, Sir William, an officer, *Henry VIII*
Britaine, Duke of, *Henry V*
Brook, false name of Ford, *Merry Wives of Windsor*
Brutus, Junius, a tribune, *Coriolanus*
Brutus, Marcus Junius, *Julius Caesar*
Buckingham, Edward Stafford, Duke of, *Henry VIII*
Buckingham, Henry Stafford, Duke of, *Richard III*
Buckingham, Humphrey Stafford, Duke of, *2 Henry VI*
Bullcalf, Peter, *2 Henry IV*
Bullen, Anne, *Henry VIII*
Burgundy, Duke of, Cordelia's suitor, *King Lear*
Burgundy, Duke of (Philip the Good), *Henry V*, *1 Henry VI*
Bushy, favourite of Richard, *Richard II*
Butts, Doctor, the King's physician, *Henry VIII*
Cade, Jack, a rebel, *2 Henry VI*
Cadwal, name taken by Arviragus, *Cymbeline*
Caesar, Octavius, *Julius Caesar*, *Antony and Cleopatra*
Caithness, Scottish nobleman, *Macbeth*
Caius, kinsman of the Andronici, *Titus Andronicus*
Caius, name taken by Kent, *King Lear*
Caius, Doctor, a Frenchman, *Merry Wives of Windsor*
Caius Cassius, *see* Cassius
Caius Ligarius, *see* Ligarius
Caius Lucius, *see* Lucius
Caius Marcius, *see* Coriolanus
Calchas, Trojan priest, *Troilus and Cressida*
Caliban, 'a savage and deformed slave', *Tempest*
Calphurnia, Caesar's wife, *Julius Caesar*
Cambio, name taken by Lucentio, *Taming of the Shrew*
Cambridge, Richard (Plantagenet), Earl of, *Henry V*
Camillo, Sicilian lord, *Winter's Tale*
Campeius, Cardinal, papal legate, *Henry VIII*
Canidius, Antony's lieutenant-general, *Antony and Cleopatra*
Canterbury, Archbishop of, *see* Bourchier *and* Cranmer

A Selective Finding List

Canterbury, Archbishop of (Henry Chicheley), *Henry V*
Canterbury, Archbishop of (William Warham), *Henry VIII*
Caphis, a servant, *Timon of Athens*
Capucius, a Spanish ambassador, *Henry VIII*
Capulet, Cousin, *Romeo and Juliet*
Capulet, Lady, Romeo's mother, *Romeo and Juliet*
Capulet, 'Old', Romeo's father, *Romeo and Juliet*
Carlisle, Bishop of, *Richard II*
Casca, a conspirator, *Julius Caesar*
Cassandra, Priam's daughter, a prophetess, *Troilus and Cressida*
Cassio, Michael, a Florentine, *Othello*
Cassius, Caius, *Julius Caesar*
Catesby, Sir William, *Richard III*
Catlin, Simon, a musician, *Romeo and Juliet*
Cato, Young, Marcus Cato's son, *Julius Caesar*
Celia, Duke Frederick's daughter, *As You Like It*
Ceres (impersonated by Ariel), *Tempest*
Cerimon, a physician, *Pericles*
Cesario, name taken by Viola, *Twelfth Night*
Charles VI, King of France, *Henry V*
Charles the Dauphin, later Charles VII of France, *1 Henry VI*
Charles the Wrestler, *As You Like It*
Charmian, Cleopatra's attendant, *Antony and Cleopatra*
Chatillon, a French lord, *King John*
Chiron, son of Tamora, *Titus Andronicus*
Cicero, *Julius Caesar*
Cimber, Metellus, a conspirator, *Julius Caesar*
Cinna, a conspirator, *Julius Caesar*
Cinna, a poet, *Julius Caesar*
Clarence, George, Duke of, *3 Henry VI*, *Richard III*
Clarence, Thomas, Duke of, *2 Henry IV*, *Henry V* (non-speaking)
Claudio, betrothed to Juliet, *Measure for Measure*
Claudio, betrothed to Hero, *Much Ado About Nothing*
Claudius, Brutus's servant, *Julius Caesar*
Claudius, King of Denmark, *Hamlet*
Cleomenes, Sicilian lord, *Winter's Tale*
Cleon, Governor of Tharsus, *Pericles*
Clifford, John (Young Clifford), *2 and 3 Henry VI*
Clifford, Thomas, Lord (Old Clifford), *2 Henry VI*
Clitus, Brutus's servant, *Julius Caesar*

Cloten, Cymbeline's stepson, *Cymbeline*
Cobweb, a fairy, *Midsummer Night's Dream*
Colville, Sir John, *2 Henry IV*
Cominius, Roman commander, *Coriolanus*
Conrade, follower of Don John, *Much Ado About Nothing*
Constable of France (Charles Delabreth), *Henry V*
Constance, Lady, Arthur's mother, *King John*
Cordelia, Lear's youngest daughter, *King Lear*
Corin, an old shepherd, *As You Like It*
Coriolanus, *see* Marcius, Caius
Cornelius, a physician, *Cymbeline*
Cornelius, a courtier, *Hamlet*
Cornwall, Duke of, Regan's husband, *King Lear*
Costard, a clown, *Love's Labour's Lost*
Court, Alexander, a soldier, *Henry V*
Courtezan, *Comedy of Errors*
Crab, a dog, *Two Gentlemen of Verona*
Cranmer, Thomas, Archbishop of Canterbury, *Henry VIII*
Cromwell, Thomas, *Henry VIII*
Curan, a courtier, *King Lear*
Curio, Orsino's attendant, *Twelfth Night*
Curtis, a servant, *Taming of the Shrew*
Dardanius, Brutus's servant, *Julius Caesar*
Dauphin, *see* Charles *and* Lewis
Davy, Shallow's servant, *2 Henry IV*
Decius Brutus, a conspirator, *Julius Caesar*
Deiphobus, son of Priam, *Troilus and Cressida*
Delabreth, *see* Constable of France
Demetrius, Roman soldier, *Antony and Cleopatra*
Demetrius, in love with Hermia, *Midsummer Night's Dream*
Demetrius, son of Tamora, *Titus Andronicus*
Dennis, Oliver's servant, *As You Like It*
Denny, Sir Anthony, *Henry VIII*
Derby, Thomas Lord Stanley, Earl of, *Richard III*
Dercetas, friend of Antony, *Antony and Cleopatra*
Desdemona, Othello's wife, *Othello*
Diana, the goddess, *Pericles*
Diana Capilet, a widow's daughter, *All's Well that Ends Well*
Dick, the Butcher of Ashford, *2 Henry VI*
Diomedes, Cleopatra's attendant, *Antony and Cleopatra*

Diomedes, Greek general, *Troilus and Cressida*
Dion, Sicilian lord, *Winter's Tale*
Dionyza, Cleon's wife, *Pericles*
Dogberry, a constable, *Much Ado About Nothing*
Dolabella, friend of Octavius, *Antony and Cleopatra*
Doll Tearsheet, *2 Henry IV*
Donalbain, son of Duncan, *Macbeth*
Dorcas, a shepherdess, *Winter's Tale*
Doricles, name taken by Florizel, *Winter's Tale*
Dorset, Thomas Grey, Marquess of, *Richard III*
Douglas, Archibald, Earl of, *1 Henry IV*
Dromio of Ephesus, and of Syracuse, twins, *Comedy of Errors*
Duke (Senior), The, *As You Like It*
Dull, Anthony, a constable, *Love's Labour's Lost*
Dumain, Captain (two), *All's Well that Ends Well*
Dumain, in love with Katharine, *Love's Labour's Lost*
Duncan, King of Scotland, *Macbeth*
Edgar, Gloucester's legitimate son, *King Lear*
Edmund, Gloucester's bastard son, *King Lear*
Edward, Earl of March, later Edward IV, *2* and *3 Henry VI*, *Richard III*
Edward, Earl of Warwick, Clarence's son, *Richard III*
Edward, Prince of Wales, son of Henry VI, *3 Henry VI*, (ghost of)
    Richard III
Edward, Prince of Wales, later Edward V, *3 Henry VI*, *Richard III*
Egeon, merchant of Syracuse, *Comedy of Errors*
Egeus, Hermia's father, *Midsummer Night's Dream*
Eglamour, Sir, a knight, *Two Gentlemen of Verona*
Elbow, 'a simple constable', *Measure for Measure*
Elinor, Queen, John's mother, *King John*
Elizabeth, Princess (afterwards Elizabeth I; non-speaking), *Henry VIII*
Ely, Bishop of (John Fordham), *Henry V*
Ely, Bishop of (John Morton), *Richard III*
Emanuel, Clerk of Chatham, *2 Henry VI*
Emilia, Iago's wife, *Othello*
Emilia, attendant on Hermione, *Winter's Tale*
Enobarbus, Domitius, Roman soldier, *Antony and Cleopatra*
Ephesus, Duke of, *see* Solinus
Eros, Antony's servant, *Antony and Cleopatra*
Erpingham, Sir Thomas, *Henry V*
Escalus, a lord, *Measure for Measure*

Escalus, Prince of Verona, *Romeo and Juliet*
Escanes, lord of Tyre, *Pericles*
Essex, Earl of (Geffrey Fitz-peter), *King John*
Euphronius, a schoolmaster, *Antony and Cleopatra*
Evans, Sir Hugh, a Welsh parson, *Merry Wives of Windsor*
Exeter, Thomas Beaufort, Duke of, *Henry V, 1 Henry VI*
Exeter, Henry Holland, Duke of, *3 Henry VI*
Exton, *see* Pierce of Exton
Fabian, Olivia's servant, *Twelfth Night*
Falstaff, Sir John, *Merry Wives of Windsor, 1 and 2 Henry IV*
Fang, a sheriff's officer, *2 Henry IV*
Fastolfe, Sir John, a cowardly knight, *1 Henry VI*
Father that has killed his son, *3 Henry VI*
Faulconbridge, Lady, *King John*
Faulconbridge, Philip, the Bastard, *King John*
Faulconbridge, Robert, *King John*
Feeble, Francis, a woman's tailor, *2 Henry IV*
Fenton, Anne Page's suitor, *Merry Wives of Windsor*
Ferdinand, Alonso's son, *Tempest*
Ferdinand, King of Navarre, *Love's Labour's Lost*
Feste, Olivia's fool, *Twelfth Night*
Fidele, name taken by Imogen, *Cymbeline*
Fitzwater, Lord, *Richard II*
Flaminius, Timon's servant, *Timon of Athens*
Flavius, a tribune, *Julius Caesar*
Flavius, a soldier (non-speaking), *Julius Caesar*
Flavius, Timon's steward, *Timon of Athens*
Fleance, Banquo's son, *Macbeth*
Florence, Duke of, *All's Well that Ends Well*
Florizel, Prince, in love with Perdita, *Winter's Tale*
Fluellen, Welsh officer, *Henry V*
Flute, Francis, a bellows-mender, *Midsummer Night's Dream*
Ford, Frank, sometimes disguised as Brook, *Merry Wives of Windsor*
Ford, Mistress Alice, Frank's wife, *Merry Wives of Windsor*
Fortinbras, Prince of Norway, *Hamlet*
France, King of, Cordelia's successful suitor, *King Lear*
France, King of, *All's Well that Ends Well*
France, King of, *see also* Charles VI, Charles the Dauphin, Lewis XI,
   Philip
France, Princess of, *Love's Labour's Lost*

Francis, a tapster, *1* and *2 Henry IV*
Francis, Friar, *Much Ado About Nothing*
Francisca, a nun, *Measure for Measure*
Francisco, a sentry, *Hamlet*
Francisco, a lord, *Tempest*
Frederick, Duke, Celia's father, *As You Like It*
Froth, 'a foolish gentleman', *Measure for Measure*
Gabriel, a servant, *Taming of the Shrew*
Gadshill, a robber, *1 Henry IV*
Gallus, a soldier (non-speaking), *Antony and Cleopatra*
Ganymede, name taken by Rosalind, *As You Like It*
Gardiner, Stephen, Bishop of Winchester, *Henry VIII*
Gargrave, Sir Thomas, *1 Henry VI*
Garter King-at-arms (Thomas Wriothesley), *Henry VIII*
Gaunt, John of, Duke of Lancaster, *Richard II*
Gertrude, Queen of Denmark, *Hamlet*
Glansdale, Sir William, *1 Henry VI*
Glendower, Owen, *1 Henry IV*
Gloucester, Earl of, *King Lear*
Gloucester, Eleanor de Bohun, Duchess of, *Richard II*
Gloucester, Eleanor Cobham, Duchess of, *2 Henry VI*
Gloucester, Richard, Duke of, later Richard III, *1*, *2*, and *3 Henry VI*,
    Richard III
Gloucester, Prince Humphrey, later Duke of, *2 Henry IV*, *Henry V*,
    1 and *2 Henry VI*
Gobbo, Launcelot, Shylock's servant, *Merchant of Venice*
Gobbo, 'Old', Launcelot's father, *Merchant of Venice*
Goffe, Matthew, *2 Henry VI*
Goneril, Duchess of Albany, Lear's eldest daughter, *King Lear*
Gonzalo, 'an honest old counsellor', *Tempest*
Goodfellow, Robin, *see* Puck
Gower, an attendant, *2 Henry IV*
Gower, an officer, *Henry V*
Gower (John), the poet, *Pericles*
Grandpré, a French lord, *Henry V*
Gratiano, Bassanio's friend, *Merchant of Venice*
Gratiano, Brabantio's brother, *Othello*
Green, favourite of Richard, *Richard II*
Gregory, Capulet's servant, *Romeo and Juliet*
Gregory, a servant, *Taming of the Shrew*

Gremio, suitor to Bianca, *Taming of the Shrew*
Grey, Lady, *see* Woodville, Elizabeth
Grey, Lord, *Richard III*
Grey, Sir Thomas, a traitor, *Henry V*
Griffith, Queen Katherine's gentleman-usher, *Henry VIII*
Groom of the Stable, *Richard II*
Grumio, Petruchio's servant, *Taming of the Shrew*
Guiderius, Cymbeline's son, known as Polydore, *Cymbeline*
Guildenstern, a courtier, *Hamlet*
Guildford, Sir Henry, *Henry VIII*
Gurney, James, Lady Faulconbridge's servant, *King John*
Hal, Prince, *see* Henry (Hal), Prince of Wales
Harcourt, an officer, *2 Henry IV*
Harfleur, Governor of, *Henry V*
Hastings, Lord, *2 Henry IV*
Hastings, Lord, *3 Henry VI, Richard III*
Hastings, a pursuivant, *Richard III*
Hecate, goddess of the moon, *Macbeth*
Hector, son of Priam, *Troilus and Cressida*
Helen, an attendant, *Cymbeline*
Helen of Troy, *Troilus and Cressida*
Helena, a physician's daughter, *All's Well that Ends Well*
Helena, in love with Demetrius, *Midsummer Night's Dream*
Helenus, a priest, son of Priam, *Troilus and Cressida*
Helicanus, Lord of Tyre, *Pericles*
Henry, Prince, later Henry III, *King John*
Henry Bolingbroke, Duke of Hereford, later Henry IV, *Richard II,*
   1 Henry IV, 2 Henry IV
Henry (Hal), Prince of Wales, later Henry V, *1* and *2 Henry IV,*
   Henry V
Henry VI, *1, 2,* and *3 Henry VI,* (corpse and ghost) *Richard III*
Henry Tudor, Earl of Richmond, later Henry VII, *3 Henry VI, Richard*
   III
Herbert, Sir Walter, a soldier, *Richard III*
Hermia, loved by Lysander, *Midsummer Night's Dream*
Hermione, Leontes's queen, *Winter's Tale*
Hero, Leonato's daughter, *Much Ado About Nothing*
Hippolyta, Queen of the Amazons, *Midsummer Night's Dream*
Holland, John, follower of Jack Cade, *2 Henry VI*
Holofernes, a schoolmaster, *Love's Labour's Lost*

A Selective Finding List

Horatio, Hamlet's friend, *Hamlet*
Horner, Thomas, an armourer, *2 Henry VI*
Hortensio, suitor of Bianca, *Taming of the Shrew*
Hortensius, a servant, *Timon of Athens*
Host of the Garter Inn, *Merry Wives of Windsor*
Hostess, *see* Quickly, Mistress
Hostilius, *Timon of Athens*
Hotspur (Henry Percy), *Richard II, 1 Henry IV*
Hubert (de Burgh), *King John*
Hume, John, a priest, *2 Henry VI*
Humphrey, Prince, Duke of Gloucester, *see* Gloucester
Hymen, god of marriage, *As You Like It*
Iachimo, *Cymbeline*
Iago, Othello's ensign, *Othello*
Iden, Alexander (later Sir), *2 Henry VI*
Imogen, Cymbeline's daughter, *Cymbeline*
Iras, attendant of Cleopatra, *Antony and Cleopatra*
Iris, a spirit, *Tempest*
Isabel of France, Richard's Queen, *Richard II*
Isabel, Queen of France, *Henry V*
Isabella, Claudio's sister, *Measure for Measure*
Jamy, Captain, a Scottish officer, *Henry V*
Jaquenetta, a wench, *Love's Labour's Lost*
Jaques, a lord, *As You Like It*
Jaques de Boys, Orlando's brother, *As You Like It*
Jessica, Shylock's daughter, *Merchant of Venice*
Joan of Arc (Joan Pucelle), *1 Henry VI*
John, Don, the Bastard, *Much Ado About Nothing*
John, Friar, *Romeo and Juliet*
John of Gaunt, *see* Gaunt
John of Lancaster, Prince, later Duke of Bedford, *1* and *2 Henry IV, Henry V, 1 Henry VI*
Joseph, a servant, *Taming of the Shrew*
Jourdain, Margery (or Margaret), a witch, *2 Henry VI*
Julia, lover of Proteus, *Two Gentlemen of Verona*
Juliet, Claudio's betrothed, *Measure for Measure*
Junius Brutus, a tribune, *Coriolanus*
Juno, a spirit, *Tempest*
Jupiter, King of the gods, *Cymbeline*
Katharine, loved by Dumain, *Love's Labour's Lost*

Katherine of France, Princess, later Queen of Henry V, *Henry V*
Katherine, Queen of Henry VIII, *Henry VIII*
Katherina Minola, the shrew, *The Taming of the Shrew*
Kent, Earl of, *King Lear*
Laertes, Polonius's son, *Hamlet*
Lafeu, an old lord, *All's Well that Ends Well*
Lartius, Titus, Roman general, *Coriolanus*
Launce, Proteus's servant, *Two Gentlemen of Verona*
Lavache, the Countess's fool, *All's Well that Ends Well*
Lavinia, Titus's daughter, *Titus Andronicus*
Lawrence, Friar, *Romeo and Juliet*
Le Beau, a courtier, *As You Like It*
Le Fer, Monsieur, a French soldier, *Henry V*
Lennox, a thane, *Macbeth*
Leonardo, Bassanio's servant, *Merchant of Venice*
Leonato, governor of Messina, Hero's father, *Much Ado About Nothing*
Leonine, Dionyza's servant, *Pericles*
Leontes, King of Sicilia, *Winter's Tale*
Lepidus, Marcus Aemilius, *Julius Caesar*, *Antony and Cleopatra*
Lewis XI of France, *3 Henry VI*
Lewis the Dauphin, later Lewis VIII, *King John*
Lewis the Dauphin, son of Charles VI, *Henry V*
Ligarius, Caius, a conspirator, *Julius Caesar*
Lincoln, Bishop of, *Henry VIII*
Lion, played by Snug, *Midsummer Night's Dream*
Lodovico, kinsman of Brabantio, *Othello*
Lodowick, Friar, role assumed by Vincentio, *Measure for Measure*
Longaville, in love with Maria, *Love's Labour's Lost*
Lorenzo, in love with Jessica, *Merchant of Venice*
Lovel, Lord ('Sir Thomas'), *Richard III*
Lovell, Sir Thomas, Chancellor of the Exchequer, *Henry VIII*
Luce, a kitchen-maid, *Comedy of Errors*
Lucentio, Bianca's suitor, *Taming of the Shrew*
Lucetta, Julia's waiting-woman, *Two Gentlemen of Verona*
Luciana, Adriana's sister, *Comedy of Errors*
Lucilius, friend of Brutus, *Julius Caesar*
Lucilius, servant of Timon, *Timon of Athens*
Lucio, 'a fantastic', *Measure for Measure*
Lucius, young servant of Brutus, *Julius Caesar*
Lucius, a lord, and his servant, *Timon of Athens*

A Selective Finding List

Lucius, Titus's eldest son, *Titus Andronicus*
Lucius, Caius, Roman ambassador, *Cymbeline*
Lucius, Young, Lucius's son, *Titus Andronicus*
Lucullus, a lord, *Timon of Athens*
Lucy, Sir William, *1 Henry VI*
Lychorida, Marina's nurse, *Pericles*
Lymoges, Duke of Austria, *King John*
Lysander, in love with Hermia, *Midsummer Night's Dream*
Lysimachus, governor of Mytilene, *Pericles*
Macduff, thane of Fife, and his Lady and Son, *Macbeth*
MacMorris, an Irish officer, *Henry V*
Maecenas, friend of Octavius, *Antony and Cleopatra*
Malcolm, later King of Scotland, *Macbeth*
Malvolio, Olivia's steward, *Twelfth Night*
Mamillius, Leontes's son, *Winter's Tale*
Marcade, a messenger, *Love's Labour's Lost*
Marcellus, a soldier, *Hamlet*
Marcius, Caius (Coriolanus), *Coriolanus*
Marcius, Young, Coriolanus's son, *Coriolanus*
Marcus Antonius, *see* Mark Antony
Mardian, a eunuch, *Antony and Cleopatra*
Margarelon, bastard son of Priam, *Troilus and Cressida*
Margaret, attendant on Hero, *Much Ado About Nothing*
Margaret Plantagenet, Clarence's daughter, *Richard III*
Margaret, Queen, *1, 2,* and *3 Henry VI, Richard III*
Maria, loved by Longaville, *Love's Labour's Lost*
Maria, attendant on Olivia, *Twelfth Night*
Mariana, friend of Diana's mother, *All's Well that Ends Well*
Mariana, of the 'moated grange', *Measure for Measure*
Marina, Pericles's daughter, *Pericles*
Mark Antony, *Julius Caesar, Antony and Cleopatra*
Martext, Sir Oliver, a country curate, *As You Like It*
Martius, son of Titus, *Titus Andronicus*
Marullus, a tribune, *Julius Caesar*
Melun, a French lord, *King John*
Menas, a pirate, *Antony and Cleopatra*
Menecrates, friend of Pompey, *Antony and Cleopatra*
Menelaus, Helen's husband, *Troilus and Cressida*
Menenius Agrippa, friend of Coriolanus, *Coriolanus*
Menteith, Scottish nobleman, *Macbeth*

Mercade, *see* Marcade
Mercutio, friend of Romeo, *Romeo and Juliet*
Messala, friend of Brutus, *Julius Caesar*
Metellus Cimber, *see* Cimber
Michael, follower of Jack Cade, *2 Henry VI*
Michael, Sir, associate of the Archbishop of Canterbury, *1 Henry IV*
Milan, Duke of, Silvia's father, *Two Gentlemen of Verona*
Miranda, Prospero's daughter, *Tempest*
Montague, 'Old' and Lady, Romeo's parents, *Romeo and Juliet*
Montague, John Neville, Marquess of, *3 Henry VI*
Montano, Governor of Cyprus, *Othello*
Montgomery, Sir John, *3 Henry VI*
Montjoy, French herald, *Henry V*
Moonshine, played by Starveling, *Midsummer Night's Dream*
Mopsa, a shepherdess, *Winter's Tale*
Morgan, name taken by Belarius, *Cymbeline*
Morocco, Prince of, suitor to Portia, *Merchant of Venice*
Mortimer, Edmund, Earl of March, *1 Henry IV*, *1 Henry VI*
Mortimer, Lady, Edmund's Welsh wife, *1 Henry IV*
Mortimer, Sir Hugh, *3 Henry VI*
Mortimer, Sir John, *3 Henry VI*
Morton, *2 Henry IV*
Moth, Armado's page, *Love's Labour's Lost*
Moth, a fairy, *Midsummer Night's Dream*
Mouldy, Ralph, *2 Henry IV*
Mowbray, John, Duke of Norfolk, *3 Henry VI*
Mowbray, Thomas, Duke of Norfolk, *Richard II*
Mowbray, Thomas, Lord, *2 Henry IV*
Mugs, a carrier, *1 Henry IV*
Mustardseed, a fairy, *Midsummer Night's Dream*
Mutius, Titus's youngest son, *Titus Andronicus*
Nathaniel, a servant, *Taming of the Shrew*
Nathaniel, Sir, a curate, *Love's Labour's Lost*
Nerissa, Portia's waiting-maid, *Merchant of Venice*
Nestor, aged Greek commander, *Troilus and Cressida*
Nicanor, a Roman spy, *Coriolanus*
Nicholas, a servant, *Taming of the Shrew*
Norfolk, Duchess of, *Henry VIII*
Norfolk, John Mowbray, Duke of, *3 Henry VI*
Norfolk, John Howard, Duke of, *Richard III*

Norfolk, Thomas Howard, 2nd Duke of, *see* Surrey, Earl of
Norfolk, Thomas Mowbray, Duke of, *Richard II*
Northumberland, Henry Percy, 1st Earl of, *Richard II, 1* and *2 Henry IV*
Northumberland, Henry Percy, 3rd Earl of, *3 Henry VI*
Northumberland, Lady, *2 Henry IV*
Nurse (Angelica), Juliet's, *Romeo and Juliet*
Nym, Corporal, *Merry Wives of Windsor, Henry V*
Oatcake, Hugh, a watchman, *Much Ado About Nothing*
Oberon, King of the Fairies, *Midsummer Night's Dream*
Octavia, Octavius's sister, *Antony and Cleopatra*
Octavius Caesar, *Julius Caesar, Antony and Cleopatra*
Oliver de Boys, Orlando's brother, *As You Like It*
Olivia, a countess, loved by Orsino, *Twelfth Night*
Ophelia, Polonius's daughter, *Hamlet*
Orlando de Boys, in love with Rosalind, *As You Like It*
Orleans, Bastard of (Dunois), *1 Henry VI*
Orleans, Duke of, *Henry V*
Orleans, Master-Gunner of, and his son, *1 Henry VI*
Orsino, Duke (or Count) of Illyria, *Twelfth Night*
Osric, a foppish courtier, *Hamlet*
Oswald, Goneril's steward, *King Lear*
Overdone, Mistress, a bawd, *Measure for Measure*
Oxford, John de Vere, Earl of, *3 Henry VI, Richard III*
Pacorus, a soldier, *Antony and Cleopatra*
Page, Anne, loved by Fenton, *Merry Wives of Windsor*
Page, Master George (or Thomas), Anne's father, *Merry Wives of Windsor*
Page, Mistress Meg, Anne's mother, *Merry Wives of Windsor*
Page, William, Anne's schoolboy brother, *Merry Wives of Windsor*
Painter, a, *Timon of Athens*
Pandarus, Cressida's uncle, *Troilus and Cressida*
Pandulph, Cardinal, *King John*
Panthino, Antonio's servant, *Two Gentlemen of Verona*
Paris, betrothed to Juliet, *Romeo and Juliet*
Paris, Priam's second son, *Troilus and Cressida*
Paris, Governor of, *1 Henry VI*
Parolles, cowardly follower of Bertram, *All's Well that Ends Well*
Patch-breech, a fisherman, *Pericles*
Patience, Katherine's lady-in-waiting, *Henry VIII*

Patroclus, friend of Achilles, *Troilus and Cressida*
Paulina, Antigonus's wife, *Winter's Tale*
Peaseblossom, a fairy, *Midsummer Night's Dream*
Pedant, *Taming of the Shrew*
Pedro, Don, Prince of Arragon, *Much Ado About Nothing*
Pembroke, William Herbert, Earl of, *3 Henry VI*
Pembroke, William Marshal, Earl of, *King John*
Percy, Henry, *see* Northumberland
Percy, Lady ('Kate'), Hotspur's wife, *1* and *2 Henry IV*
Percy, Thomas, Earl of Worcester, *1 Henry IV*
Perdita, Leontes's daughter, *Winter's Tale*
Peter, Nurse's servant, *Romeo and Juliet*
Peter, a servant, *Taming of the Shrew*
Peter, Friar, *Measure for Measure*
Peter of Pomfret, a prophet, *King John*
Peto, companion of Falstaff, *1* and *2 Henry IV*
Petruchio, follower of the Capulets, *Romeo and Juliet*
Petruchio, Katherina's suitor, *Taming of the Shrew*
Phebe, loved by Silvius, *As You Like It*
Philario, friend of Posthumus, *Cymbeline*
Philarmonus, a soothsayer, *Cymbeline*
Philemon, Cerimon's servant, *Pericles*
Philip, a servant, *Taming of the Shrew*
Philip, King of France, *King John*
Philo, friend of Antony, *Antony and Cleopatra*
Philostrate, Theseus's Master of the Revels, *Midsummer Night's Dream*
Philotus, a servant, *Timon of Athens*
Phrynia, a prostitute, *Timon of Athens*
Pierce (Piers) of Exton, Sir, *Richard II*
Pilch, a fisherman, *Pericles*
Pinch, a schoolmaster and exorcist, *Comedy of Errors*
Pindarus, a slave, *Julius Caesar*
Pisanio, Posthumus's servant, *Cymbeline*
Pistol, Ancient (Lieutenant), *2 Henry IV*, *Henry V*, *Merry Wives of Windsor*
Poet, a, *Timon of Athens*, *Julius Caesar*
Poins, Edward (Ned), *1* and *2 Henry IV*
Polixenes, King of Bohemia, *Winter's Tale*
Polonius, Lord Chamberlain, *Hamlet*

A Selective Finding List

Polydore, name taken by Guiderius, *Cymbeline*
Pompeius, Sextus (Pompey), son of Pompey the Great, *Antony and Cleopatra*
Pompey Bum, a bawd, *Measure for Measure*
Popilius Lena, a senator, *Julius Caesar*
Portia, Brutus's wife, *Julius Caesar*
Portia, loved by Bassanio, *Merchant of Venice*
Posthumus Leonatus, Imogen's husband, *Cymbeline*
Potpan, a servant, *Romeo and Juliet*
Priam, King of Troy, *Troilus and Cressida*
Proculeius, *Antony and Cleopatra*
Prospero, formerly Duke of Milan, *Tempest*
Proteus, a gentleman, loved by Julia, *Two Gentlemen of Verona*
Publius, a senator, *Julius Caesar*
Publius, Marcus's son, *Titus Andronicus*
Puck (or Robin Goodfellow), *Midsummer Night's Dream*
Pyramus, played by Bottom, *Midsummer Night's Dream*
Quickly, Mistress, *1* and *2 Henry IV*, *Henry V*, *Merry Wives of Windsor*
Quince, Peter, a carpenter, *Midsummer Night's Dream*
Quintus, son of Titus, *Titus Andronicus*
Rafe, a servant, *Taming of the Shrew*
Rambures, a French lord, *Henry V*
Ratcliff, Sir Richard, follower of Richard, *Richard III*
Rebeck, Hugh, a musician, *Romeo and Juliet*
Regan, Duchess of Cornwall, Lear's second daughter, *King Lear*
Reignier, Duke of Anjou, King of Naples, *1 Henry VI*
Reynaldo, Polonius's servant, *Hamlet*
Richmond, Henry, Earl of, *see* Henry Tudor
Rinaldo, the Countess's steward, *All's Well that Ends Well*
Rivers, Lord (Anthony Woodville, Lord Scales), *3 Henry VI*, *Richard III*
Robert, a servant, *Merry Wives of Windsor*
Robin, an apprentice, *2 Henry VI*
Robin, Falstaff's page, *Merry Wives of Windsor*
Rochester, Bishop of, *Henry VIII*
Roderigo, in love with Desdemona, *Othello*
Rogero, a gentleman, *Winter's Tale*
Rosalind, loved by Orlando, *As You Like It*
Rosaline, loved by Berowne, *Love's Labour's Lost*
Rosencrantz, a courtier, *Hamlet*
Ross, Lord, *Richard II*

Ross, Thane of, *Macbeth*
Rousillon, Countess of, *All's Well that Ends Well*
Rugby, John, Dr Caius's servant, *Merry Wives of Windsor*
Rumour, the presenter, *2 Henry IV*
Rutland, Edmund, Earl of, *3 Henry VI*
Salanio, friend of Antonio, *Merchant of Venice*
Salarino, friend of Antonio, *Merchant of Venice*
Salerio (perhaps a mistake for Salanio or Salarino), *Merchant of Venice*
Salisbury, William Longsword, Earl of, *King John*
Salisbury, John Montacute, Earl of, *Richard II*
Salisbury, Thomas Montacute, Earl of, *Henry V*, *1 Henry VI*
Salisbury, Richard Neville, Earl of, *2 Henry VI*
Sampson, a servant, *Romeo and Juliet*
Sandys, Lord, *Henry VIII*
Saturninus, Emperor of Rome, *Titus Andronicus*
Say, Lord, *2 Henry VI*
Scales, Lord, *2 Henry VI*
Scarus, friend of Antony, *Antony and Cleopatra*
Scroop, Henry, Lord, of Masham, *Henry V*
Scroop, Richard, Archbishop of York, *1* and *2 Henry IV*
Scroop, Sir Stephen, *Richard II*
Seacole, Francis, a scribe, *Much Ado About Nothing*
Seacole, George, a literate watchman, *Much Ado About Nothing*
Sebastian, name taken by Julia, *Two Gentlemen of Verona*
Sebastian, Viola's twin brother, *Twelfth Night*
Sebastian, Alonso's brother, *Tempest*
Seleucus, Cleopatra's treasurer, *Antony and Cleopatra*
Sempronius, a lord, *Timon of Athens*
Sempronius, kinsman of the Andronici, *Titus Andronicus*
Servilius, servant of Timon, *Timon of Athens*
Seyton, Macbeth's armourer, *Macbeth*
Shadow, Simon, *2 Henry IV*
Shallow, Robert, 'a country justice', *2 Henry IV*, *Merry Wives of Windsor*
Shylock, a usurer, *Merchant of Venice*
Sicilius Leonatus, Posthumus's father, and his dead wife and sons, *Cymbeline*
Sicinius Velutus, a tribune, *Coriolanus*
Silence, a country justice, *2 Henry IV*
Silius, an officer, *Antony and Cleopatra*

A Selective Finding List

Silvia, the Duke of Milan's daughter, *Two Gentlemen of Verona*
Silvius, a shepherd, *As You Like It*
Simonides, Thaisa's father, King of Pentapolis, *Pericles*
Simpcox, Saunder, and Mrs Simpcox, *2 Henry VI*
Simple, Peter, Slender's servant, *Merry Wives of Windsor*
Siward, Earl of Northumberland, *Macbeth*
Siward, Young, *Macbeth*
Slender, Abraham, Shallow's cousin, *Merry Wives of Windsor*
Sly, Christopher, 'a drunken tinker', *Taming of the Shrew*
Smith, the Weaver, *2 Henry VI*
Snare, an officer, *2 Henry IV*
Snout, Tom, a tinker, *Midsummer Night's Dream*
Snug, a joiner, *Midsummer Night's Dream*
Solanio, friend of Antonio, *Merchant of Venice*
Solinus, Duke of Ephesus, *Comedy of Errors*
Somerset, Edmund Beaufort, 2nd Duke of, *2 Henry VI*
Somerset, Henry Beaufort, 3rd Duke of, and Edmund, 4th Duke of, confused, *3 Henry VI*
Somerset, John Beaufort, Earl of, later 1st Duke of, confused with Edmund, 2nd Duke of, *1 Henry VI*
Somerville, Sir John, a Lancastrian, *3 Henry VI*
Son that has killed his father, *3 Henry VI*
Soundpost, James, a musician, *Romeo and Juliet*
Southwell, John, a priest, *2 Henry VI*
Speed, Valentine's servant, *Two Gentlemen of Verona*
Stafford, Sir Humphrey, *2 Henry VI*
Stafford, Lord, a Yorkist, *3 Henry VI*
Stafford, William, *2 Henry VI*
Stanley, Sir John, *2 Henry VI*
Stanley, Thomas, Lord, Earl of Derby, *Richard III*
Stanley, Sir William, *3 Henry VI*
Starveling, Robin, a tailor, *Midsummer Night's Dream*
Stephano, servant of Portia, *Merchant of Venice*
Stephano, a 'drunken butler', *Tempest*
Strato, Brutus's servant, *Julius Caesar*
Suffolk, Charles Brandon, Duke of, *Henry VIII*
Suffolk, William de la Pole, Earl of, later Duke of, *1* and *2 Henry VI*
Sugarsop, a servant, *Taming of the Shrew*
Surrey, Thomas Fitzalan, Earl of (non-speaking), *2 Henry IV*
Surrey, Thomas Holland, Duke of, *Richard II*

Surrey, Thomas Howard, Earl of, later Duke of Norfolk, *Richard III*,
    Henry VIII
Talbot, John, Lord, later Earl of Shrewsbury, *1 Henry VI*
Talbot, John ('Young'), *1 Henry VI*
Tamora, Queen of the Goths, *Titus Andronicus*
Taurus, Octavius's lieutenant-general, *Antony and Cleopatra*
Tearsheet, Doll, *2 Henry IV*
Thaisa, Pericles's wife, *Pericles*
Thaliard, Lord of Antioch, *Pericles*
Thersites, Achilles's fool, *Troilus and Cressida*
Theseus, Duke of Athens, *Midsummer Night's Dream*
Thidias, *Antony and Cleopatra*
Thisby, played by Flute, *Midsummer Night's Dream*
Thomas, Friar, *Measure for Measure*
Thump, Peter, Horner's servant, *2 Henry VI*
Thurio, suitor of Silvia, *Two Gentlemen of Verona*
Thyreus, *see* Thidias
Timandra, a prostitute, *Timon of Athens*
Time (as Chorus), *Winter's Tale*
Titania, Queen of the Fairies, *Midsummer Night's Dream*
Titinius, friend of Brutus, *Julius Caesar*
Titus, a servant, *Timon of Athens*
Tom, Poor, name taken by Edgar, *King Lear*
Topas, Sir, impersonated by Feste, *Twelfth Night*
Touchstone, Duke Frederick's jester, *As You Like It*
Tranio, Lucentio's servant, *Taming of the Shrew*
Travers, a servant, *2 Henry IV*
Trebonius, a conspirator, *Julius Caesar*
Tressel, a gentleman, *Richard III*
Trinculo, a jester, *Tempest*
Tubal, friend of Shylock, *Merchant of Venice*
Tybalt, Juliet's cousin, *Romeo and Juliet*
Tyrrel, Sir James, *Richard III*
Ulysses, Greek commander, *Troilus and Cressida*
Ursula, attendant on Hero, *Much Ado About Nothing*
Urswick, Sir Christopher, a priest, *Richard III*
Valentine, a gentleman, *Two Gentlemen of Verona*
Valentine, kinsman of the Andronici, *Titus Andronicus*
Valentine, attendant on Orsino, *Twelfth Night*
Valeria, friend of Virgilia, *Coriolanus*

Varrius, friend of Pompey, *Antony and Cleopatra*
Varrius, friend of the Duke (non-speaking), *Measure for Measure*
Varro, Brutus's man, *Julius Caesar*
Varro, *Timon of Athens*
Vaughan, Sir Thomas, *Richard III*
Vaux, Sir Nicholas, *Henry VIII*
Vaux, Sir William, *2 Henry VI*
Venice, Duke of, *Merchant of Venice, Othello*
Ventidius, one of Antony's generals, *Antony and Cleopatra*
Ventidius, a debtor, *Timon of Athens*
Verges, a constable, *Much Ado About Nothing*
Vernon, a Yorkist, *1 Henry VI*
Vernon, Sir Richard, follower of Hotspur, *1 Henry IV*
Vincentio, Duke of Vienna, *Measure for Measure*
Vincentio, Lucentio's father, *Taming of the Shrew*
Viola, twin sister of Sebastian, *Twelfth Night*
Violenta (non-speaking), *All's Well that Ends Well*
Virgilia, Coriolanus's wife, *Coriolanus*
Voltemand, a courtier, *Hamlet*
Volumnia, Coriolanus's mother, *Coriolanus*
Volumnius, friend of Brutus, *Julius Caesar*
Wall, played by Snout, *Midsummer Night's Dream*
Walter, a servant, *Taming of the Shrew*
Wart, Thomas, a recruit, *2 Henry IV*
Warwick, Earl of, a Yorkist, *2 and 3 Henry VI*
Warwick, Earl of, *2 Henry IV, Henry V, 1 Henry VI*
Weird Sisters, *Macbeth*
Westminster, Abbot of, *Richard II*
Westmoreland, Ralph Neville, 1st Earl of, *1 and 2 Henry IV, Henry V*
Westmoreland, Ralph Neville, 2nd Earl of, *3 Henry VI*
Whitmore, Walter, *2 Henry VI*
William, a yokel, *As You Like It*
Williams, Michael, a soldier, *Henry V*
Willoughby, Lord, *Richard II*
Wolsey, Cardinal, *Henry VIII*
Woodville, Elizabeth, Lady Grey, later Queen of Edward IV, *3 Henry VI, Richard III*
Woodville, Lieutenant of the Tower, *1 Henry VI*
Worcester, Thomas Percy, Earl of, *1 Henry IV*
York, Duke of, *see* Aumerle

York, Cicely Neville, Duchess of, *Richard III*
York, Duchess of, *Richard II*
York, Edmund of Langley, Duke of, *Richard II*
York, Richard, Duke of, *Richard III*
York, Richard Plantagenet, Duke of, *1, 2* and *3 Henry VI*
York, Richard·Scroop, Archbishop of, *Richard II*
York, Thomas Rotherham, Archbishop of, *Richard III*

FURTHER READING

So much has been written about Shakespeare that we can list only some of the more important sources of information. The principal encyclopaedic guide is *The Reader's Encyclopaedia of Shakespeare* (also published as *A Shakespeare Encyclopaedia*), edited by O. J. Campbell and E. G. Quinn (New York, 1966). Also useful is *A Shakespeare Companion 1564–1964*, by F. E. Halliday (Harmondsworth, 1964). These may be supplemented by the essays in *A New Companion to Shakespeare Studies*, edited by Kenneth Muir and S. Schoenbaum (Cambridge, 1971). The major work on Shakespeare's sources is *Narrative and Dramatic Sources of Shakespeare*, edited by Geoffrey Bullough, 8 vols. (London, 1957–75). The most recent detailed study of Shakespeare's life is S. Schoenbaum's *William Shakespeare: A Documentary Life* (Oxford, 1975; compact edition, 1977). A useful bibliography is David Bevington's *Shakespeare* (Goldentree Bibliographies, Arlington Heights, Illinois, 1978).

Information about editions of Shakespeare is given in the body of this *Dictionary*. For English readers, the best single-volume edition is probably that edited by Peter Alexander (London, 1951). The American tradition favours annotated, student-type editions; the Riverside, edited by G. Blakemore Evans and others (Boston, Mass., 1974), contains much useful ancillary material, but its highly conservative treatment of the text is not to everyone's taste. The Pelican *Complete Works*, edited by Alfred Harbage and others (Baltimore and London, 1969) is more economically presented. The most detailed scholarly one-play-per-volume edition at present in progress is the new Arden, available in both hard-back and paper-back. The New Penguin (paper-back) offers readable Introductions, helpful annotation, and, for some plays, more up-to-date treatment. The American Pelican and Signet editions are conveniently presented paper-back texts with Introductions and annotations.

The major overall study of Shakespeare on the stage is still G. C. D. Odell's *Shakespeare – from Betterton to Irving*, 2 vols. (New York, 1920). Robert Speaight's *Shakespeare on the Stage* (London, 1973) carries the story forward to more recent times. An excellent study with a more critical bias is Richard David's *Shakespeare in the Theatre* (Cambridge, 1978). *Shakespeare in Music*, edited by Phyllis Hartnoll (London, 1964) and *Shakespeare and the Artist*, by W. M. Merchant (Oxford, 1959), are the most valuable treatments of their subjects.

Critical studies abound. A good general introduction, linking the work with the life and background, is M. M. Reese's *Shakespeare: His World and his Work* (revised edition, London, 1980). Stanley Wells's *Shakespeare: the Writer and his Work* (London, 1978) offers a more concise survey. Other standard studies are mentioned in the *Dictionary* under A. C. Bradley, W. H. Clemen, Samuel Taylor Coleridge, Harley Granville-Barker, Samuel Johnson, G. Wilson Knight, E. M. W. Tillyard, G. Bernard Shaw, Elmer Edgar Stoll, and others. The annual publication *Shakespeare Survey* (Cambridge) and the American *Shakespeare Quarterly* (Washington, D.C.) offer the means of keeping abreast of Shakespeare studies.